Unsettled Ground

UNSETTLED GROUND

The Whitman Massacre and Its Shifting Legacy in the American West

CASSANDRA TATE

SASQUATCH BOOKS

SEATTLE

Printed in Canada

SASQUATCH BOOKS with colophon is a registered trademark of Penguin Random House LLC

24 23 22 21 20   9 8 7 6 5 4 3 2 1

Editors: Gary Luke and Jennifer Worick
Production editor: Rachelle Longé McGhee
Cover painting: Pobytov/DigitalVision Vectors/Getty Images
Design and maps: Tony Ong

Library of Congress Cataloging-in-Publication Data
Names: Tate, Cassandra, author.
Title: Unsettled ground : the Whitman Massacre and its shifting legacy in the American West / Cassandra Tate.
Other titles: Whitman Massacre and its shifting legacy in the American West
Identifiers: LCCN 2019052745 (print) | LCCN 2019052746 (ebook) | ISBN 9781632172501 (hardcover) | ISBN 9781632172518 (ebook)
Subjects: LCSH: Whitman Massacre, 1847. | Cayuse Indians–Oregon–History–19th century. | Cayuse Indians–Washington (State)–History–19th century. | Cayuse Indians–Missions–Oregon. | Cayuse Indians–Missions–Washington (State) | Waiilatpu Mission (Wash.) | Oregon–History–19th century. | Washington (State)–History–19th century. | Whitman Mission National Historic Site (Wash.) | Whitman, Marcus, 1802-1847–Statues.
Classification: LCC E99.C32 T38 2020 (print) | LCC E99.C32 (ebook) | DDC 979.7/48–dc23
LC record available at https://lccn.loc.gov/2019052745
LC ebook record available at https://lccn.loc.gov/2019052746

ISBN: 978-1-63217-250-1

Sasquatch Books
1904 Third Avenue, Suite 710
Seattle, WA 98101

SasquatchBooks.com

FOR GLENN

CONTENTS

AUTHOR'S NOTE ABOUT NOMENCLATURE

I use the word "Indian" to refer to the indigenous people of the Northwest, in keeping with the preference of staff at the Confederated Tribes of the Umatilla Indian Reservation (CTUIR). Because of the great variation in the spellings of the names of individual Indians as recorded by Euro-Americans in the nineteenth century, I also generally defer to the CTUIR for the preferred spellings.

TIMELINE

October 18, 1805: Cayuse and Walla Walla people meet explorers Lewis and Clark near the mouth of the Walla Walla River, in the tribes' first direct encounter with Euro-Americans.

1818: Cayuse and Walla Walla leaders grant fur traders Alexander Ross and Donald McKenzie permission to build what becomes Fort Walla Walla near the site of the meeting with Lewis and Clark.

March 1, 1833: The New York–based *Christian Advocate and Journal* publishes a report claiming that four Indians from the West had traveled to Saint Louis to seek "the white man's Book of Heaven."

August 12, 1835: Rev. Samuel Parker and Marcus Whitman arrive at the American Fur Company's annual rendezvous in Wyoming, intending to scout locations for missions in the West, under the sponsorship of the Boston-based American Board of Commissioners for Foreign Missions (ABCFM).

February 19, 1836: Newlyweds Marcus and Narcissa Whitman leave New York to become missionaries in Oregon Country. They are joined later by fellow missionaries Henry and Eliza Spalding and William Henry Gray.

September 12, 1836: The missionary party arrives at Fort Vancouver. Narcissa and Eliza remain there for eight weeks while their husbands begin building two separate mission stations, 120 miles apart.

December 10, 1836: Marcus Whitman escorts Narcissa to a rudimentary house he has built on Cayuse land near present-day Walla Walla. Three months later, Narcissa gives birth to their only child, a daughter named Alice Clarissa.

August 1838: Four additional missionary couples arrive in Oregon Country under the sponsorship of the ABCFM. Members of the expanded missionary community quarrel almost constantly about goals, strategy, and personal habits.

June 23, 1839: The Whitmans' young daughter, Alice Clarissa, drowns. Narcissa, deeply depressed, withdraws from missionary work.

September 14, 1842: Whitman receives orders from the American Board to close his mission. After riding to Boston to appear before the board in person, he successfully appeals the decision.

May through September 1843: Returning west, Whitman helps guide the first large wagon train on what becomes known as the Oregon Trail.

April 1844: Two Cayuse men who had received medical treatment from Whitman die; their relatives accuse him of causing the deaths.

April and November 1845: In a series of confrontations with Whitman, Cayuse leaders demand that he pay them for the use of their land and accuse him of being willing to use poison to kill Indians in order to seize it.

June 1846: The Senate ratifies a treaty setting the border between British Canada and the United States at the forty-ninth parallel, a move that opens Oregon Country to increasing colonization by Americans.

Fall 1847: An estimated four thousand emigrants reach Oregon Country by wagon train. Their arrival coincides with a virulent outbreak of measles among the Cayuse.

November 29, 1847: A small group of Cayuse attacks the Whitman Mission, killing Marcus and Narcissa Whitman, five adult male emigrants, and two teenage boys; four more men will be killed over the next week, for a total of thirteen dead.

August 14, 1848: Congress responds to news of the so-called "Whitman Massacre" by establishing the Territory of Oregon as a federal entity and dispatching federal troops to fight in the "Cayuse War."

April 1850: Five Cayuse men surrender to Oregon Territorial Authorities. They are charged with murder in connection with the attack on the Whitman Mission, given a brief trial, convicted, and hanged.

June 9, 1855: At the Walla Walla Treaty Council, representatives of the Cayuse, Walla Walla, and Umatilla reluctantly sign a treaty ceding 6.4 million acres of their homelands in return for a 510,000-acre reservation in eastern Oregon.

December 1859: Rev. Cushing Eells establishes Whitman Seminary as a "living monument" to his former missionary colleague, Marcus Whitman. Initially a private school for precollege students, it becomes Whitman College in 1882.

November 28 and 29, 1897: Stephen B. Penrose, president of Whitman College, organizes a two-day commemoration of the fiftieth anniversary of the attack on the Whitman Mission.

August 1936: Walla Walla business leaders raise enough money to establish the Whitman Mission National Monument (later expanded and renamed the Whitman Mission National Historic Site).

May 22, 1953: A bronze statue depicting Marcus Whitman as a muscular frontiersman is dedicated in the National Statuary Hall in the US Capitol.

August 11, 1978: The American Indian Religious Freedom Act is enacted, requiring federal agencies to "protect and preserve" traditional spiritual and cultural practices.

November 14 and 15, 1997: Whitman College, the Whitman Mission National Historic Site, and representatives of the Confederated Tribes of the Umatilla Indian Reservation mark the 150th anniversary of the attack on the Whitman Mission with a symposium titled "Examining the Collision of Cultures in an Age of Multiculturalism: The Whitman Tragedy 1847–1997."

July 31, 1998: The Tamástslikt Cultural Institute—the only tribally owned museum and interpretive center on the Oregon Trail—opens near Pendleton.

October 2017: A Marcus Whitman statue in Walla Walla and a romanticized portrait of Narcissa Whitman at Whitman College are vandalized.

January 2019: A Seattle legislator introduces a bill to replace the statue of Marcus Whitman in the US Capitol, arguing that "Marcus Whitman does not meet the standards of being one of our state's top honorees."

INTRODUCTION

Marcus Whitman was a Protestant missionary who might have been only a historical footnote had not he, his wife Narcissa, and eleven others been killed by Cayuse Indians during an attack on his mission near present-day Walla Walla, Washington, in 1847. Instead, he became one of the most memorialized figures in the Northwest. A county, a college, a national forest, half a dozen public schools, and numerous other enterprises—from an upscale hotel in Walla Walla to a church in Des Moines—carry his name. The Washington legislature once considered a measure to rename the iconic Mount Rainier in his honor. His former mission is a National Historic Site. His statue stands in the National Statuary Hall in the Capitol Building in Washington, DC, nine feet of gleaming bronze on a seven-ton block of polished granite, depicting a muscular, buckskin-clad frontiersman with a ripped torso and linebacker thighs. He appears to be striding resolutely along an unbroken trail, one foot higher than the other, buckskin fringe and kerchief flying, a Bible in one hand, saddlebags and a scroll in the other. His strong jaw is neatly bearded, his flowing locks topped by a beaver-skin hat. If the National Statuary Hall had a hunk contest, he'd be the winner, hands down.

The statue embodies Whitman's place in the mythology of the West, not the realities of his life. The only feature that can be verified as historically accurate are the saddlebags, which were copied from a pair used by Whitman when he was an itinerate physician in upstate New York. He left them behind when he was appointed a missionary in 1835. They ended up a century later in the collections of the Presbyterian Historical Society in Philadelphia. Sculptor Avard Fairbanks, who was commissioned to create the statue in 1950, studied them when he was designing what is otherwise a fanciful depiction of Marcus Whitman. Even the quotation carved into the granite pedestal—"My Plans Require Time and Distance"—is a paraphrase of something Whitman wrote, not his exact words.

The bronze Whitman was unveiled on May 22, 1953. More than three hundred people attended the ceremonies, including most of Washington State's congressional delegation, dozens of other dignitaries, four distant descendants of the Whitman family, and one dove, who flew in through a window and fluttered around throughout the services.[1] Supreme Court Justice William O. Douglas, a graduate of Whitman College in Walla Walla (and eventual liberal icon), gave the main dedication speech. He described Whitman as a "dynamic man of boundless energy" who "brought thousands into the region beyond the old frontier." Like most of the other speakers, Douglas emphasized Whitman's role in promoting the settlement of the West by whites, praised his vision and fortitude, called him a martyr, and deplored the "treachery" of the Indians who killed him. Washington governor Arthur Langlie was unable to attend but sent word that "it is a privilege for the citizens of Washington . . . to offer to the people of the United States this visible monument to one who lived humbly and died nobly in pursuit of happiness and freedom for his fellow men." Langlie said that Whitman had made "tragic sacrifices," he had "died a martyr," and "America honors itself by honoring him."[2]

The story of the "Whitman Massacre" was a standard part of the curriculum for schoolchildren throughout the Northwest in the 1950s. I was introduced to it as a sixth-grader in Seattle. It was a simple tale, with sharply defined heroes and villains and thrilling touches of mayhem and gore. Marcus and Narcissa Whitman were brave, noble pioneers who came west to "save" Indians. It was never clear to me what the Indians were being saved from, or whether they wanted to be saved, or what they thought about the missionaries, or why they attacked the mission, but they were not the focus of the story that we were told. The emphasis was on the white people. Marcus was strong and handsome; Narcissa was beautiful and saintly; they were "massacred" by brutal, ungrateful "savages." I was left with an indelible image of Narcissa's long, white throat being slashed by a knife, sending a river of blood down the front of her billowing gown.

Actually, she was shot, but memory and story and history and fact have a fluid relationship. Heroes rise and fall to the rhythms of what scholars call "the politics of memory." New facts are revealed, old ones dissected, and stories reshaped (and sometimes forgotten altogether) as political and social conditions change. The initial narrative, or "memory," about the Whitmans—as told by whites— emphasized their religiosity. It reflected the evangelical values of dominant voices in the mid-nineteenth century, a time of intense religious revivalism in the United States. By the end of the century, after two major economic crises and associated social and political upheavals, a new version of the story had emerged. Grounded in nostalgia for an idealized past, it celebrated the Whitmans as heroic pioneers who had helped a young, expansionist nation realize its dreams of Manifest Destiny. A competing narrative, one that included the voices and perspectives of the Cayuse and other indigenous peoples, began to develop in the late 1960s. Books such as Dee Brown's *Bury My Heart at Wounded Knee* and films such as *Soldier Blue* and *Little Big Man* helped foster public interest in uncovering the history of the West from Indian points of view.

In the 1980s the National Park Service, which operates the Whitman Mission National Historic Site, stopped commemorating the annual anniversary of the attack on the mission; redesigned its displays to give more attention to the Cayuse and a more balanced assessment of their interactions with the Whitmans; and phased out use of the word "massacre" in favor of more neutral language. The word appeared five times in a four-page brochure distributed by the Park Service in the late 1950s. In contrast, it was not used at all in brochures available in 1997, the 150th anniversary of what instead was called the Tragedy at Waiilatpu. Today the tendency is to see the Indians, not the missionaries, as the martyrs.

We seem to live in a binary world, where the lines between good and bad are clearly drawn, without much room for nuance. For more than a century after their deaths, Marcus and Narcissa Whitman were venerated by non-Indians as heroic pioneers who had given their lives to bring Christianity and "civilization" to the West. In more recent years, however, they've been demonized as cultural imperialists and agents of genocide. They received too much credit in the first instance, and too much blame in the second. They were complicated, imperfect people: idealistic but culturally arrogant, courageous but inflexible; and it was the way they died, more than what they did in life, that guaranteed them a place in the history of the Northwest.

The Whitmans left comfortable homes in upstate New York in 1836 to become missionaries in what was then called Oregon Country—a vast region (consisting of the present-day states of Washington, Oregon, Idaho, and parts of Montana and Wyoming) that relatively few Americans had ever seen. They were joined by another missionary couple, Henry and Eliza Spalding. They reached their destination after an arduous, seven-month, three-thousand-mile journey. Narcissa and Eliza were the first women known to have crossed the continent from coast to coast. They traveled much of the way on horseback, riding sidesaddle.

Whitman established a mission on Cayuse land at a place he thought was called Waiilatpu (pronounced "way-EE-let-pu"). Henry

Spalding picked a site 120 miles to the northeast, at Lapwai, among Nez Perce Indians in present-day Idaho. Relations between the Whitmans and their hosts were initially cordial, but disappointment and disillusionment built up over time, on both sides. The Whitmans expected the Cayuse to be eager to convert to Christianity, take up farming, and live like white people. The Indians were interested in some aspects of the newcomers' culture and religion but only to supplement, not replace, their traditional beliefs and way of life. Long-simmering tensions erupted in violence on November 29, 1847, ending with the deaths of the Whitmans and eleven other Americans.

The attack was a pivotal event in Northwest history. One immediate effect was the passage of a long-delayed bill establishing the Territory of Oregon, a measure that extended federal authority over the region. The bill had been stalled for more than two years by a debate over whether slavery would be permitted in the new territory. In the end, it was not. Meanwhile, the superintendent of Indian affairs issued an order declaring that the Cayuse had "forfeited" their rights to their ancestral homelands. He encouraged settlers to file claims to Cayuse lands and stipulated that the claims would not be undercut by any future treaties with the Indians. The "massacre" became a rallying cry for a two-year war of harassment and retribution against not only the Cayuse but any Indians suspected of being allies of or sympathetic to the Cayuse. Finally, in the spring of 1850, five Cayuses surrendered to the territorial government in Oregon City and were hanged, after a brief, cursory trial.

The Whitman story was burnished and romanticized for generations after their deaths, at least in the version told by non-Indians, but it has now largely faded from public memory. Although Whitman retains his place in the National Statuary Hall—at least as of this writing—and his name remains attached to monuments, plaques, and highway signs from upstate New York to the Northwest coast, many people don't know who he was.

This book takes a new look at the Whitmans, the Cayuse, and the shifting legacy of the events at Waiilatpu. One of my goals is to slice through the myths, lies, and misconceptions that have built up around the story over the past 170 years. Narcissa Whitman did not have her throat sliced, as I once imagined. She was not scalped, as Richard Neuberger, then a young freelance writer and later a US senator from Oregon, reported in 1938, in particularly lurid prose ("Narcissa's blond scalp eventually dangled against the greasy thigh of a Cayuse warrior").[3] She was not "shot a dozen times . . . men whipping her laid-bare back while she was still breathing," her head "a cracked melon," as in a scene conjured by an Idaho writer in 2019.[4] Marcus Whitman did not convince the US government to fend off British claims to the Northwest and thereby "save" Oregon Country for American settlers. The Cayuse attack on the Whitman Mission was not unprovoked.

The key figures in this tale were neither heroes nor villains but simply human beings, caught in a web not entirely of their making. Their lives played out in ways that profoundly shaped the history of the Northwest and continue to influence it to this day. What follows is, to the best of my research and knowledge, an evenhanded account of what happened and why, and how the narrative changed with each new generation of storytellers. It's a complex tale of arrogance, fortitude, naïveté, and misunderstandings. It can be seen as a singular American tragedy but also as representative of the tangle of cultural myopia and conflict that marked each wave of American incursion into the West.

My dissection of the story begins with the incident that wrapped Marcus and Narcissa Whitman in a cloak of martyrdom and put their names in the history books and on the roadside markers: the November 1847 attack at Waiilatpu.

CHAPTER ONE

THE ATTACK

It is my painful task to make you acquainted with a horrid massacre which took place yesterday at Waiilatpu, about which I was first apprised early this morning by an American who had escaped, of the name of Hall, and who reached this place half naked and covered with blood.

—*William McBean, Fort Walla Walla, to Hudson's Bay Company Board of Management, Fort Vancouver, November 30, 1847*

The attack began shortly after the noon meal on November 29, 1847—around 1:00 p.m., according to some accounts; closer to 2, according to others. In the moments before the first blows were struck and the first screams were heard, Mary Ann Bridger, the twelve-year-old daughter of mountain man James F. "Jim" Bridger and a Flathead Indian woman, was in the kitchen in the large, T-shaped Mission House, washing dishes. John Sager, seventeen, the oldest of a family of seven children who had been adopted by the Whitmans after the deaths of their parents on the Oregon Trail in 1844, also was in the kitchen, winding brown twine for brooms. Narcissa Whitman was

Canadian artist Paul Kane drew this sketch of the Whitman Mission in July 1847, four months before a group of Cayuses attacked the mission, killing Marcus and Narcissa Whitman and eleven others. *Used with permission of the Royal Ontario Museum © ROM; 946.15.318.*

helping two of John's sisters bathe in a wooden tub in the living room. Marcus Whitman sat nearby, reading. A carpenter named Josiah Osborn was repairing floorboards in a large corner room that had once been reserved for use by Indians but had recently been turned over to him and his family. Some of the mission children were in the schoolroom with their teacher. Outside, three newly arrived emigrant men had hoisted a steer on a derrick and were butchering it. A small group of Cayuse Indians stood a short distance away, watching. It was a cold, overcast day.

More than seventy people had settled in for the winter at the Whitman Mission at Waiilatpu, most of them emigrants who had arrived that fall and were too weary, sick, or destitute to continue their journey west until the spring. Five families were crammed into a building called the Emigrant House, along with three single men. A family of seven had makeshift quarters in the blacksmith shop. The Whitmans, their wards (including Mary Ann Bridger, two other métis or mixed-race children, and the seven Sager orphans), the Osborn family, and half a dozen other people lived in the main Mission House. The newest occupant was ten-year-old Eliza Spalding (named after her mother). Her father, Henry Spalding, one of Whitman's fellow missionaries, had brought her to the mission to attend school just one week earlier. Two other emigrant families, with a total of eleven people, were sharing a cabin at the mission's sawmill in the foothills of the Blue Mountains, twenty miles away.

It's not clear how many people were occupying two nearby Cayuse villages headed by a man named Tiloukaikt (the most common spelling of his name). The entire Cayuse tribe, divided among three major bands, probably consisted of fewer than five hundred men, women, and children. Tiloukaikt's band had been decimated by an outbreak of measles that began in the fall of 1847. "We have the measles all about us," Marcus Whitman wrote to a missionary colleague at The Dalles.[1] Measles also swept through the mission community, sickening several young adults and at least a dozen children, but only one (Josiah Osborn's six-year-old daughter) had died. In contrast, mortality among the Indians—who had no acquired immunities against any of the infectious diseases introduced by Euro-Americans—was shockingly high. An estimated thirty Indians living near the mission, mostly children, died between the first week of October and the end of November.[2] The fact that nearly all of Whitman's white patients recovered while his Indian patients did not led some Cayuses to suspect that he was using poison to deliberately kill Indians.

Henry Spalding spent about a week in the area after bringing Eliza to the mission on November 22, 1847. He visited one of Tiloukaikt's villages on November 23. That day, "three Indians died, including a child," he wrote. "It was most distressing to go into a lodge of some ten fires and count twenty or twenty-five, some in the midst of measles, others in the last stages of dysentery, in the midst of every kind of filth, of itself sufficient to cause sickness, with no suitable means to alleviate their inconceivable sufferings, with perhaps one well person to look after the wants of two sick ones."[3] Two days later, Spalding traveled to another village. "Found the Indians everywhere sick with the measles, dying from one to three daily," he wrote.[4] On the evening of November 27, Spalding and Whitman left Waiilatpu together to visit a Cayuse community on the Umatilla River, twenty-five miles south, in response to reports of illness there. Whitman returned to the mission late the next day. Spalding, injured in a fall from his horse, stayed behind—a move that probably saved his life.

Three children from Tiloukaikt's band were buried on the morning of November 29, one of them reportedly a son of the headman. Two of Tiloukaikt's other children had died earlier, as had the wife of Tomahas (also spelled Tamáhus), another Cayuse leader. Sometime after the burials, a group of Cayuses—fourteen to eighteen, by most estimates—armed themselves with clubs, tomahawks, guns, and knives; covered the weapons with blankets; and went to the mission complex. Most gathered around the derrick where the steer was being butchered. Whitman noticed their presence but did not think it unusual because, as Catherine Sager put it later, Indians "always came around on such days to get what was thrown away."[5] Two Indians pounded on the back door of the kitchen at the Mission House, then pushed their way in and asked for medicine. People in adjoining rooms heard loud voices. Some of them swore later that the voices were those of Tiloukaikt and Tomahas.

Roused by the noise, Whitman went to the kitchen, telling Narcissa to bolt the door behind him. Mary Ann Bridger, who had spent half her life with the Whitmans, was the only eyewitness to what happened in the kitchen after that. She said that when Whitman turned toward a cupboard, presumably to get the medicine, one of the Indians drove a tomahawk into his head. Mary Ann fled outside and ran around the building to the front, screaming. Whitman lay on the floor, a deep gash on the back of his head, three slashes across his face. John Sager had been shot by a rifle and his throat was cut. Still alive, both Whitman and Sager would linger for hours before dying.[6] The rifle shot may have been a signal. Outside, Cayuses near the butchered steer pulled out weapons they had hidden beneath blankets and began firing. "All over the place was heard at once the firing of guns, the yelling and war whoops of the Indians," Eliza Spalding wrote in a memoir published in 1916. "Dear reader, for years the firing of a gun or sudden shout brought up vivid memories of that terrible hour and place."[7]

Twenty people who survived the attack eventually wrote about or were interviewed about what they saw—or *thought* they saw. Most survivors, like Eliza, were children at the time and did not publicly recount their experiences until many years later. It's impossible to know the degree to which their stories were colored by trauma or by what they had been told or by the simple haze of time. As historian Ari Kelman, in a book about the Sand Creek Massacre, has noted: "Scenes of violence, especially mass violence, are notorious for breeding unreliable and often irreconcilable testimony."[8] The historical record also includes reports by several people who were not at the mission on the day of the attack but became closely involved in subsequent events, including a Catholic priest who arrived two days later and helped bury the dead; Hudson's Bay Company officials at Forts Walla Walla and Vancouver; and Henry Spalding. The details in these various accounts, whether written within a few days of the attack or decades later, are often contradictory, sometimes lurid, and consistently ethnocentric.

The Cayuse perspective is difficult to recover. Non-Indians—explorers, fur traders, missionaries, settlers, government agents—left diaries, letters, periodicals, books, and other written records that historians can mine today. The Cayuse, like other indigenous peoples, recorded their history orally. But that oral tradition was weakened after the attack. "People wouldn't talk about it publicly," Roberta Conner, director of the Tamástslikt Cultural Institute, remarked in 2018. "We got stuck with the 'murderer' label. It was a source of shaming for a long, long time."[9] The Cheyenne and Arapaho who survived the Sand Creek Massacre of 1864 (when American troops attacked a peaceful village in Colorado and slaughtered hundreds) had grief and outrage to keep alive their stories about what had happened, to be passed down through the generations. That wasn't the case when it came to the Cayuse and the Whitmans. Consequently, important information is missing from the historical record. What's clear, however, is that the Whitman Mission was engulfed by violence in an outburst that began in the early afternoon of November 29, and the first target was the man who had once promised to "save" the Indians.

The first gunshots were followed by panic and confusion. In the schoolroom of the Mission House, teacher Lucian Saunders looked out the window and saw a wounded man running toward the house, his arm hanging limp at the elbow and covered in blood. Saunders, a lawyer from Oskaloosa, Iowa, had arrived at Waiilatpu in October 1847 with his wife, Mary, and their five children. Whitman was impressed by his credentials and had convinced him to spend the winter teaching school at the mission. According to one of the students, when Saunders saw what was happening outside, he ran out of the room and down the stairs, saying something like "I must go to my family." With that, "we boys went to the window and saw that the Indians had dropped their blankets and were running about with their weapons in their hands, shooting and shouting."[10]

The wounded man was Nathan Kimball, one of the three emigrants who had been butchering the steer. He had been shot in the arm. One of the other men, William Canfield, had a wound from a gunshot in his side. The third, a bachelor named Jacob Hoffman, was dead. Walter William Marsh, a widower with two children, was also dead, shot as he ran from the gristmill where he had been working. Saunders had been overtaken, seized, and clubbed to death by two Indians as he tried to reach the Emigrant House—about four hundred feet from the Mission House—where his family and many of the other women and children were. Matilda Sager, who was eight years old at the time, claimed more than seventy years later that Saunders had been beheaded and that she had seen his body, "lying there with his head severed."[11] Matilda was the third and last of the Sagers to publish her memoirs; she may have felt pressure to outdo her two older sisters by spicing her account with gruesome but invented details. Still, by any measure the attack was brutal. Many of the killings were done at close quarters, with hatchets and clubs, not with bullets fired at a sanitary distance. The first outsider on the scene, the Jesuit missionary Father Jean B. A. Brouillet, said he saw three victims whose skulls had been crushed.

The scene in the Mission House was chaotic. Ten-year-old Elizabeth Sager leaped naked from the tub in the living room. Her twelve-year-old sister, Catherine, who had just finished dressing, ran toward the door. Narcissa wailed something about being a widow but then composed herself. She called Catherine back and told Elizabeth to put on her clothes. Kimball burst into the room, holding his bleeding arm. Elizabeth remembered him saying, "The Indians are killing us. I don't know what the damned Indians want to kill me for—I never did anything to them. Get me some water." The incongruity of hearing a swear word in the Whitmans' living room made the little girl giggle. She expected Narcissa to chastise him for cursing and was surprised when she said nothing and instead got water and began washing Kimball's arm.[12]

Several emigrant women had rushed into the living room when the firing began. Narcissa told one of them—Margaret Osborn, the carpenter's wife—to go back into the former "Indian Hall" with her husband and children and lock the door. Then Narcissa and two of the other women dragged Marcus from the kitchen into the adjacent dining room and laid him on the floor, putting a pillow under his head. Narcissa got a towel and some ashes to try to staunch the flow of blood and asked if there was anything else she could do for him. He whispered "No."[13]

The Cayuses were well-organized, well-armed, and focused. With the single exception of Narcissa Whitman, they targeted only the male "Bostons" (a term widely used among Northwest tribes for Americans) at the mission. A French Canadian hired hand and three métis boys were not molested. The initial assault probably lasted less than fifteen minutes.[14] When it ended, three men were dead and six others seriously wounded (including John Sager who, at seventeen, would have been considered fully grown by the Indians). Only one of the whites managed any kind of a defense. Jacob Hoffman struck at his attackers with his axe before he was killed. A tailor who had been at work in the Emigrant House on a new Sunday suit for Marcus Whitman was fatally wounded when an Indian stepped into his room and shot him point-blank. Andrew Rogers, a young would-be minister who had lived at Waiilatpu for two years, had been at the river filling a pail with water and was shot in the wrist while sprinting back toward the Mission House. He crashed into the exterior door to the dining room, breaking the glass in the upper half, before the door was unbolted and he tumbled inside. When he saw Whitman lying on the floor, he asked if he was dead. Whitman reportedly answered with a weak "No." If he spoke again, no one heard him.

Narcissa was standing by the door, looking through the broken glass, when she was shot. Some of the witnesses said she was shot in the right shoulder; some said the right side; others said the left breast. She shrieked, clutched her wound, and sank to her knees. Rogers helped her to her feet. She and the rest of the frightened group—thirteen in all, including three children who had been sick in bed with measles—retreated to a dormitory on the second floor. Marcus Whitman, now unconscious, was left below.

The schoolchildren, meanwhile, had fled to a loft above the schoolroom. Eliza Spalding described the loft as a makeshift affair, consisting of just "a few boards overhead," with no staircase or ladder to reach it. Some of the older boys hurriedly pushed a table to the center of the room, piled some books on it, climbed up, and pulled in the younger children. Francis Sager, at fifteen the oldest in the group, then "told us all to ask God to save us," according to his sister Matilda.[15]

Among the children who were huddled in the loft were the three métis boys: thirteen-year-old John Manson and his eleven-year-old brother, Stephen, whose father, a French Canadian employee of the Hudson's Bay Company, had brought them to the mission to attend school a few weeks earlier; and a boy Narcissa had named David Malin, about eight, who had lived with the Whitmans for five years. During a lull following the gunshot that wounded Narcissa, Joseph Stanfield, a French Canadian who worked for the Whitmans, came into the schoolroom and called up into the loft, telling the Manson brothers and David to come down. Stanfield assured them that because they were part Indian, they would not be harmed. He helped them down, then took them to the lodge of Nicholas Finlay (sometimes spelled Finley), a former fur trapper. Finlay and his Cayuse wife, Josephte, lived about a quarter mile east of the mission. Later, some of the survivors would claim that the lodge had served as the headquarters for the Cayuses who planned and carried out the attack; others would say that Finlay and his wife helped restrain some of the Indians and protected the women and children who became hostages.

With the departure of the three boys, the only member of the mission community who was fluent in Nez Perce—the primary language of the Cayuse—was ten-year-old Eliza Spalding. She had been born on Nez Perce land at the Spalding Mission at Lapwai, in present-day Idaho, and had grown up among Nez Perce Indians, close relatives of the Cayuse. She would be called upon to serve as interpreter as events unfolded over the next days and weeks.

As dusk fell, a little after 4:00 p.m., some of the Cayuses broke into the main floor of the Mission House, smashing windows and doors, plundering the pantry, scattering books and papers, taking coveted items like pots and pans, and tossing aside the rest. Josiah Osborn, his wife, Margaret, and their three surviving children— Nancy, seven; John, three; and Alexander, two—heard the commotion from where they cowered in their room in the northwest corner of the building. Osborn had lifted up some loose floorboards, and the family had crawled into a three-foot-high space below. "In a few moments our room was full of Indians, talking and laughing as if it were a holiday," Nancy Osborn said in an account written in 1912, sixty-five years after the attack. "The only noise we made was by my brother Alex, two years old. When the Indians came into our room and were directly over our heads, he said, 'Mother, the Indians are taking all of our things.' Hastily she clapped her hand over his mouth and whispered that he must be still."[16] Matilda Sager, hiding with other schoolchildren in the loft upstairs, remembered hearing the sound of dried berries rattling on the floor of the pantry as Indians emptied storage containers.[17]

At some point—the eyewitness accounts are contradictory, and none pinpoint the time—a Cayuse named Tamsucky came to the base of the stairway and called up to the people in the rooms above. Speaking in English, he said the Indians were planning to burn down the Mission House and that Narcissa and all those who were with her should leave immediately. Catherine Sager thought that Narcissa seemed eager to believe that "God maybe has raised us up a friend."[18] Accompanied by Rogers and most of the others, Narcissa slowly came down the stairs. She reportedly averted her face when she saw her husband's bloodied, mutilated head. Weak from loss of blood herself, she sank down onto a settee in her wrecked living room.

The schoolchildren also left their refuge in the loft and went downstairs, escorted by Joseph "Joe" Lewis, a man of French Canadian and

Indian heritage who had briefly worked for Whitman. As they passed through the kitchen, the children saw the body of John Sager. Eliza Spalding described him as "lying in a huddled heap, his throat cut from ear to ear, not yet dead."[19] After John had been attacked, hours earlier, he had had enough presence of mind to stuff a part of a woolen scarf that he had been wearing into the gash in his neck. Approaching his older brother's body, Francis Sager impulsively leaned over and pulled at the scarf, unleashing a gush of blood. John died soon afterward. The wounded Kimball stayed behind, in the upstairs dormitory, along with Catherine Sager, her two youngest sisters, and another of the Whitmans' wards, Helen Mar Meek (nine-year-old daughter of mountain man Joseph L. "Joe" Meek and a Nez Perce woman). The two young Sager girls and Helen were all sick with measles.

It was now almost dark. Of the fourteen male "Bostons" on the premises when the attack began, one had escaped and was on his way to Fort Walla Walla, a Hudson's Bay Company fur trading post at the confluence of the Walla Walla and Columbia Rivers, about twenty-five miles west of the mission. Two others had managed to hide. Two young emigrant men were seriously ill and bedridden, possibly with measles; the Indians ignored them for the moment. The rest of the men were either dead or wounded.

In her account of the day's events, Eliza said she and the other schoolchildren were standing outside the Mission House when she heard Tamsucky tell Narcissa Whitman and Andrew Rogers that the Indians wanted all the survivors to go into the Emigrant House. "Mrs. Whitman said, 'No, we are afraid,'" Eliza wrote. He tried to reassure her, saying, "You will not be molested and we are sorry for what has been done." Narcissa said she was too weak to walk on her own. Tamsucky ordered that she be carried out on the settee. Joe Lewis picked up one end, Rogers took the other end despite his wounded arm, and together they carried Narcissa from the living room through the kitchen and out the north door into the main yard.

A short distance from the house, Lewis dropped his end of the improvised litter and jumped out of the way. A group of Cayuses "raised the yell," wrote Eliza, and began firing. Rogers looked up, said "Oh, my God," and collapsed.[20] Lorinda Bewley, a young emigrant woman who followed Rogers out of the Mission House, said the ball that hit him passed so close to her that it stung her fingers. (Rifles fired spherical lead balls in those days; pointed bullets were not yet in use.[21]) Two balls struck Narcissa, one of them smashing into her cheek.[22]

Although mortally wounded, Rogers would live for several more hours. Narcissa was apparently killed instantly. The schoolchildren, watching from where they had been lined up against the Mission House, saw her body as it rolled from the settee into the mud. Eliza Spalding said one Indian grabbed Narcissa's hair, raised her head, and beat her dead face with a war club. Matilda Sager said the Indian used a riding whip, not a club.[23] They agreed that there were no tears or shrieks from the children; they were all stunned, even the youngest, into silence.

Joe Lewis's role in the attack on the Whitman Mission is unclear. Some of the survivors said he had been an agitator, goading the Cayuse to violence because of an undying hatred for whites. Born in Canada to a European father and a Delaware mother, he was said to have fought with the US Army under Major John C. Fremont in California during the Mexican-American War in 1846. He joined an emigrant train at Fort Hall in present-day Idaho in 1847 and arrived at Waiilatpu in either late October or early November. Whitman hired Lewis as a laborer, although he privately described him as "a worthless vagabond, not worth the food he eats."[24] Lewis allegedly told some Cayuses that he had overheard conversations between the Whitmans and Henry Spalding in which the missionaries talked about poisoning Indians and argued about whether they should be poisoned quickly or gradually. Yet the Cayuse did not appear to trust Lewis completely, and at least one taunted him for not having taken an active part in the killings. Perhaps in response, Lewis raised a pistol and turned it on Francis Sager.

At fifteen, Francis, like his seventeen-year-old brother John, would have been considered an adult. Lewis pulled Francis from where he had been standing, in the line of schoolchildren, between Eliza and his sister Matilda. Nancy Osborn, hidden with her family beneath the floorboards in the Mission House, said she heard Francis cry out, "Oh Joe, don't shoot me."[25] There was a single gunshot. Francis "fell at our feet," wrote Eliza, adding, "I was sure our time had come. I put my apron over my face. I did not want to see the guns pointed at us."[26]

But there was no more gunfire that day. The Indians ushered the schoolchildren and most of the other survivors into the Emigrant House and then returned to their villages. Nathan Kimball, Catherine Sager, and the three sick girls remained in the dormitory. The dead were left where they had fallen. "As soon as it became dark," wrote Nancy Osborn, "the Indians left for their lodges. . . . Everything became still. It was the stillness of death." From their hiding place in the old Indian room, the Osborns heard the moans of the dying Rogers, lying just six feet away. "We heard him say, 'Come Lord Jesus, come quickly.' Afterward he said faintly, 'Sweet Jesus.' Then fainter and fainter came the moans until they ceased all together."[27] The day ended with nine people dead—one woman, six men, and two teenage boys.

The first news of the attack reached the outside world the next morning, when Peter D. Hall pounded on the gate at Fort Walla Walla. Hall, an emigrant from Illinois, had been installing a floor in the second story of the Mission House when the initial shots were fired.

Mary Saunders (the schoolteacher's wife) said she saw him climb out a windowsill, slide down the building, and run toward the willows along the Walla Walla River. Several Indians chased after Hall, but he escaped.[28] William McBean, the Hudson's Bay Company trader who was in charge of the fort, had reasons to resist taking him in. With only five men to help him defend the post, McBean did not want to appear to be siding with the Americans against the Cayuse. He said later that at Hall's request, he had given him a coat, blanket, tobacco, and other supplies and seen him rowed to safety across the Columbia River, away from any pursuing Indians.[29] Hall was never seen or heard from again. Some believe he drowned; others that he was ambushed by a Cayuse who had followed him. In any case, Hall is sometimes counted as a fourteenth victim of the "Whitman Massacre." He left behind a wife and five daughters, who, along with some forty others, were held as hostages by the Cayuse.

William Canfield, one of the men who had been wounded in the early minutes of the attack, waited until nightfall to leave where he was hiding, in the blacksmith shop, and try to escape. He told his wife that his life would be in danger if the Indians found him. He said he wanted to warn the Spaldings in case the Cayuse attack was part of a general Indian uprising. Although he had never been to the Spalding Mission, about 120 miles to the northeast, Canfield knew the general direction and the trail was fairly well marked. He arrived there on December 4, some four and a half days later.

The Osborn family also slipped away from the mission during that first night. The moon had risen by the time they crept out from under the floorboards; although in its last quarter, it provided enough light for them to make their way to the river and begin walking the twenty-five miles to Fort Walla Walla. They had gone just a few miles when Margaret Osborn collapsed. She had given birth two weeks earlier (to an infant who lived for only a few hours). She may also have been recovering from measles. Her husband, Josiah, left her hidden in some brush with Nancy and their two-year-old son; and then he walked on, carrying three-year-old John on his back. He stumbled into the fort on the morning of December 2. With help from a Walla Walla Indian who was working as a guide for McBean, Josiah returned and rescued the rest of his family the next day. McBean, still wary about antagonizing the Cayuse, reluctantly allowed the Osborn family to stay at the fort. Even though the Indians returned to their own lodges each night, leaving the mission unguarded, none of the other survivors of the assault tried to escape. Most of them were women and children. They were strangers in that land; they would not have known which way to go to find help. They chose to stay put and hope for rescue.

Two more men were killed on the morning of November 30, the day after the initial attack. The first was Nathan Kimball, who had found refuge in the Mission House after being shot during the initial burst of gunfire. After spending a restless night in the dormitory with Catherine Sager and the three feverish girls, Kimball wrapped a blanket around himself as a sort of disguise and left to get water from the river. He had filled a bucket and started back toward the house when he was seen, shot again, and this time killed. Later that morning, twenty-four-year-old James Young, who had been working with his father and two brothers at the sawmill in the Blue Mountains, was shot as he approached the mission with a wagonload of lumber. Joe Stanfield, the Whitmans' French Canadian laborer, found Young slumped on the ground with a bullet in his head. Stanfield buried the young man where he lay.

After the death of Kimball, Joe Lewis and several Cayuses climbed the stairs to the second floor of the Mission House and found Catherine Sager and the three other girls trembling in a corner, the younger ones crying. When Lewis asked why the girls were crying, Catherine said they were hungry, thirsty, and frightened. The Indians brought them food and water and tried to calm their fears by telling them, through Lewis, that they would be taken to Fort Walla Walla soon, but meanwhile they should join the women and the other children in the Emigrant House.

At that point the Cayuse probably did not intend to hold the survivors as hostages. Tiloukaikt, head of the two villages closest to the mission, made a point of telling Mary Saunders that she and the others would soon be on their way to Fort Walla Walla. Again that night the Cayuse returned to their lodges, leaving the survivors unguarded but fearful. "Before night all the Indians went away to their own village and we were left in peace until the morrow," wrote Mary Saunders. "But the dead still lay unburied and no woman dared to go out of the house to mourn over her loved ones or to care for their remains. To add horror to the situation, the Indian dogs howled all night long."[30]

Father Brouillet arrived the next morning, on December 1. The Catholic priest had established a mission on the Umatilla River, about twenty-five miles southwest of Waiilatpu, just a few days earlier. He had heard about the ravages of measles among Tiloukaikt's people and decided to visit "for the purpose of baptizing the infants and such dying adults as might desire this favor." He reached Tiloukaikt's main village, about three miles east of Waiilatpu, late on the evening of November 30 and learned to his shock what had happened the day before. He baptized three sick children at daybreak and prepared to travel on to the Whitman Mission. Two of the children died before he left.[31]

Brouillet described what he saw at Waiilatpu in a letter to officials at Fort Walla Walla, dated March 2, 1848: "Ten dead bodies lying here and there, covered with blood and bearing the marks of the most atrocious cruelty—some pierced with balls, others more or less gashed by the hatchet. Dr. Whitman had received three gashes on the face. Three others had their skulls crushed so that their brains were oozing out."[32] The women in the Emigrant House were sewing "winding sheets" (shrouds) for the dead from a bolt of muslin that Tiloukaikt had brought them. Joe Stanfield had begun digging a mass grave. Brouillet, two Walla Walla Indians, and a Cayuse elder that the whites called Chief Beardy helped finish the grave. The survivors watched and wept as the dead were placed in a wagon—"all piled up like dead animals," one of the Sager girls recalled—and then buried in a shallow trench, six feet long, twelve feet wide, and four feet deep.[33]

Six days later, the two young men who had been sick at the time of the initial attack—Amos Sales, in his early twenties, and Crockett Bewley, eighteen-year-old brother of Lorinda—were dragged from their beds, beaten with clubs, and tomahawked to death.[34] Eliza Spalding thought the men were killed because they had begun to recover and the Indians "were afraid they might skip out some night."[35] There were reports that one of Tiloukaikt's sons, known to the whites as Edward, had consulted a "great chief" at the Umatilla who told him the men's diseases would spread if they were allowed to live. Historian Clifford Drury, author of numerous books about the missionaries, attributed the deaths to tension between Tiloukaikt and the young warriors, including his son. "The murder of James Young on the day after Tiloukaikt had promised that there would be no more killings, was evidently done without the chief's knowledge or consent," he wrote. "The murder of the two sick men, Sales and Bewley, took place when Tiloukaikt was away and his son Edward was seemingly in charge."[36]

There was no more killing after that. Marcus and Narcissa Whitman were dead, along with eleven others. Peter Hall was missing and presumed dead. Hannah Louise Sager and Helen Mar Meek both died of measles not long after being taken to the Emigrant House. William Canfield was safe at Lapwai. The Osborn family was recovering at Fort Walla Walla. Tiloukaikt had sent three Cayuses to the sawmill to bring the people there down to the mission.

The group included Elam Young (James's father) and his two surviving adult sons, and Joseph Smith, an emigrant from Illinois, and his wife and five children. They arrived just after dark on December 7, several hours after the deaths of Sales and Bewley. On the whispered advice of some of the emigrant women, the men told the Cayuses they were British ("King George Men"), not "Bostons."[37]

The Cayuses put the men to work at the gristmill, grinding corn and wheat. The women sewed and cooked. According to Mary Saunders, eight to ten "young chiefs" came to the mission daily for meals. Three young women, including Lorinda Bewley, were claimed as wives. A total of forty-five people were held captive for a month and then ransomed by Peter Skene Ogden, a Hudson's Bay Company official from Fort Vancouver, at a cost of sixty-two blankets, sixty-two cotton shirts, twelve muskets, six hundred rounds of ammunition, thirty-seven pounds of tobacco, and some smaller items.[38]

But that was not the end of the story, or the beginning.

CHAPTER TWO

THE IMPERIAL TRIBE

This is the country of the Cayouses.

—*Narcissa Whitman, October 18, 1836*

Roberta Conner was a seventh-grader in the small town of Coulee Dam in north-central Washington when, as far as she can recall, she heard about the "Whitman Massacre" for the first time. It was 1968. The story was a standard unit in the Washington State history curriculum for public school students. It was not something her Cayuse, Nez Perce, and Umatilla relatives ever talked about. The classroom lesson was brief and left her with only a vague impression of martyred missionaries and "murdering Cayuses." But she remembers reacting to it with a certain skepticism. "It always felt, to me, very peculiar that the only martyrs in history were white people," she says.[1]

Conner has devoted much of her professional life to telling more nuanced stories about the indigenous peoples of the Columbia Plateau. An enrolled member of the Confederated Tribes of the Umatilla Indian Reservation, she was born in 1955 in Salem,

Oregon, and grew up mostly in the Pendleton area. When she was thirteen, her Nez Perce grandmother gave her the name Sisaawipam, a Sahaptin word that a linguist told Conner may have had something to do with people coming out of "the cold place"—possibly a reference to the time when glaciers were melting and Ice Age floods were thundering over the Columbia Plateau. She graduated from Pendleton High School in 1973, from the University of Oregon with a degree in journalism in 1977, and from Willamette University with a master's in management in 1984. She worked for an Indian nonprofit in Seattle and for the Small Business Administration in Denver and Sacramento before becoming the founding director of the Tamástslikt (pronounced Tah-MUST-licked) Cultural Institute in 1998. The institute, on the Confederated Tribes' reservation near Pendleton, is the only tribally owned museum and interpretive center on the Oregon Trail.

A compact woman, about five feet five, Conner has long, gray hair, which she usually wears pulled back from her face, held in place by barrettes or twisted into a French bun. She lives on 352 acres near Pendleton, where she raises horses and enjoys the comings and goings of mice, skunks, hawks, deer, coyotes, and elk, among other creatures. She is thoughtful, articulate, and direct. She also has a personal connection to the Whitman story. Among her ancestors are the first three people to be accepted into a church founded by Marcus Whitman and Henry Spalding at Lapwai: James Conner, a mountain man (with a Nez Perce wife) who helped guide the missionaries to Oregon Country; Tuitekes, son of a Cayuse man and a Nez Perce woman, who was given the name Joseph when he was baptized; and Tamootsin, a Nez Perce, baptized as Timothy. Conner points out that of the three, only Timothy remained faithful to the church. James Conner was excommunicated for polygamy, failure to observe the Sabbath, operating a still, and various other transgressions. Joseph, father of the legendary Chief Joseph—whose eloquence in defeat after the Nez Perce War of 1877 made him a national hero—renounced Christianity in 1863, after the federal government reduced the size of the Nez Perce reservation by some six million acres and opened the land to miners and settlers.

Conner doesn't remember hearing any of her relatives talk about the Whitmans when she was growing up. Not many people publicly admitted to Cayuse heritage. "There was a stigma about being Cayuse," she commented in 2018. "We were the shame of the region. Only in the last twenty years has it become more common for people to identify as Cayuses."[2] Part of the challenge of telling the story today is that oral traditions were fractured; Indian people who had direct knowledge of what happened wouldn't talk about it, leaving only a few "threadbare oral histories" and accounts by white people. Still, one thing is certain: "By the time the Whitmans arrived, we had been welcoming strangers here for more than three decades, going back to Lewis and Clark in 1805. There's a ton of hospitality and generosity that precedes the violence. That's an imbalance in the story. We had been taking care of these precarious travelers in our homeland for a long time before we killed the Whitmans."[3]

The people who became known as Cayuse were given that name by French Canadian fur traders, who called them Cailloux, meaning "Rock People," because of the rocky nature of parts of their homeland. Fur trader Alexander Ross spelled it Cayouse. To the botanist and explorer David Douglas, they were the Kyeuuse or the Kyuuse. Early emigrants thought they were Cai-uses, Skyuse, Kaius, Kioos, Kiusas, and other variants. Their own name for themselves may have been Liksiyu.[4] To their Nez Perce neighbors, they were Weyiiletpuu or Waiilatpu: the People of the Place of Waving Grass (often incorrectly translated as "Place of the Rye Grass").[5]

Great Basin wild rye (*Leymus cinereus*) is one of dozens of native grasses and sedges that flourished on the flatlands and rolling hills in Cayuse country. Ice Age floods shaped much of this landscape, drilling deep crevices into ancient basalt, stripping away topsoil in some areas, piling it up in others, plucking huge chunks of rock from basalt cliffs along the Columbia River, leaving behind shallow caves that Plateau Indians later used for shelter and storage. Geologists believe that the Northwest was pummeled by a hundred or more "mega floods" originating from Glacial Lake Missoula in Montana during the last Ice Age alone. Floodwaters backed up at Wallula Gap, the only outlet for water draining from the entire Columbia Basin to the sea, creating temporary lakes that inundated the Walla Walla Valley alone with up to 250 feet of water. Flood-borne sediments settled out of these lakes, becoming part of the rich topsoil that supports the farms, orchards, and ranches of the Walla Walla, Yakima, and Willamette Valleys today. The sediment is also the basis for the quality of the acclaimed wines produced in the Mid-Columbia Basin. Wine grapes require soil that is both fast-draining and water-retentive, characteristics provided by the fine-grained sand and silt in the flood deposits.

Geologists say that one of those floods, maybe twelve thousand to fifteen thousand years ago, stripped away most of a thick outcropping of basalt downstream from Wallula, leaving two massive pillars that overlook Washington State Route 730, two miles south of US Highway 12. According to a Cayuse legend, the pillars are actually the work of the trickster Coyote. One day, it is said, Coyote saw three beautiful Cayuse sisters building a fish trap in Nch'i-Wána (literally the Big River, now called the Columbia). He tricked them into marrying him. For a while, all was well, but eventually he became jealous of his wives. He turned one of the sisters into a cavern and the other two into basalt pillars on the south side of the river. Then he turned himself into a large rock on the north side, so that he might keep an eye on them forever. Canadian artist Paul Kane saw the pillars and heard the story about the "Rocks of the Ki-use girls" when he passed through the region in July 1847.[6] The pillars—shown on maps as the "Cayuse Sisters" or the "Twin Sisters"—still stand sentinel near the river, but the cavern beneath them was inundated by the completion of McNary Dam in 1954.

The Cayuse were the masters of this land when the first whites saw it, in the early 1800s. Their skill in breeding and raising horses ("cayuse" continues to be used as the name of a fast, sure-footed horse in the West) gave them wealth and influence over other indigenous peoples. They were tough, hard-minded traders and much feared as warriors. Scottish-born Alexander Ross, who helped build the area's first trading post in 1818, described them as "by far the most powerful and warlike" of the tribes on the Columbia Plateau—the region bordered by the Rockies on the east, the Cascades on the west, the Deschutes River drainages to the south, and the Okanogan highlands near the Canadian border to the north. They "regulate all the movements of the others in peace and war, and as they stand well or ill disposed toward their traders, so do the others," wrote Ross.[7] David Douglas, encountering a group of "Kyeuuse" at The Dalles in 1826, called them "the terror of all other tribes west of the mountains."[8] Thomas J. Farnham, a would-be colonizer who traveled through the country a decade later, gave them the label later used by many others: "the imperial tribe" of Old Oregon.[9]

In earlier days, before horses entered their world, the Cayuse were river people, living in small villages clustered along the Walla Walla, Umatilla, and other drainages south of the Columbia.[10] Extended families shared rectangular, A-framed longhouses, held up by driftwood logs and covered with tule mats. Tule (pronounced "too-lee") is a type of sedge that swells when wet. During winter rains, gaps between water-swollen tules would close, creating a snug, waterproof structure. The lodges were disassembled and reassembled on new sites as needed. People traveled by canoe or on foot. They

Cayuse leader Paul Showaway and his daughter in front of their tule lodge at Thorn Hollow winter camp on the Cayuse, Umatilla, and Walla Walla Indian Reservation, 1901. Many Cayuse held on to traditional practices even after being forced onto the reservation. *Lee Moorhouse Collection, PHO36_4259, Special Collections and University Archives, University of Oregon, Eugene.*

had dogs but no other domesticated animals. Some of the dogs were trained to haul firewood and other supplies in backpacks or on a travois (a type of sled, framed by two poles in the shape of an isosceles triangle). Like other indigenous people on the Plateau, the Cayuse were seasonally mobile, harvesting wild foods as they became available, following a way of life handed down through generations, over thousands of years.

People lived in autonomous villages or bands, bound by language, social customs, and shared purpose. There was no single, politically unified "tribe." Headmen were selected on the basis of experience and abilities. Conflicts were resolved by a council of elders and headmen; decisions were arrived at by consensus. Women advised but did not directly participate in councils. Polygamy was common, although generally the province of headmen and others with status and influence. There were strong taboos against marrying blood relatives, including cousins, which meant that people often went outside their local communities to find partners. The resulting bonds of kinship created extensive social networks among Plateau peoples.

In the spring, when the salmon began running, people left their winter villages and moved to favorite fishing sites on the Big River. Men used traps, nets, and spears to harvest salmon as they swam upstream to spawn. Women gutted, cleaned, and spread the fish on platforms to dry. Dried fish was a staple in winter, when other food was scarce. Family groups and small bands moved on to other locations as roots, tubers, nuts, berries, and other plants ripened. The diet included more than a hundred species of plants. A mainstay was camas (*Camassia quamash*), a lily-like bulb that reminded some Euro-Americans of potatoes and others of onions. By late May, camas was in bloom, turning meadows and marshlands into seas of blue. The main harvest began in summer. Women pried the entire plant from the ground, using elkhorns or pointed hardwood sticks; removed the largest bulbs; and replanted the rest, to be harvested again the next year.

Camas fields were not farmed in the conventional sense, but they were cultivated, usually by family groups that returned to the same areas year after year. Controlled burns helped reduce weeds and brush. Nutritional studies have shown that camas has more than twice as much calcium and four times as much iron as potatoes and nearly 40 percent more protein per pound than steelhead trout.[11]

Anthropologist Eugene Hunn has estimated that plant foods provided about 60 percent of the total indigenous diet. Harvesting them required detailed knowledge of the land and its resources and rhythms.[12] Places were named after the natural resources found there (as in "Place of Waving Grass" and "Place of Balsamroot Sunflower"), in contrast to the Euro-American convention of putting the names of people on the landscape. This intimate familiarity with the land may have helped the Cayuse see how horses could thrive on the region's grasslands.

According to oral tradition, the Cayuse acquired their first horses sometime in the 1730s, as a result of what had originally been a war party against the Shoshone (also called Snake) Indians. Approaching a group of Shoshones on a tributary of the Snake River, Cayuse scouts were bewildered to see their enemies riding what appeared to be elk or large deer. Closer investigation revealed that the prints left by the hooves of the mysterious animals were not split, like those of other hooved mammals, but were solid and round. The Cayuse chief arranged a truce and asked to trade for some of the strange creatures. It is said that he and his warriors gave away all they had and returned home, nearly naked, with a mare and a stallion—descendants of horses that had been reintroduced into the New World by the Spanish.

The Cayuse response to those first horses reflected their ability to adapt to changing circumstances and take advantage of new opportunities. People who were hidebound by tradition would not have traded everything they had for something they had never seen before; or, later, be as eager to acquire the guns, metal, cloth, and other new technology offered by Euro-American fur traders; or, still later, be as receptive to the missionaries who showed up in their homeland.

Cayuse herds increased rapidly—a combination of selective breeding (inferior horses were gelded), periodic raids on other tribes, and the abundance of good grazing land. By the early 1800s, an individual who owned only fifteen to twenty horses was considered poor; wealthy families controlled two thousand or more. Cayuse-bred horses were unprepossessing in appearance—they tended to be short and stocky—but they were famed for their speed, endurance, and agility.

Horses led to what historian Theodore Stern has called "a revolution in perspective" for the Cayuse.[13] No longer restricted to what they could carry or what their dogs could pull, they moved into new territories, traveling as far east as the Great Plains and as far west as California to hunt, trade, fight, and capture slaves.[14] A horse with a travois could easily haul several hundred pounds, much more than a dog. The seasonal migrations now included annual trips across the Rocky Mountains to hunt buffalo. This brought the Cayuse into contact with Midwestern tribes. They soon incorporated elements of Plains culture into their own, adopting new styles of clothing and personal ornamentation, methods of hunting, and ways of packing and transporting goods. They added conical teepees, sometimes covered with buffalo hides, to their housing options, although tule mats remained the covering of choice.

Horses improved the range and effectiveness of war parties, making it possible for the Cayuse to dominate their sedentary neighbors on the Columbia. They claimed suzerainty over The Dalles, the great fishery and trade emporium of the Columbia, forcing the weaker bands in that area to pay them tribute in the form of salmon and other goods. "For years to come," wrote historians Robert Ruby and John Brown, "they would not let its salmon eaters, teeth worn and eyes blinded by river sand, forget their inferiority."[15] This domination

Edward S. Curtis titled this 1909 photograph of a young Cayuse woman on horseback "Holiday Trappings." The Cayuse have a proud tradition of bedecking themselves and their horses with finery on gala occasions. *Library of Congress, Prints and Photographs Division, Edward S. Curtis Collection, LC-USZ62-115021.*

continued into the 1840s. Henry K. W. Perkins, a Methodist missionary at Wascopam, near The Dalles, described the "Kaius" as "the elite of the country." They "consider the fishers along the river as their humble servants, and there is no end of their acts of injustice and oppression toward them," he wrote.[16]

The increased mobility led to even tighter social and political connections between the Cayuse and Indian peoples throughout the Plateau, especially the Walla Walla, to the north; the Umatilla, to the southwest; and the Nez Perce, whose homeland lay to the east of Cayuse country. Intertribal boundaries were permeable. Combined parties camped together at fishing stations in Cayuse country on the Grande Ronde River or in Nez Perce country on the

Wallowa; hunted together; intermarried; spoke each other's languages; and joined together in raids and war parties, particularly against the Shoshonean tribes to the south. Today, it is rare to find a member of the Confederated Tribes of the Cayuse, Umatilla, and Walla Walla who does not have ancestors from two or three or more tribal groups.[17]

Over time, the Cayuse became so closely affiliated with the Nez Perce that they lost their original language. Linguists divide the languages of the Plateau into two main families: Sahaptian (spoken by the Nez Perce, Walla Walla, Umatilla, Yakama, and others); and Salishan (spoken by the Flathead, Coeur d'Alene, Spokane, and others).[18] The Cayuse language was an "isolate," unrelated to either of the major groups. By the early 1800s most Cayuse spoke Nuumiipuutin, the Sahaptin language of the Nez Perce.[19] Marcus Whitman noted in 1837 that younger Cayuse did not understand the language of their ancestors at all. A linguist who visited the Confederated Tribes reservation in 1888 found only six people who spoke what has since been designated an extinct language.[20]

By making it easier to travel, horses greatly expanded the aboriginal trade network that was centered at Celilo Falls, the first of a ten-mile series of cataracts and cascades known collectively as The Dalles of the Columbia, where the river narrowed and squeezed and punched its way through the Cascade Mountains. For thousands of years Indians had gathered to fish, trade, gamble, and socialize at Celilo and adjacent sites. Horses extended the reach of this network, stretching it from Alaska to California and a thousand miles to the east. A dizzying array of goods could be found at what came to be called the Wall Street of the West: buffalo robes, grizzly claws, and parfleches (containers made of rawhide) from the Great Plains; obsidian and pipestone from the Great Basin; parrot feathers and turquoise from the Southwest; whale oil and ornamental shells (including the prized dentalium) from the Pacific coast. Manufactured goods made their way into the interior through coastal trade with European and American ships that came in search of sea otter and other furs. Cloth, metal, beads, and other items from distant factories ended up at the trade marts on the Columbia long before the first white people were seen there.[21]

It was not just white people's goods that flowed more freely into the Plateau after the horse revolution, but also their pathogens. Contact or "crowd" diseases such as smallpox and measles evolved along with the earliest civilizations in the Old World. People of European heritage had developed some degree of immunity to contagious diseases through long exposure, but the New World was "virgin soil"—that is, populated by people who had no experience with Old World viruses. The first smallpox pandemic (an epidemic that spreads beyond its initial point of infection) hit the Northwest around 1780. The consensus among anthropologists and ethnobiologists is that it broke out among tribes on the Great Plains and was carried west along trade routes. Historian Elliott West points out that it is not a coincidence that the pandemic occurred after the horse culture was fully established across the West. Earlier outbreaks, before horses, moved so slowly that the contagion burned itself out before reaching fresh populations. In contrast, "travel by hooves got the infection into virgin soil in time to set its horrors loose."[22]

It's not possible to know exactly how many Plateau Indians died during that first pandemic, but anthropologist Robert Boyd has concluded that the mortality rate was at least 30 percent, killing perhaps twenty-five thousand people.[23] A second pandemic, a generation later, may have been even more deadly. Drawing from oral histories, accounts by early white observers, and other sources, Boyd estimated that up to 45 percent of the regional population died as a result of smallpox by 1802, leaving only about forty thousand people alive out of a pre-epidemic population of some one hundred eighty thousand.[24] If the numbers are uncertain, the impact is clear. Whole villages were wiped out. Communities lost their leaders, their elders, their youngest members. Illness and death were traditionally understood as the result of spiritual transgression. Smallpox cut like a scythe through long-standing ideas about how the world was ordered, creating what Eugene Hunn called "a spiritual apocalypse."[25]

Plateau people had not yet had any direct contact with Euro-Americans. They did not associate the devastating new diseases with outsiders. "We had no belief that one Man could give [disease] to another, any more than a wounded Man could give his wound to another," one informant told fur trader David Thompson.[26] Instead, they seemed to interpret the epidemics as evidence that relations with the spirit world were out of whack and something drastic was needed to restore balance. Historian Christopher Miller has argued that the epidemics shattered old belief systems and gave rise to "a new thought pattern," based on prophecies that a powerful supernatural being would soon come to the earth, bringing an end to the world as it was known. But after that, one prophet predicted, "all the spirits of the dead" would be resurrected. "Then things will be made right and there will be much happiness." As Miller noted, there were remarkable similarities between the apocalyptic visions of the Indian prophets and the millennial preachings of the missionaries who showed up on the Plateau a few decades later.[27]

A central element in the new Plateau worldview was attributed to a Spokane prophet named Yureerachen (Circling Raven), whose son died of smallpox in 1782. Yureerachen is said to have retreated to a mountaintop after his son's death, where he had a vision of the coming of "white-skinned ones."[28] When he came down from the mountain, he reportedly proclaimed: "Soon there will come from the rising sun a different kind of men from any you have yet seen, who will bring with them a book, and will teach you everything, and after that the world will fall to pieces."[29] He assured his followers that the men would be friendly and would open the way to a restored and better world. To hasten their arrival, the people were to participate in a ceremony that came to be known as the Prophet Dance. Variations of the Prophet Dance spread across the Plateau, some coinciding with the smallpox epidemic of the 1780s, others appearing after the second epidemic, around 1800.[30] What all these prophetic movements seemed to have in common was a belief that a new kind of person would come soon from the east and great changes would follow.

Members of Meriwether Lewis and William Clark's Corps of Volunteers for Northwestern Discovery were the first "white-skinned ones" to have direct contact with the Cayuse and their neighbors. The expedition (which included Clark's black slave, York, a Shoshone woman named Sacagawea, and her young child) reached Plateau country in October 1805, a month after stumbling, half-starved, out of the Bitterroot Mountains onto the Weippe Prairie. A group of Nez Perce Indians there gave them food and valuable information about the region's geography, and helped them make canoes for the passage down the Clearwater and Snake Rivers to the Columbia and on to the coast. Two Nez Perce guides accompanied the party downriver. The guides were often sent ahead to announce the group's approach and prepare for ceremonial meetings. As word spread, hundreds of Indians gathered along the route, curious about the bearded strangers.

On October 18 members of the expedition camped near the mouth of the Walla Walla River, where a delegation of local Indians, probably including Cayuse, greeted them. The explorers' knowledge of which people they were meeting was not very precise. For one thing, they were in a hurry. For another, they were hearing languages they had never heard before, spoken by people with a tradition of intermarriage and cross-cultural connection. The leader of the group was a man the captains called Yelleppit or Yel-lep-pet. Clark described him as a "Great Chief" and "a bold handsom Indian, with a dignified countenance about 35 years of age, about 5 feet 8 inches high and well perpotiond [*sic*]." It's possible he was actually a Cayuse named Ollicutt (also spelled Allowcatt), who had a role in the fur trade a few years later. The word *yelépt* means "friend, blood brother" in Nez Perce and is similar to a Sahaptin word for "trading partner." He could have been simply trying to describe his role, not tell the captains his name. What seems clear is that this leader recognized the Americans as potentially valuable partners in trade.[31]

Yelleppit welcomed the party by sending over a gift of firewood (including dried sagebrush and willow), an important gesture in a virtually treeless land. The next morning, the captains reciprocated by giving him a small medal stamped with a portrait of President Thomas Jefferson, a handkerchief, and a string of wampum (beads made from the shells of East Coast mollusks). Yelleppit tried to persuade the captains to stay for at least another day, "a request that betrayed something more than just native curiosity about whites," in the words of Lewis and Clark scholar James Ronda. "The chief had his eye on the weapons and goods carried by the explorers."[32] The captains hurried on but promised to return in the spring, on their way back east.

As promised, the expedition returned in late April 1806. Clark marveled at the size and condition of the horse herds grazing on the hillsides as they traveled upriver. "It astonished me to See the order of their horses at this Season of the year," he wrote, "when I know they had wintered on dry grass of the plains and at the Same time rode with greater Severity than is Common among ourselves. I did not See a Single horse which Could be deemed pore, and maney of them were very fat."[33]

They reached Yelleppit's village, consisting of fifteen large tule mat lodges, on the evening of April 27. The headman told his people to offer the visitors fuel and food. He set an example by personally delivering an armful of wood and a platter of roasted fish. The bargaining began the next morning. Yelleppit opened the session by presenting Clark with "a very eligant white horse."[34] Clark offered his sword in return, along with some musket balls and a little gunpowder. By this point the Americans—who had come as explorers, not traders—had few items left to give to Indians. Yelleppit accepted the gifts and exacted an agreement that the expedition would stay at least another day. That evening, the headman hosted a grand feast and dance. Several hundred Indian men, women, and children attended, including a large contingent of Yakamas from neighboring villages to the north. Clark reported that much of the dancing was led by a shaman who had predicted the coming of people from the east. "We were told [he] was a Medesene man & Could foretell things," Clark wrote. "That he had told of our Comeing into their Country and was now about to Consult his God the moon if what we Said was the truth &c. &c."[35]

The Cayuse, in particular, had reasons for being interested in these powerful strangers. Their herds had multiplied, but they themselves had not. The population was probably not much more than five hundred at the time of first contact with non-Indians.[36] Mere accumulation of horses would not be enough to maintain their position of dominance; they needed new sources of power. White people had weapons that far surpassed the power of bows and arrows. They had blankets, beads, kettles, axes, knives, shiny medals, and other goods that not only made daily life more comfortable but also served as a way to display wealth and status. The very fact that white people had access to such wondrous things suggested, as historian Alexandra Harmon put it, that "they had relations with one or more particularly powerful non-mortal beings, and it behooved Indians to learn what they could about those beings and the way to get that power."[37] At least six of the members of the Lewis and Clark expedition could write, making strange marks on paper, a novelty with its own kind of magic. All this made the Cayuse receptive to the next wave of outsiders who came to their country—the fur traders.

The first to arrive was David Thompson, a London-born surveyor, mapmaker, and partner in the Montreal-based North West Company. Thompson was mapping the lower Columbia with a crew of seven other "Nor'Westers" in July 1811 when he met "the Chief of all the Shawpatin Tribes" near the junction of the Snake and Columbia Rivers. Thompson didn't identify him by name, but this "chief" may have been the same man Lewis and Clark called Yelleppit. Thompson thought he was "about forty years of age, say six feet in height, of a mild manly countenance good features and every way a handsome man, clean and well dressed." As translated by Thompson's interpreter, the man said his people needed "a Lodge for trading" so they could get guns, steel-tipped arrows, axes, knives, and "many other things which you have and which we very much want." Thompson promised that such a lodge would be built as soon as the fastest, safest way to deliver the goods could be found. He passed out tobacco and other gifts to seal the deal. He also put up a pole with a British flag and a sign, dated July 9, 1811, basically claiming exclusive rights to the fur trade north of the Columbia on behalf of Great Britain and "the N.W. Company of Merchants from Canada."[38]

A group of traders and clerks from John Jacob Astor's Pacific Fur Company found Thompson's flag and sign about a month later, to their surprise and irritation. Astor had become one of the wealthiest men in America through a business that began with a single fur shop in New York. In 1810 he sent two expeditions to the Northwest—one by ship, the other overland—in an effort to expand his global fur empire. The ship (the *Tonquin*) left New York in September 1810 and arrived at the mouth of the Columbia six months later, after a voyage that underscored some of the difficulties of supplying distant outposts in the West with manufactured goods from the East. Eight sailors died while trying to guide the *Tonquin* over the treacherous Columbia Bar, where the great river poured into the sea. Astor's overland party did not reach the coast until the following spring, after an excruciating journey that took the lives of five men.

The Astorians built a small compound, grandly named Fort Astoria, on the south bank of the Columbia, where the modern city of Astoria, Oregon, is now located. Then they sent a contingent upriver to establish trading relationships with Indians in the interior. The party included Alexander Ross, a twenty-seven-year-old Scotsman who left a job teaching school in Canada to seek his fortune in the fur business. On August 12, Ross and his companions encountered a group of about fifteen hundred Cayuses ("Cajouses," in his spelling), Nez Perces ("Shaw Haptens"), and Walla Wallas, camped at the mouth of the Walla Walla River. The Indians welcomed the traders with a grand procession: men and women dressed in their finest white deerskins, faces painted, clothing and moccasins richly decorated with beads, porcupine quills, and other ornaments. Ross noticed that the warriors, especially the Cayuse and Nez Perce, carried guns. After the procession the headmen and others of high status sat down with the traders, passed a ceremonial pipe, and gave speeches indicating a wish for peace, friendship, and white men's goods.[39]

Two days later, the Astorians found Thompson's flag, hoisted in the midst of an "immense" assembly of Indians, including some from the Walla Walla encampment. The Indian leaders said Thompson (known to them as "Koo-Koo-Sint," or "Stargazer") had given them presents to ensure that the Americans did not trade above the Snake River.

However, if the Americans gave them more than Thompson had, they could go where they pleased. The Indians were playing one group of outsiders (soon to be known as "Bostons") against another ("King George Men"), in a subtle dance born of long experience in intertribal trading.[40]

The outbreak of war between the United States and Britain in 1812 put an end to John Jacob Astor's ambitions in the Northwest. He liquidated the Pacific Fur Company in 1813 and sold its assets, including Fort Astoria, to the North West Company. Fort Astoria became Fort George. Many of the Astorians, including Ross, went to work for their former rival. But the long-promised trading post would not be built until 1818, a delay due in part to the theft of a silver goblet.

The goblet was a prize possession of John Clarke, a Pacific Fur Company partner. In late May 1813, Clarke and a dozen or so associates were en route to the coast with a load of furs when they met with a band of "Catatouch" Indians (actually Palouses). A vain, pompous man by all accounts, Clarke kept the goblet in a traveling case and liked to show it off. On this occasion he passed it to the headman, who passed it, like a precious pipe, to other warriors in a ceremonial circle. Everyone admired it. In the morning, however, the silver goblet was gone. Although it was later recovered, Clarke ordered that the suspected thief (who turned out to be a visiting Nez Perce) be hanged. The suspect's lodge was dismantled and the lodge poles used to make a scaffold in the shape of a tripod. The Indians watched, horrified, as the man was hanged on June 1, 1813. Then they mounted their horses and sped away, to spread the word about what had been done.[41]

Relationships between the fur traders and all the Sahaptian-speaking people on the Plateau remained tense for several years. At one point Ross and three of his men faced a council of chiefs from the Cayuse, Nez Perce, and four other "warlike" tribes. The Indians assailed the traders as "the men who kill our relations, the people who have caused us to mourn." An exchange of valued items was a customary way of resolving tensions after an incident non-Indians might classify as murder. In this case, the traders had to give up nearly all the goods they had with them before they were allowed to leave.[42]

In 1818, Cayuse and Walla Walla leaders granted Ross and his fellow Nor'Wester Donald McKenzie permission to build a post near the mouth of the Walla Walla, but only after extended negotiations. The chiefs demanded, first, that all the assembled Indians be given gifts. Next, they insisted that the traders pay for the timber they needed to build the post. Finally, they asked that the traders not provide any weapons to their enemies.[43] Ross distributed tobacco and other gifts, paid for the timber, promised to trade guns only to the Cayuse's allies, and was allowed to proceed with the construction of what was initially called Fort Nez Percés. The local inhabitants clearly had mixed feelings about having contact with new people who had proven to be dangerous and unpredictable. Alexandra Harmon, writing about the Indians of Puget Sound, made an observation that perhaps applied as well to the Cayuse: "To indigenous people, the King George men and Bostons were in many respects repulsive. Some were unnaturally pale; some had hairy faces. . . . They spoke languages as incomprehensible as birds' chirping. Nevertheless, the villagers respected the newcomers' manifest ability to acquire extraordinary riches and approved their interest in trading."[44]

Fort Nez Percés was located on the east bank of a bend in the Columbia, a half-mile above the mouth of the Walla Walla, on a wind-swept, grassy plain. The Columbia at that point was broad and placid, reminding Ross of a lake more than a river. To the south lay "wild hills and rugged bluffs" and "two singular towering rocks"— the basalt pillars known to whites as the Cayuse Sisters (and as Wáatpatukaykas, or Standing for the Spirits Place, to the Cayuse). Horses roamed over the plains; flocks of geese and other fowl flew overhead; salmon and sturgeon ruffled the river. Ross thought the country was "delightful beyond description."[45] But it was also virtually without timber. The crew of ninety-five laborers, sent up from Fort George (the former Astoria), had to travel up to one hundred miles to find wood and raft it back for the fort's double palisade, storehouse, and interior buildings.

Ross was named chief trader and stayed on in that position even after the North West Company was forced to merge with the London-based Hudson's Bay Company in 1821. The fort, known as Fort Walla Walla after the merger, became one of the most important trading posts in the interior. The shelves held an astonishing array of goods—"wool, flannel, calico, tobacco twists, tea bricks, sugar cones, mouth harps, thimbles, beads, nails, metal cups and kettles, guns, ball and powder, dice, needles, and hats"—in addition to knives and axes.[46] The Cayuse initially traded beaver they had caught for these desirable commodities.[47] As they trapped out the beaver in their own territory, they became middlemen, obtaining pelts from other Indians (mostly Spokane and Flathead—the Nez Perce thought that hunting small fur-bearing animals was a task suited only for women and slaves). The Cayuse also found a lucrative market for their horses. In the days before a cattle industry was established in Oregon Country, horses were an important source of meat as well as transportation. Records kept by the Hudson's Bay Company show that more than seven hundred were slaughtered to feed personnel at Fort Walla Walla between 1822 and 1825.[48]

Three decades after the Spokane prophet predicted the arrival of "a different kind of men from the rising sun," parts of his prophecy had come true. The fur trade had brought many different kinds of people into Plateau communities, greatly increasing the racial and ethnic diversity. The chief traders were mostly English or Scottish. The labor force included French Canadians, Iroquois, and other eastern Indians, along with Hawaiians (called Kanakas or Owyhees), recruited by ships' captains on their way to the Northwest coast. Many of the men, including the chief traders, entered into common-law marriages with Indian women. Native wives were invaluable assistants on the frontier. They set up and dismantled camps; collected firewood; gathered roots, berries, and other foods; cooked; cleaned and packed the furs; and made moccasins, snow-shoes, and clothing. They also helped strengthen social ties between the traders and local people. Both the North West Company and the Hudson's Bay Company accepted and even encouraged these relationships, although there were no priests or ministers to solemnize them in the Euro-American fashion. The traders' métis (mixed-race) children, connected to two worlds, often grew up bilingual and took on roles as interpreters.

A primary communication tool between these disparate groups was Chinook Jargon, a simple trade argot of about one thousand words, based on the Chinookan spoken by indigenous people on the lower Columbia but including terms from English, French, Nootkan, Russian, and other languages. The grammar was easy to learn. The vocabulary was limited but functional enough for basic commerce. Authorities differ on the origin of the jargon but agree that it was disseminated by the fur trade. Missionaries and settlers would rely on it long after the traders were gone.

The fur trade also introduced elements of Christianity to the Plateau. Members of the eastern Iroquois Confederacy, long exposed to Catholic doctrine, traveled west with the traders, lived with local Indians, and taught them prayers, rituals, and Bible stories. In 1823 the Hudson's Bay Company mandated that everyone at its forts, including non-Indians, attend Sunday services.[49] Rudimentary instruction in western religion was considered useful in promoting "good conduct and right living" among the Indians, and the whites were supposed to model good behavior.[50] Many traders were practicing Christians themselves and took their beliefs with them into Indian country. David Thompson and Alexander Ross were both devout Protestants. Pierre Pambrun, a French Canadian who took over as head of Fort Walla Walla in 1832, was an active promoter of Catholic doctrine. Each winter he taught the Lord's Prayer, translated into Chinook Jargon, to one of the chiefs. The Indians would dance in cadence while the chief chanted the prayer, blending new practices and old rituals.[51]

John K. Townsend, a young American naturalist who visited a large Cayuse village on the Umatilla River in July 1836, was surprised to learn that Indians there gathered for "divine service" every day at sunrise and again in the evening.[52] Narcissa Whitman remarked on the same thing shortly after she and her husband, Marcus, established their mission at "Wieletpoo" a few months later. "The Cayuses as well as the Nez Perces are very strict in attending to their worship which they have regularly every morning at day break & eve at twilight and once on the Sab," she wrote. "They sing & repeat a form of prayers very devoutly after which the Chief gives them a talk."[53]

If parts of the Indian prophecies had come true, others were yet to be fulfilled. For people who were, in scholar Christopher Miller's words, "looking forward to the end of the world" and its subsequent renewal, the pace must have been frustratingly slow.[54] The prophet had spoken of "a book" and men who "will teach you everything." Perhaps it was a quest for those last two elements that led four Plateau Indians to travel to Saint Louis with an American fur caravan in the fall of 1831. It's also possible that they undertook the journey for simple economic reasons. The Hudson's Bay Company had steadily reduced its terms of trade, charging more for what it sold to Indians and paying less for what the Indians offered in trade. The delegates to Saint Louis might have been seeking American traders who could undercut their British competitors. Whatever their actual objectives, the story that eventually began to circulate was that Indians in the West wanted missionaries to come and teach them about "the white man's Book of Heaven." It was this "Macedonian cry" (a reference to the Apostle Paul, who dreamed that a stranger asked him to "Come over to Macedonia and help us") that brought the Whitmans and their fellow missionaries to Oregon Country.

Historian Alvin Josephy has pieced together what little is known about the four men. Their leader was a Nez Perce called Speaking Eagle, about forty-four years old. Traveling with him was Man of the Morning, also in his forties, the son of a Nez Perce buffalo hunter and a Flathead woman. Two young Nez Perces, Rabbit Skin Leggings and Horns Worn Down, both about twenty, completed the group. They all came from an area in present-day Idaho where many people still warmly remembered the 1805 and 1806 visits of Lewis and Clark.[55] The travelers arrived in Saint Louis in October 1831 and found their way to the house and office of William Clark, then superintendent for Indian affairs for western tribes.

Clark was in no mood to be gracious to his visitors. The Indian Removal Act, forcing Indians in the southeast to move to land west of the Mississippi River, had been signed into law by President Andrew Jackson just one year earlier. Clark was inundated by Indians protesting the policy. He made only two brief references to the people from the Plateau, whom he mistakenly identified as "Shoshones." In a report to Lewis Cass, secretary of war, dated November 20, 1831, Clark said he was "surrounded" by hundreds of Indians, "all expecting a satisfactory adjustment of their difficulties," including some "from west of the Rocky Mountains."[56] In a private letter to Cass a few days later, Clark complained about being "harassed by Indians from different directions" and mentioned in passing that "a deputation of Shoshones are here."[57]

The four Indians spoke no English, and Clark understood virtually nothing of their language. They tried to communicate their thoughts with sign language. Before they could make any real progress, the two senior members of the delegation became sick and died. Both were given last rites by a Catholic priest and buried in the Saint Louis parish cemetery.[58] The other two travelers stayed until the following spring, when they left Saint Louis on the steamboat *Yellowstone*. The artist George Catlin was on board and painted their portraits while they traveled up the Missouri toward their homeland. One of them died before they reached the mouth of the Yellowstone River; the other apparently reached home safely but then vanished from the historical record.[59]

Among the people thronging William Clark's quarters in the fall of 1831 were six Wyandot Indians from Ohio, a tribe facing forced removal to Kansas. Their spokesman was William Walker. Fifteen months later, Walker wrote a letter to Gabriel P. Disoway of New York City, a major financial backer of the Methodist Missionary Society. The Wyandot party had arrived in Saint Louis shortly after the four Nez Perces. Walker said that he had seen one of the Indians, who was quite ill. He also said Clark had told him the Indians had wanted to get "a book containing directions" about the proper way to worship "the supreme Being." Disoway sent Walker's letter to the *Christian Advocate and Journal and Zion's Herald*, a widely distributed weekly published in New York City by the Methodist Episcopal Church. The paper printed the letter, along with a lengthy and florid elaboration from Disoway, on March 1, 1833. The crux was that "these wandering sons of our native forests" were in desperate need of missionaries who would have "the courage to penetrate into their moral darkness." A subsequent editorial asked: "Who will respond to the call from beyond the Rocky Mountains?"[60] The *Christian Advocate* published a number of other enthusiastic and woefully uninformed letters in the following weeks and months. Not one seriously challenged the idea that tens of thousands of Indians in the West were yearning for Christian conversion. "This credulity might seem touching or amusing," historian Albert Furtwangler observed, "but it soon carried dozens of young men and women into months of hardship, sickness, and frustration, and led many of them and their children into early graves."[61]

The first to respond to the call were Methodists: Jason Lee, a tall, black-bearded, thirty-one-year-old minister; his twenty-seven-year-old nephew, Daniel Lee; and three associates. Traveling west with an expedition led by Boston merchant Nathaniel J. Wyeth, they reached a Cayuse village on the Walla Walla River in August 1834. The Cayuse greeted them warmly, gave them horses, and urged them to stay. "The hospitality shown us was worthy of their pretensions as a governing tribe," Daniel Lee remembered.[62] The Methodists, however, moved on and eventually built a mission in the Willamette Valley.

The next year, Rev. Samuel Parker, a Presbyterian, passed through on reconnaissance for the Boston-based American Board of Commissioners for Foreign Missions. Again, Cayuse headmen welcomed the stranger. Parker told them he had come to select a site for a mission that would include a school and a "preaching house." He promised that every year a ship loaded with trade goods would arrive, and the contents would be divided among the Indians as payment for the use of their land. This promise would prove to have serious repercussions in years to come, after the Cayuse welcomed the Whitmans into their realm and waited for payments that never came.

CHAPTER THREE

THE MISSIONARIES

These people who came west to "civilize" the heathen—
what made them decide to do that? To me it's completely
irrational to go into somebody else's country and try to
tell them how to think, how to pray, how to live, how to
raise their children.

—*Roberta Conner, director, Tamástslikt Cultural Institute*

Marcus and Narcissa Whitman and most of their fellow missionaries came from an area of western New York widely known as the
Burned-over District because of the waves of evangelistic fervor that
swept over it in the nineteenth century. The phrase was attributed to
Charles G. Finney, a Connecticut-born preacher who pioneered the
kind of religious revivals that became commonplace in the region
during the 1820s and 1830s. The revivals were characterized by fiery
sermons, public confessions of sin, weeping, praying, and collec-
tive conversions. Some lasted for weeks—to the point, it was said,
that there was little "fuel" (unsaved souls) left to "burn" (convert

to Christianity). These events particularly enthralled Narcissa, but both she and Marcus had what is known as a conversion experience during a revival, as did Henry and Eliza Spalding. All four of them embraced the "Great Commission"—a biblical mandate to "go ye into all the world, and preach the gospel to every creature"—a standard exhortation from the revivalist pulpit.

The upsurge in evangelism coincided with an accelerated movement of Euro-Americans westward. In 1830 the United States was still a small country, consisting of only twenty-four states (all but two of them east of the Mississippi River), and the borders with British Canada and Mexico were in dispute. But there were those who believed it was the nation's "manifest destiny" to colonize all the land from coast to coast, as far north as the fifty-fourth parallel and deep into Mexican territory to the south. That the land was already occupied, and had been for thousands of years, was not a deterrent. Estimates of the indigenous population then living within what is now the continental United States vary wildly and amount to little more than guesses. Lewis Cass, secretary of war under President Andrew Jackson from 1831 to 1836, used the number 313,130 (including 105,060 Indians east of the Mississippi and another 208,070 to the west). Other calculations ranged from 472,000 to nearly 600,000 total. Not in dispute was the fact that the population had been decimated since the arrival of non-Indians. "That the Indians have diminished, and are diminishing, is known to all who have directed their attention to the subject," wrote Cass, a central figure in the implementation of the Indian Removal Act. The law, signed by Jackson in 1830, authorized the president to negotiate treaties with eastern tribes to relocate them west of the Mississippi, outside the existing borders of the United States. "And these are the remnants of the primitive people, who only two centuries ago, possessed this vast country; who found in the sea, the lakes, the rivers, and forests, means of subsistence sufficient for their wants," Cass added.[1]

Cass was among those who defended the Indian Removal Act as a benevolent measure. By forcing Indians to move away from areas of white settlement, he argued, the government could ensure that at least some "remnants" of the population would survive. Otherwise, they would be doomed to extinction. George Catlin, a Pennsylvania-born artist who spent years painting Indians of the Great Plains, went a step further. He called for the creation of a sort of theme park—a vast western preserve where Indians could live in unmolested harmony with nature, and tourists could stop by to view the quaint ways of the "specimens." Catlin seized upon this idea during a trip to the Dakotas in 1832 and continued to refine it as he traveled around the Plains throughout the decade, painting Indians and collecting artifacts. He presented a fully articulated vision in his 1841 masterwork, *Letters and Notes on the Manners, Customs and Condition of the North American Indians*. He imagined "a magnificent park, where the world could see for ages to come, the native Indian in his classic attire, galloping his wild horse, with sinewy bow, and shield and lance, amid the fleeting herds of elks and buffaloes." It would be "a nation's Park, containing man and beast, in all the wild and freshness of their nature's beauty!"[2]

Catlin was a sentimentalist, full of romanticized regrets about the dismal prospects facing the "children of the forest."[3] Evangelicals like the Whitmans and their associates were determined to save Indian souls and believed the best way to do that was to strip them of every vestige of their traditional way of life. They were convinced that if Indians were to survive in a country increasingly dominated by whites, and eventually enjoy a satisfactory afterlife, they had to live like white people: learn English, cut their hair, wear European clothing, become farmers, and convert to Christianity. "We point them with one hand to the Lamb of God," Henry Spalding wrote, "and with the other to the hoe."[4]

Three prevailing principles guided the missionaries: that Christianity equaled civilization and vice versa; that "the dear heathen" were living in a savage and degraded state because they did not know God; and before the Indians could fully know God, they needed to embrace white culture. Eliza Spalding wrote about her eagerness to bring "the blessings of civilization and religion" to Indians.[5] Henry Spalding insisted: "The only thing that can save them from annihilation is the introduction of civilization."[6] Few Euro-Americans at the time would have questioned the assumption that Christianity was the basis for "civilization." As historian Elliott West has observed, "religious conversion and cultural transformation were parts of one process, fully entangled."[7] The two objectives fed each other. The initial impulse that motivated these missionaries was evangelistic. They were idealists who deeply believed that the unsaved would spend eternity in the fires of hell if they were not converted to Christianity. But over time, they became unapologetic agents of what some scholars today call "settler colonialism." Marcus Whitman put it bluntly in an 1844 letter to relatives in New York: "I have no doubt our greatest work is to be to aid the white settlement of this country and help to found its religious institutions."[8]

People who knew Marcus Whitman said he looked something like his brothers and nephews. In photos, the faces of these men are characterized by sharp cheekbones, overhanging eyebrows, thin lips, downturned mouths, and large, angular noses. None of them bear any resemblance to the hunky figure memorialized in bronze and representing Washington State in the US Capitol's National Statuary Hall. Some acquaintances said that Whitman was tall; others that he was of medium height. Some remembered his eyes as blue; others, gray. There was general agreement that he was lean ("raw boned," by

Paul Kane created these small pencil sketches sometime during his two-year odyssey to document indigenous life in the Northwest in the 1840s. He never identified the subjects, but in 1968, an amateur historian and Whitman enthusiast in New York argued that they could have been Marcus and Narcissa Whitman. *Used with permission of the Royal Ontario Museum © ROM; 946.15.293 and 946.15.299.*

one account), with slightly stooped posture.[9] He suffered frequent bouts of ill health; his initial application to become a missionary in 1834 was rejected because he was considered too frail. He occasionally wore leather "pantaloons" when riding horseback in Oregon Country, but he would have been appalled to be portrayed in buckskins—a material he associated with "heathen" culture. He preferred to dress in the woolen coats and trousers favored by the professional men of his era. An inventory of his clothing after his death included a "superfine" coat valued at $45 ($1,250 in 2020 dollars) and a "silk velvet vest" valued at $8 ($222). His total wardrobe was worth more than $325 (nearly $10,000)—making him considerably better dressed than the frontiersman on the pedestal in Statuary Hall.[10]

Marcus Whitman was born in a log cabin in Federal Hollow (later renamed Rushville), in the Finger Lakes region of upstate New York, on September 4, 1802, the third of Beza and Alice Green Whitman's six children. Federal Hollow, located on land that had once been farmed by Seneca Indians, had been chartered as a town just a few years earlier. Beza, a shoemaker and tanner, and Alice, both natives of western Massachusetts, moved to the settlement in the fall of 1800. Beza built the town's first tannery, producing the leather that he used in his shoemaking business. He was prosperous enough to move his growing family from the log cabin into a large frame house five years later. The family lived in only part of the house; the rest of the building was used as an inn and tavern. Alice managed the tavern and also helped out in the little shop, opposite the house, where Beza made shoes.

Growing up in rustic conditions in a newly settled village, Marcus acquired skills in self-sufficiency that would serve him well on the western frontier. He chopped wood, tended animals, learned basic carpentry, and helped his parents with other chores. "I was accustomed to tend a carding machine when I was a boy," he recalled in a letter written in 1846, referring to a device used to prepare wool for spinning.[11] As historian Clifford Drury has pointed out, Whitman rarely reflected on his past. Of his 175 surviving letters, this was the only one to mention an experience in early boyhood. That reticence might be partly explained by the emotionally challenging circumstances of his later childhood.

Beza Whitman died on April 7, 1810, at age thirty-seven, leaving Alice with five children under age twelve. A few months later she sent Marcus, then eight, to live with his grandfather, Samuel Whitman, and uncle, Freedom Whitman, in the village of Cummington, in western Massachusetts. Alice, according to one of her grandchildren, "never spent any time in sentiment."[12] The boy's new guardians were devout Baptists. Marcus described them as "pious" men who "gave me constant religious instruction and care."[13] He lived with these relatives for five years. He was thirteen when he returned to Federal Hollow for the first time since leaving home, arriving at the family house unexpectedly around twilight and knocking on the door. No one recognized Marcus, including his mother. He was a total stranger to his seven-year-old sister, also named Alice, who had been only two years old when he left. As his sister told the story to her own daughter many years later, when Marcus saw his mother, he said, "How do you do, Mother?" She replied, "I'm no mother to you," and he burst into tears.[14]

During her son's absence, Marcus's mother had remarried and given birth to two more children. Her new husband, Calvin Loomis, had taken over Beza's businesses: the tannery, the shoe shop, and the tavern. Marcus stayed only about three weeks before returning to Massachusetts. His grandfather arranged for him to live with a family in Plainfield, near Cummington, where Marcus attended a school taught by the pastor of the local Congregational church. Among his fellow students was the abolitionist John Brown. During this period Marcus embraced the Calvinistic theology that would govern the rest of his life.

At age seventeen Marcus had a conversion experience. "I was awakened to a sense of my sin and danger and brought by Divine grace to rely on the Lord Jesus for pardon and salvation," he wrote, in words typical of other "converts" in the Burned-over District.[15] He wanted to become a minister. However, both the Congregational and the related Presbyterian denominations required that their ministers be well-educated, with four years of college and at least two years in a theological seminary before they could be ordained. Six years of schooling would be expensive, and Whitman's family could give him little, if any, financial help. In addition, his mother, who was not particularly devout and never joined a church, was not sympathetic to his ministerial ambitions. He would later chastise her for insufficient piety.[16]

When he was eighteen, Whitman moved back to his hometown (which by then had been renamed Rushville). He lived in his mother's house and worked in his stepfather's tannery and shoe shop until he "attained his majority" (in the terminology of the day) on his twenty-first birthday. At that point, Whitman apprenticed himself to a local doctor—the first step toward becoming a physician. In contrast to the lengthy training needed to become an ordained minister, a license to practice medicine could be obtained after only two years of "riding" with a doctor and a sixteen-week session at a medical school.

Whitman completed his apprenticeship and enrolled for the fall term at the College of Physicians and Surgeons in Fairfield, New York, in 1825. His education there consisted mostly of reading textbooks and listening to lectures. There were virtually no laboratory facilities and no hospital or clinic nearby where students could gain hands-on experience. Cultural taboos restricted the use of human bodies for dissection. Under a law passed by the New York State Legislature in 1820, unclaimed bodies of convicts who had died in the Auburn State Prison could be given to Fairfield College for dissection, but it was still rare for students to have legal access to a cadaver. Anatomy, like other subjects in the medical school, was taught mostly by lectures. Whitman finished his term on January 23, 1826, and received a medical license the following May. He had not yet earned the right to put MD behind his name: the doctor of medicine degree required a second sixteen-week course at a medical school. He would return to Fairfield for a second term in 1831. Meanwhile, he temporarily took over a medical practice in Pennsylvania for a former classmate, then opened a practice of his own in a village west of Niagara Falls in Canada.

Whitman did not, however, give up his dream of becoming a minister. After less than two years in Canada, he returned to Rushville and began studying theology under Rev. Joseph Brackett, pastor of the Rushville Congregational Church. "I had not continued long when for want of active exercise I found my health become impaired by a pain in the left side which I attributed to an inflammation of the spleen," he wrote. He "resorted to remidies [sic] with apparently full relief" and resumed his studies, but the pain persisted. Eventually, "I found I was not able to study & returned to the practice of my profession."[17] Whitman's biographer, Clifford Drury, speculates that Whitman probably realized he was too old, at twenty-eight, to spend years studying for the ministry. He could go back to medical school for another four months, earn his MD degree, and make a reasonable living as a doctor.

Whitman reenrolled in the college at Fairfield in the fall of 1831. He completed another course of lectures; submitted a thesis on the topic of "caloric" (referring to the causes of heat in the body); and, on January 24, 1832, was awarded his degree. By the standards of his day, Whitman was a well-trained physician. Licensed in both New York state and in Canada, he had spent several years practicing medicine in frontier communities and was now fully credentialed. He established a practice in Wheeler, New York—a hamlet of about twenty-five families, forty miles south of Rushville. Initially, he lived in the home of an elder of the Wheeler Presbyterian Church. At some point Whitman bought a 150-acre farm, about midway between Wheeler and the nearby town of Prattsburg, and built a log cabin there.

As an itinerant country doctor, Whitman traveled widely around the region, on horseback, with his medical supplies in saddlebags. One of his staple "medications" was calomel, a compound of mercury and chlorine, which was widely used as a purgative in the nineteenth century. Medical theory of the era held that disease was often caused by an excess of blood or other bodily fluids. Whitman frequently bled his patients (as well as himself) and administered purgatives in an effort to restore balance to the body's "humors." Like other small-town doctors, he served as his own pharmacist. He bought drugs in crude form in bulk, pulverized them with a mortar, and produced his own pills. He owned a set of amputating knives and surgical saws. He also had a dental kit that included peg-type false teeth.

At thirty, Whitman was socially reserved, with what many thought a stern demeanor. His surviving letters, both personal and professional, reflect a man with a strong sense of purpose. He also could be thin-skinned, defensive, and, especially in his later years, self-aggrandizing. He wrote well but spelled badly. His social life revolved around the church. He was a trustee of the Wheeler Presbyterian Church, taught Sunday school, was active in the American Bible Society, and regularly attended sunrise prayer meetings with other young men. Rev. Joel Wakeman, a Presbyterian minister and friend of Whitman's, remembered him as "a strong temperance man" who campaigned tirelessly against the use of alcohol.[18] Whitman probably did not approve of his mother's tavern business.

Not long after moving to Wheeler, Whitman began to consider the possibility of becoming a medical missionary. He was heavily influenced by Elisha Loomis, a native of Rushville who had served as a missionary in Hawaii for the American Board of Commissioners for Foreign Missions. The first organized missionary society in the United States, founded in 1810 and based in Boston, the board sponsored Presbyterian and Congregational missions around the world. After Loomis returned to Rushville in 1832, he often spoke in area churches, proselytizing about mission life. He found a receptive listener in Marcus Whitman.

Whitman first applied for a position as a missionary with the American Board in the spring of 1834. The board asked whether he would accept an appointment to the Marquesas Islands in the South Pacific. He declined, saying he had "some fears of a hot climate."[19] After several exchanges of letters, the board rejected his application, partly because of concerns about Whitman's health and partly because he was single (the board preferred to send only married men to its missions, hoping to shield them from temptations involving native women). He reapplied six months later, at the urging of Rev. Samuel Parker, a preacher from Ithaca, New York, who was on a one-man campaign to send missionaries to "save" Indians in the West.

Parker had been galvanized by the story of the four Indians who had shown up in Saint Louis in a supposed search for the "white man's Book of Heaven." He was fifty-five years old, with a sick wife, three children, and no wilderness experience. Nonetheless, he asked the American Board to send him to Oregon Country in the spring of 1834. The board, citing Parker's age and family responsibilities, declined. Described by a colleague as someone who was "exceedingly set in his opinions" and "inclined to self-applause," Parker tried to make it on his own.[20] He got as far as Saint Louis but had to turn back.

The board was not eager to establish a mission in Oregon. For one thing, its financial resources for new enterprises were limited. It was already supporting eighty individual outposts in Africa, China, India, and elsewhere around the world. Board members seemed ready to cede Oregon to one of their evangelical rivals, the Methodist Mission Board, sponsored by the Missionary Society of the Methodist Episcopal Church. A party of Methodists led by Rev. Jason Lee was already on its way to Oregon, with an expedition organized by Nathaniel Wyeth, a Boston ice merchant who hoped to make a fortune in the fur trade. Lee and his associates would establish a mission in the Willamette Valley, near present-day Salem, in September 1834.

Meanwhile, Parker continued badgering the board until it finally agreed to sponsor an exploratory journey to Oregon, but only if he could recruit volunteers and raise most of the money himself. Parker was nearing the end of a mostly fruitless tour of churches in western New York in late November 1834 when he stopped in Wheeler. Whitman was among those who heard him speak. The two men later met privately. "I have had an interview with the Rev. Samuel Parker upon the subject of Missions and have determined to offer myself to the Am. Board to accompany him on his Mission beyond the Rocky Mountains," Whitman wrote in a December 2, 1834, letter to the board. "My health is so much restored that I think it will offer no impediment," he added.[21]

After leaving Wheeler, Parker traveled about forty-five miles west to Amity, a rustic village on the Genesee River. Speaking in a log building that served as both schoolhouse and church, he repeated his plea for missionaries to go to Oregon. His audience included Narcissa Prentiss, a twenty-six-year-old unmarried Sunday school teacher who had recently moved to Amity with her parents and siblings. She too volunteered. Parker thought it unlikely that the American Board would accept an application from a single woman. Nonetheless, he sent a query to David Greene, secretary of the board. "Are females wanted?" he asked. "A Miss Narcissa Prentiss of Amity is very anxious to go to the heathen. Her education is good—piety conspicuous," Greene demurred, writing, "I don't think we have missions among the Indians where unmarried females are valuable just now."[22]

Narcissa Prentiss was a model of piety. She had her first conversion experience when she was eleven and another at sixteen. Her mother, a devout pillar of Presbyterianism, did not allow her to read novels or other "light and vain trash," but Narcissa found stimulation and escape in romanticized biographies of such women as Harriet Newell, a missionary who went to India with her husband in 1812 and died an early, celebrated death.[23] She avidly read letters from missionaries published in the monthly *Missionary Herald*. She began to think about becoming a missionary herself when she was still in her early teens. "I frequently desired to go to the heathen," she wrote in a letter to the American Board, although initially "only half-heartedly." Narcissa vividly remembered the date when she decided to "consecrate" herself "without reserve" to missionary work: "the first Monday of Jan. 1824," after a revival.[24] When Samuel Parker showed up in her local church a decade later, she was ready to answer the call.

Narcissa was born on March 14, 1808, in Prattsburg, the third of nine children (and the eldest daughter) of Stephen and Clarissa Prentiss. Her parents were among the town's first settlers. Stephen had cleared land for a small farm there in 1805; he later took over the operation of a sawmill and gristmill. A carpenter, he used lumber from the sawmill to build houses for the community. Sometime before Narcissa's birth, he built a modest frame house, a story and a half high, for his growing family. The house still stands, although in a different location, and is maintained as a historic site in Prattsburg (now spelled Prattsburgh).

Rev. Joel Wakeman, who knew both the Whitman and the Prentiss families, described Stephen Prentiss as tall, "a little inclined to corpulency," and "remarkably reticent for a man of his intelligence and standing." Stephen served one term as a county judge and thereafter claimed the title Judge Prentiss. His business activities included, for a while, a distillery, much to his wife's disapproval. Clarissa was "fleshy and queenly in her deportment," someone who "possessed great weight of Christian character." Both were reserved and solemn in public. "It was a rare thing," Wakeman wrote, for either to "indulge in laughter."[25]

Clarissa took the lead in her family's religious life. She became a charter member of the Prattsburg Presbyterian Church when it was built in 1807 and later helped organize the Female Home Missionary Society of Prattsburg. She enrolled all her children in the local Youth Missionary Society. Stephen helped build the church but did not join it until 1817. He left after just a few years, in a tussle that may have involved the issue of temperance, and did not return to the fold until 1831. He had given up his interests in the distillery by then, apparently fearing the effect of drinking on his sons.[26]

Prattsburg in the 1820s was a fairly isolated community, with a population of about fourteen hundred. Roads were primitive, manufactured goods hard to come by. Families had to be self-sufficient. Narcissa learned how to weave and spin, sew, cook over an open fire, and make soap and candles. She was comparatively well-educated for a woman of her generation. She was a member of the first class of women to be enrolled in the Franklin Academy, a church-affiliated secondary school in Prattsburg. She completed one twenty-one-week term in April 1828, when she was twenty, and returned for a second term two years later. Among her fellow students at that time was an aspiring missionary named Henry Harmon Spalding.

Narcissa's surviving letters and journal show that she was a graceful, accomplished writer. In different circumstances and in a different era, she might have found success in the literary world. But her options were limited. She briefly taught kindergarten in two nearby schools, but by 1832 she was living at home and helping her mother with household chores. She spent most of her twenties "waiting the leadings of Providence concerning me," as she put it.[27]

The average American woman in the 1830s was married by twenty-one; Narcissa was approaching spinsterhood as she waited for directions from Providence.

Narcissa's friends and acquaintances described her as a woman of medium height, about five feet five and, like her mother, somewhat "fleshy." She had fair skin, gray-blue eyes, and thick, tawny hair, which she parted in the middle and wore in a tight bun at the back of her neck. Her eyes often troubled her; she needed glasses for reading and sewing. She had erect posture and usually dressed severely, in plain, high-necked, long-sleeved, full-skirted dresses. She was widely admired for the quality of her singing voice—a clear, strong soprano, which she used to good effect in church services. "She was not a beauty," wrote Rev. Wakeman, "and yet when engaged in singing or conversation there was something in her appearance very attractive."[28]

As the eldest daughter in a large family, Narcissa had many household responsibilities and few idle hours. Her social life, like Marcus's, revolved around the church. She taught Sunday school. She hosted women's prayer meetings in her home. She continued to dream of becoming a missionary in an exotic place. Still, she could do little to shape her own future beyond hope for a marriage proposal from a man who shared her values. As she discovered, single women did not receive appointments from the American Board. If Narcissa were to "go to the heathen," she would have to do so as the wife of a missionary.

⁓

In mid-January 1835, Marcus Whitman learned that the board had appointed him as an "assistant missionary" to accompany Parker on a scouting expedition to the West in the spring. He made arrangements to sell his farm and close his medical practice. He then briefly visited Parker, who had returned to his home in Ithaca; Parker told him about the would-be female missionary in Amity and suggested he call on her. Whitman had already indicated that he was willing to "take a wife, if the service of the board would admit."[29] When he found out that Narcissa was willing to go to Oregon, he may have seen it as a sign that Providence intended them to go together as husband and wife.

Marcus Whitman and Narcissa Prentiss were born within twenty-five miles of each other and had spent most of their lives in the same general area of New York. Marcus had once attended a prayer meeting in the Prentiss home, but Narcissa was living and teaching kindergarten in a nearby community at the time.[30] They apparently did not meet each other until February 21, 1835, when Marcus arrived in Amity. They spent only a few hours together, spread out over the next two days, but by the time he left, they were engaged. The two would not see each other again for nearly a year.

In Saint Louis, Whitman and Parker met with officials of the American Fur Company and received grudging permission to travel with the company's caravan to the Rocky Mountain rendezvous, an annual gathering of trappers, traders, and Indians. The two men hoped to find Indian guides there who could help them explore the region and locate potential mission sites. From Saint Louis they took a steamboat to Liberty, Missouri, about four hundred miles upriver, where the caravan was being assembled. Writing to Narcissa on April 30, 1835, shortly before the caravan left Liberty, Whitman said he thought the trip across the Great Plains and over the Rockies would be easier than he and Parker had expected. "Many obstacles to our journey as conceived by us do not exist," he wrote. "We are assured of abundant protection until we shall have passed the mountains, and beyond the mountains we are told we shall not have much to fear from the Indians."[31]

The caravan that year included about sixty rough-edged, hard-drinking, unchurched fur traders, hunters, and voyageurs, hauling tons of supplies to exchange for pelts at the rendezvous. The missionaries disapproved of their intemperate habits, and the men, in turn, resented the presence of the missionaries. "Very evident tokens gave us to understand that our company was not agreeable, such as the throwing of rotten eggs at me," Whitman wrote to Greene, the board's secretary, with what might have been a touch of dry humor.[32] Parker was even more disliked. A Hudson's Bay Company trader memorably described him as "a missionary from the United States of the presbiterian [sic] persuasion who sends us all to Hell—honest man—with as little ceremony as I would (at this moment for I am very hungry) drive a rump steak into my bread basket."[33]

Whitman gained a measure of respect after an outbreak of cholera forced the caravan to halt for about three weeks near present-day Council Bluffs, Iowa. More than a dozen men, including the caravan's commander, were sickened, and three eventually died.[34] Whitman had had no direct experience treating the disease—a severe infection of the intestines, spread by contaminated food or water—but he knew enough to associate it with lack of cleanliness. He recommended that the men be moved from a camp in a low-lying area bordering the Missouri River to "a clean and healthy situation" on higher ground. In a letter to Narcissa, he attributed the outbreak to the traders' consumption of alcohol and dirty water. "It is not strange that they should have the cholera," he wrote, "because of their intemperance, their sunken and filthy situation."[35]

The caravan reached the rendezvous site, on the Green River in western Wyoming, on August 12, 1835, several weeks later than expected, due in part to the cholera outbreak. Thousands of Indians and several hundred trappers were waiting, impatiently. It would have been an impressive sight: Indians, trappers, and too many horses to count, in a shifting mosaic of color and motion, spread out over a long, broad meadow. If Whitman was awed, he didn't confide it in his travel diary. "Arrived at rendezvous on Green river," he reported, laconically. "Most of the traders and trappers of the mountains are here, and about two thousand Shoshoni or Snake Indians, and forty lodges of Flathead & Napiersas [Nez Perce], and a few Utaws [Utes]."[36]

News that a doctor had arrived spread quickly. The next day, Whitman removed a three-inch iron arrowhead from the back of Jim Bridger, one of the most celebrated "mountain men" of the frontier era. The operation—performed without anesthesia—was not an easy one for either patient or physician. The arrowhead had been lodged in Bridger's body for three years, a reminder of a skirmish with Blackfeet Indians. It had hooked into a bone and "a cartilaginous substance" had grown around it. Its removal impressed the trappers and Indians who gathered around to watch. Whitman also dug an arrowhead from the shoulder of one of the caravan's hunters. After that, Parker wrote, "calls for medical and surgical aid were almost incessant."[37] Both Jim Bridger and another mountain man, Joe Meek, would later send their young, mixed-race daughters to school at the Whitman Mission.

Neither Whitman nor Parker had direct, firsthand knowledge about the Indians that they hoped to evangelize. Their primary source of information turned out to be Sir William Drummond Stewart, a Scottish nobleman who had been adventuring in the American West for three years. Stewart had worked, traveled, and formed friendships with a number of luminaries in the fur trade, including Bridger and Meek. He had attended two previous rendezvous and had a trader's understanding of the social geography of the region. Stewart told the missionaries that the Flathead and Nez Perce were "very friendly to the whites and not addicted to steal," that they lived in "fertile vallies [sic] capable of good cultivation," and that any missionaries who settled among them "would be free from hostile attacks from other tribes."[38]

Apparently on Stewart's advice, Whitman and Parker met with a group of Nez Perce and Flathead headmen on August 16. Through an interpreter—a trapper named Charles Compo, a French Canadian married to a Nez Perce woman—they received the impression that the Indians were eager to have missionaries come and live on their lands. The headmen "expressed great pleasure in seeing us and strong desires to be taught," Whitman wrote in his travel diary, later sent to the American Board.[39] He and Parker decided to split up. Whitman would return east with the fur company and arrange to bring a party of missionaries to Oregon the next year; Parker would continue traveling west, scouting locations.

Parker, escorted by Compo, Compo's wife, and a group of Nez Perces, left a few days later. Whitman stayed on for another week. During that time he met a Nez Perce boy named Tackitonitis (also written "Tack-i-too-tis") who spoke a little English. Whitman wanted to take him east so he could learn more English and serve as an interpreter for the missionaries. After some discussion, the boy's father agreed. Whitman immediately began trying to acculturate the youth, renaming him "Richard." A few days later, another Nez Perce father asked whether his son, Ais, could go too. Whitman agreed; he called this boy John.

Whitman and the two young Nez Perces left the rendezvous with the caravan on August 27, 1835. About four and a half months later they arrived in Amity, where Whitman learned that the Prentiss family had moved six miles north to the small village of Angelica. He and the boys reached Angelica around December 10. After a brief visit with Narcissa, Whitman sent the boys to one of Parker's relatives in Ithaca and hurried sixty miles north to his mother's home in Rushville. He spent the rest of the winter there, working on arrangements for what was now officially the American Board's Oregon Mission.

Whitman's most pressing concern was to find at least one other couple who could go to Oregon. Board secretary David Greene provided him with a few names, including Rev. and Mrs. Oliver S. Powell of Amity, friends of Narcissa. They were ruled out because Mrs. Powell had recently given birth. Another missionary couple who had expressed an interest decided instead to go to Astoria, on the Northwest coast. In a letter dated December 30, 1835, Greene offered Whitman some advice about the qualifications of suitable companions but didn't give him any more names. Whitman would have to do his own recruiting.

It turned out that few prospective missionaries were willing to accept an assignment in Oregon. Exotic locations overseas—in Africa, China, India, the "Sandwich Islands" (Hawaii), and elsewhere—had more appeal. Most assignments were in densely populated areas, offering more evangelical bang for the buck, as it were: potential converts could number in the thousands instead of the hundreds. The fact that Whitman wanted to take women on an overland trip across the Rockies proved another barrier to his recruitment efforts. Greene, for one, wasn't sure it was a good idea. "Have you carefully ascertained & weighed the difficulties in the way of conducting females to those remote & desolate regions and comfortably sustaining families there?" he asked.[40]

In a two-thousand-word appendix to his travel journal, mailed to the board from Rushville on December 17, Whitman expressed confidence that a wagon could be taken over the mountains, that women could ride in it whenever they wanted, that the missionaries could take cows and cattle with them on the journey so they could have milk and meat when they reached their destination, and that they could quickly become self-sufficient with a little bit of help from the Hudson's Bay Company. It would not be the last time that Whitman demonstrated unfounded optimism in his approach to the Oregon Mission.

Whitman had promised to bring the Nez Perce boys back to their families by summer, which meant he would need to be on his way to the Missouri frontier by mid-February 1836. With just a few weeks left to find at least one other married couple to go with him and Narcissa to Oregon, he turned to Henry Spalding, who had just been appointed as a missionary to the Osage Indians in what is now eastern Kansas. Of all the missionaries who went to Oregon under the auspices of the American Board, Spalding had the roughest start in life. He was born to an unmarried mother in a log cabin near Wheeler on November 26, 1803. His father never acknowledged him. His mother gave him up when he was little more than a year old, binding him over to foster parents. When he was seventeen, his foster father became enraged over something, whipped him, and threw him out of the house. Years later, Spalding bitterly recalled trudging down the road to a neighbor's house, "sad, destitute, 17, crying, a cast off bastard wishing myself dead."[41]

A schoolmaster named Ezra Rice took him in. Spalding stayed with him for four years, working for his room and board and attending the "common school" where Rice taught. Spalding's education was limited; at twenty-one he read with difficulty and had only a rudimentary command of grammar and arithmetic. He was also tenacious, hardworking, and determined to make a better life for himself. In the fall of 1825 he enrolled in the Franklin Academy, a newly established college preparatory school in Prattsburg. He was older than most of his classmates, socially inept, almost cripplingly shy, terrified of public speaking, and undoubtedly poorly dressed. Pressed for money, he dropped out after just one twenty-one-week term.

Missionary Henry Harmon Spalding, photographed in New York in 1871 by famed Civil War photographer Mathew Brady. After the deaths of the Whitmans in 1847, Spalding became a tireless champion of the idea that Marcus Whitman had "saved" Oregon. *Presbyterian Historical Society, Philadelphia, Pennsylvania.*

He worked as a farm laborer, picked up occasional stints as a primary school teacher, saved money, and eventually returned to the academy. With help from a tuition waiver and a small scholarship from the American Education Society, he was able to complete a full two years at Franklin, graduating in 1831.

Spalding had his first spiritual awakening during a revival at the Prattsburg Presbyterian Church in 1825. He had a second three years later, when he read a religious tract titled "The Conversion of the World or the Claims of Six Hundred Millions, and the Ability and Duty of the Churches Respecting Them." The message, in eighty-five hundred words, was that Christians had an obligation to see that the gospel was preached to the entire world, in preparation for Armageddon ("end times"), the Second Coming of Christ, and the creation of a world without sin or disease for the righteous. Spalding read and reread the tract and vowed to become a missionary. Neither he nor his fellow missionaries were aware that Indian prophets on the Columbia Plateau had similar views about a time when "the world will fall to pieces," after which a powerful nonmortal being would appear and show the way to a restored and better world.

In 1830, when Spalding was beginning his final year at the Franklin Academy, he asked an acquaintance if she knew of any pious young women who might be interested in missionary work. She put him in touch with Eliza Hart, the daughter of a prosperous farmer in Holland Patent, about 140 miles east of Prattsburg. Eliza, four years younger than Spalding, had all the advantages he lacked: a stable home, loving parents, brothers (three), sisters (two), and a wide circle of friends. What they had in common was a deep religiosity. Eliza had been "born again" at age eighteen. She was a member of the Presbyterian Church in Holland Patent, "of a serious turn of mind," known for pressing religious tracts on her associates.[42] She was attending a seminary for young women around the time that she began writing to Spalding. They corresponded for a full year before they met in person, when Spalding called on Eliza at her parents' home, in October 1831, shortly after he graduated from the academy.

Spalding was a sharp-featured man, muscular from the farmwork he did to earn money during the summers, with deep-set eyes, thick brows, a high forehead, and a hairline that was in full retreat by the time he was thirty. Photos taken in later life show him with a full, bushy beard, streaked with gray, and a scowl that would do justice to an Old Testament prophet. A word often used to describe Henry Spalding was "severe." He had a reputation for being rigid, abrasive, quick to take offense, and slow to let go of a grudge. Eliza was a gentler soul, intelligent but self-effacing. Whatever she thought of his personality, she agreed to continue writing to him.

Like Whitman, Spalding wanted to enter the ministry. His degree from the Franklin Academy allowed him to enroll as a junior in Western Reserve College, a small, Presbyterian-affiliated school in Hudson, Ohio. All but one of the six faculty members were clergymen. Most were fervent abolitionists. Spalding disapproved of their activism. In a letter to Eliza's father, he complained that the "raging" about abolition "has about ruined this college."[43] But he appreciated the school's mix of vocational and classical instruction. All students were required to work at least two hours a day in the college shops. He learned how to make barrels, build furniture, and run a printing press—practical skills that would serve him well in Oregon.

Spalding visited Eliza again in Holland Patent at the end of his first year at Western Reserve. He apparently proposed; she accepted and returned with him to Ohio. There is little record of this interlude in their lives. Eliza may have attended a school for young women. She told her family that Spalding was tutoring her in algebra and astronomy. He graduated in August 1833 with a thesis titled "Claims of the Heathen on the American Churches" and began making plans to attend Lane Theological Seminary, near Cincinnati.[44] He was giving some thought to becoming a missionary in China. Meanwhile, Spalding wrote to Eliza's father, formally asking permission to marry her. He made his case in very dry terms. "My anticipations in relation to Sister Eliza have been more than realized," he wrote, adding that marriage "will not at all retard our studies." Eliza was somewhat more effusive. "I trust, dear parents, that you will not hesitate to grant the request Mr. Spalding has now made," she wrote in a note at the bottom of Spalding's letter. "I have found in him a kind and affectionate friend, one in whose society I should consider it a high privilege to spend the days of my earthly pilgrimage."[45] They were married on October 13, 1833, in Hudson. Spalding refused to spend the $40 it would have cost them to travel to her parents' home for the wedding.

They rented a house near the seminary and took in boarders to make ends meet. Eliza served them "good, plain fare"—no tea, coffee, or sweets, which were considered "stimulants" and thus threats to temperance. The school, headed by Rev. Lyman Beecher (father of *Uncle Tom's Cabin* author Harriet Beecher Stowe), permitted women to attend classes. Eliza studied Greek and Hebrew, among other subjects. She also attended Beecher's weekly lectures on theology. She probably had the broadest education of all the women in the Oregon Mission and would prove to be the most adept linguist.

Spalding completed his studies, was ordained, and applied to the American Board for an appointment as a missionary in August 1835. He submitted two letters of recommendation. One, signed by two of his former pastors, said he had "a strong and vigorous constitution," had been "inured to hardship from infancy," and was "a person of undoubted piety." The other, from Artemas Bullard, head of the Foreign Mission Society of the Presbyterian Church, was something less than a full-throated endorsement. Bullard described Spalding as "not remarkable for judgment & commonsense . . . too much inclined to denounce or censure those who are not as zealous

& ardent as himself . . . a little too much inclined to be jealous." He went on to say that he thought Spalding might mellow over time. As for Eliza, Bullard wrote: "His wife is very highly respected & loved by a large circle of friends. . . . She is one of the best women for a missionaries [*sic*] wife with whom I am acquainted."[46]

The American Board's requirements for missionaries were minimal. Applicants needed only to be pious, married, and in reasonably good health. There was no expectation that candidates demonstrate cultural sensitivity, adaptability, humility, or language skills. Spalding met the standards. He was assigned to a station among the Osage Indians, who had been forced to leave their homelands in the Mississippi River Valley and move west of the Missouri. Eliza's father was not happy about the news but gave them a horse and a light wagon as a going-away gift.[47] They were in Prattsburg in October 1835, preparing to leave for the Osage station, when Eliza gave birth to a stillborn daughter. She was still recovering two months later when Marcus Whitman asked them to change their plans and go to Oregon instead.

Many years after the deaths of all the principals, a story emerged that Henry Spalding had once been in love with Narcissa Prentiss, had proposed to her, and had been spurned. It was hinted at in a 1911 history of Oregon; elaborated on in *Waiilatpu: Its Rise and Fall*, a work of historical fiction published in 1915; and widely accepted as fact by the 1950s, as in this passage from a book published by the University of Nebraska Press in 1956 and reissued in 1979: "An illegitimate child, obsessed with shame and a feverish desire to right himself by righting the world, Spalding some years before had proposed to Narcissa and had been rejected. Later the tall, dour youth had married Eliza Hart, as dark and scrawny as Narcissa was golden and buxom."[48]

It is true that Narcissa and Henry knew each other. They had been members of the same church in Prattsburg. Narcissa had attended one twenty-one week term at the Franklin Academy when Spalding was finishing his education there. But the evidence of a thwarted romance is ambiguous at best. Clifford M. Drury, dean of the historians of the missionary era, flatly dismissed the idea in his biography of Spalding, published in 1936, but found it credible when he published a biography of Whitman, one year later. Drury said he changed his mind largely on the basis of "new evidence"—a letter written by Harriet Prentiss Jackson, Narcissa's youngest sister, to Eva Emery Dye, a writer of historical fiction. According to Drury, the letter included the following claim about Spalding: "He was a student when a young man in Franklin Academy, Prattsburg the place of our nativity, and he wished to make Narcissa his wife, and her refusal of him caused the wicked feeling he cherished toward them [Marcus and Narcissa] both."[49] The letter was reportedly written in 1893, more than sixty years after the purported proposal, by a sister who would have been too young to know much about events at the time. It's not clear whether Drury ever actually saw such a letter or simply heard something about it secondhand. In any case, no such document is on file today in the archives of the Oregon Historical Society, where Drury said it was located.[50]

Drury also reinterpreted a remark that Spalding made when he first heard that Narcissa was engaged to Marcus Whitman and planning to become a missionary in Oregon. By his own account, Spalding told friends at the time that he would not go on any mission with Narcissa because he questioned her judgment. Drury decided the remark meant that Spalding was still jealous and bitter because she had refused his proposal. But it could have meant simply that he thought Narcissa was not suited for life as a missionary—and indeed, it would turn out that she was not.

The Spaldings were making final arrangements before leaving for their assignment with the Osages when they received a letter from Whitman, begging them to go to Oregon instead. Whitman did not hide his desperation. The American Board would not send a mission to Oregon unless at least one member of the party was an ordained minister. Further, it was imperative that the party leave within a few weeks in order to connect with the fur company's caravan in Saint Louis. The caravan would not adjust its schedule to accommodate any missionaries, and the missionaries would not be able to make the journey without the guidance and protection of the caravan. Spalding continued to plan for his original post but notified the board that he would join the Whitman party if necessary. "If the Board and Dr. Whitman wish me to go to the Rocky Mountains with him, I am ready," he wrote to Greene on December 28, 1835. "Act your pleasure."[51]

Greene expressed some reservations about Spalding's suitability for a mission in Oregon. "I have some doubt whether his temperament well fits him for intercourse with the traders and travellers in that region," he wrote to Whitman. However, "as to laboriousness, self-denial, energy and perseverance, I presume that few men are better qualified than he."[52] By the time Whitman received that letter, in mid-February 1836, the Spaldings had already left Prattsburg for what they still assumed would be a mission in Kansas. Whitman raced after them and begged them to change their plans. Henry left the decision to Eliza. She decided that "duty seemed to require" a new "place of destination."[53] The Spaldings agreed to wait for the Whitmans in Cincinnati and travel together across the continent. Marcus then returned to Angelica to marry Narcissa.

The wedding took place on the evening of February 18, 1836, in the Angelica Presbyterian Church. She was almost twenty-eight;

he was thirty-three. Narcissa wore a dress of black bombazine (a fabric made of tightly woven silk and wool), which she took with her to Oregon. Tackitonitis, the Nez Perce youth that Whitman had renamed "Richard," was among the wedding guests. The couple had been engaged for a year but had spent only a few hours in each other's company. They had agreed to marry "somewhat abruptly," Narcissa reportedly told an acquaintance later, "and must do our courtship now we are married."[54]

The ceremony ended with a hymn titled "Yes, My Native Land! I Love Thee!" As the song built, through stanzas that included the refrain "Can I leave thee, can I leave thee / Far in heathen lands to dwell?," the congregation was overcome with emotion. In the morning the couple would set off for a distant land that was not yet part of the United States. No white woman had yet crossed the continent. It seemed unlikely that either Marcus or Narcissa would ever return to their "native land" again. One by one, according to a story that was told later, the voices faltered, until only Narcissa could be heard, in a clear soprano, singing the last verse: "Let me hasten, let me hasten / Far in heathen lands to dwell."[55]

The next day, the Whitmans left on the first leg of their long journey to Oregon.

The Columbia River

Snake River

17
15
16
14
13
12
10
11
9
8

THE WHITMAN ROUTE, 1836

1 Angelica
2 Rushville
3 Pittsburgh
4 Cincinnati
5 St. Louis
6 Liberty
7 Platte River Crossing
8 Joined caravan
9 Fort William
   (Fort Laramie)

10 South Pass
11 Rendezvous
12 Fort Hall
13 Fort Boise
14 Blue Mountains
15 Fort Walla Walla
16 The Dalles
17 Fort Vancouver

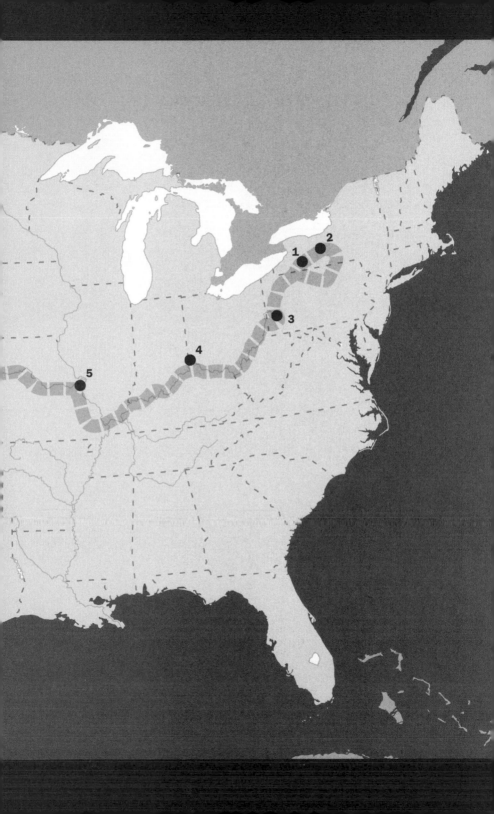

CHAPTER FOUR

DESTINATION OREGON

Never send another mission over these mountains if you value life and money.

—*Henry Spalding to David Greene, July 8, 1836*

I see no reason to regret our choice of a journey by land.

—*Marcus Whitman to David Greene, July 16, 1836*

Marcus and Narcissa Whitman left Angelica on the morning of February 19, 1836, one day after their wedding. It was the beginning of a journey that would take them far beyond the world they had known—beyond friends and family; beyond amenities such as daily postal service and readily available books and newspapers; beyond towns, well-traveled roads, schools, shops, and churches filled with the like-minded. Henry and Eliza Spalding had begun their own journey a few days earlier. The two couples would meet in Cincinnati in mid-March and proceed from there to Oregon

Country, some three thousand miles and seven months of hard travel away. It was a daunting and dangerous trip, from one coast to the other, across formidable mountains and undammed rivers; a trip never before attempted by white women and completed by relatively few men.

A deep sense of purpose gave these missionaries the courage, and the hubris, to trade familiar comforts for an uncertain future. They were driven by the belief that they had a divine mandate to "save the heathen." Eliza Spalding put it this way, in a diary entry after a painful farewell to her family: "I trust that it is the love of Christ which has constrained me to break away from the fond embrace of parents, brothers and sisters, and made me, not only willing, but anxious to spend and be spent in laboring to promote my Master's cause among the benighted Indians."[1]

The weather was cold and snowy. Whitman hired a private sleigh to take him and Narcissa to Ithaca (about one hundred miles east), where they retrieved "John," one of the two Nez Perce boys he had brought back from the rendezvous the year before. The other boy, "Richard," had stayed with one of Whitman's brothers in Rushville. After returning to Rushville from Ithaca, Narcissa had a "pair of Gentleman's boots" made for her in the Whitman family's shoe shop. After a few days of final goodbyes, they left with the two boys and traveled some three hundred miles south to Pittsburgh, where they boarded the steamboat *Siam*, bound for Cincinnati on the Ohio River. At the suggestion of her mother, Narcissa began keeping a travel diary. "We left Pittsburgh this morning at ten o'clock and are sailing at the rate of thirteen miles an hour," she wrote on March 15, 1836, in her first entry. "It is delightful passing so rapidly down the waters of the beautiful river." She enjoyed the "imposing scene" created by the parade of "stately" steamboats on the river, the "agreeable" motion of the *Siam*, and the pleasures of a private stateroom, "where we can be as retired as we wish."[2]

The Spaldings were waiting when the Whitmans and their wards arrived in Cincinnati on March 17. The two couples spent several days there together, making travel arrangements and looking for last-minute recruits for the Oregon Mission. Narcissa noted that "our two Indian youth attracted the gaze and admiration" of Cincinnati's "disciples of Jesus," but "our expectations were not realized"—they could find no one willing to join them on "our journey into the wilderness."[3]

Neither Narcissa nor Eliza—who met for the first time in Cincinnati—recorded their initial impressions of the other. Eliza made a bland reference on March 22, when she wrote "To day we leave Cincinnati in Company with Dr. and Mrs. Whitman, who are to be associated with us in laboring to erect the standard of the cross on heathen ground. . . . May God bless us in our intercourse with each other." Narcissa did not write anything about Eliza until nearly a month after she had met her, and then it was mostly in the context of comparing her health with that of the other woman's. "My health was never better than since I have been on the river," she wrote on April 7. "I think I shall endure the journey well—perhaps better than any of the rest of us. Mrs. Spalding does not look nor feel quite healthy enough for our enterprise." After more comments on her own well-being, Narcissa added this about Eliza: "I like her very much. She wears well upon acquaintance. She is a very suitable person for Mr. Spalding—has the right temperament to match him. I think we shall get along very well together; we have so far."[4]

In Cincinnati the party boarded another steamboat for the 270 or so nautical miles up the Mississippi River to Saint Louis, the last large town on the frontier. Spalding boasted, in a report to the American Board of Commissioners for Foreign Missions, that he had obtained passage for the entire group of six, including food for a voyage that was expected to last about a week, for only $95. "It seems to me now that we are on the very borders of civilization,"

Narcissa wrote on March 30. If she had any fears or second thoughts about what lay ahead, she did not express them. Instead, she struck a positive note: "I have not one feeling of regret at the step which I have taken, but count it a privilege to go forth in the name of my Master, cheerfully bearing the toil and privation that we expect to encounter." Narcissa was writing for an audience she knew would include her family, friends, and neighbors. She may have deliberately struck an upbeat tone to reassure people back home and encourage at least some to come west too.[5] Eliza's words were more introspective—intended for self-reflection rather than for an audience. Yet she too seemed undaunted. "The waters of the grand Ohio are rapidly bearing me away from all I hold dear in this life," she wrote, a few days after leaving Cincinnati. "Yet I am happy; the hope of spending the remnant of my days among the heathen, for the express purpose of pointing them to 'the Lamb of God who taketh away the sins of the world,' affords me much happiness."[6]

The missionaries hoped to reach Saint Louis by Sunday, March 27, but they were still eighty-five miles away that morning. They insisted they could not violate the biblical commandment to rest on the Sabbath. There would be times, in the months to come, when they would have to travel on Sundays or be left behind in wild country, but in this case they asked to be put ashore. The captain of the *Junius* let them off at the small riverfront town of Chester, Illinois. They spent the day with an elderly minister and his small flock. On Monday another steamboat, the *Majestic*, arrived unexpectedly; they boarded and continued on to Saint Louis.

Like other steamboats of its era, the *Majestic* had tall, twin smokestacks; an upper deck with staterooms that could accommodate up to 150 passengers; a lower deck for those who couldn't afford a private sleeping room; galleries for strolling on the upper deck; and a richly decorated saloon (the main reception area, also used as a dining hall). The Whitmans and the Spaldings each had spacious staterooms. The two Nez Perce boys slept on the lower deck. The boat offered a degree of luxury that none of these passengers had experienced before, but Narcissa was the only one to comment on it. "Since we came on board we have come on very pleasantly, our accommodations are better here than on any previous boat," she wrote. The amenities included "excellent cooks" and "servants who stand at our elbows ready to supply every want." Steamboat travel also meant enforced leisure. Narcissa took advantage of it by drinking in the "beautiful landscapes" that fringed the river, "on the one side high and rugged bluffs, and on the other low plains."[7]

The party arrived in Saint Louis on March 29. A letter from the War Department was waiting for Whitman and Spalding, granting them official permission "to reside in the Indian country among the Flat Head & Nez Percés Indians." Their wives were not mentioned. Narcissa had hoped that some letters from home would be delivered to her in Saint Louis and was disappointed that there were none. "Why have they not written, seeing it is the very last, last time they will have to cheer my heart with intelligence from home, home, sweet home, and the friends I love," she wrote, adding: "*But I am not sad.* My health is good. My mind completely occupied with present duty and passing events."[8]

Saint Louis in 1836 was a bustling, polyglot community of some fourteen thousand people, about 20 percent of whom were slaves. It would have been impossible for visitors to ignore the imprint of slavery on the city's landscape. Slave auctions were held regularly on the steps of the county courthouse and at other sites along the busiest streets, in full view of passersby. Newspaper advertisements seeking the return of runaway slaves or offering slaves for sale or hire were commonplace. Businesses or individuals could "rent" slaves with specific skills such as printing, blacksmithing, or carpentry. Many slaves worked on steamboats as crew, or on the riverfront as laborers. The Whitmans and Spaldings were members of churches that were at least nominally abolitionist (and both Henry and Eliza had been students at Cincinnati's Lane Theological Seminary when it was headed by Lyman Beecher, an incendiary abolitionist), but apparently none of them had any direct contact with slavery until they reached Saint Louis. Myra Eells, who traveled the same route two years later as part of a group sent out to "reinforce" the Oregon Mission, was horrified to find that the chambermaid on their steamship was a slave owned by the captain. "To-day have my feelings moved almost to indignation on account of the wretchedness of slavery," she wrote.[9] The Whitmans and Spaldings left no record of their reaction to the slaves in Saint Louis, or elsewhere.

Both couples visited the newly constructed Saint Louis Cathedral, with a mix of curiosity and revulsion. To evangelical Protestants in the mid-nineteenth century, Catholicism represented the seat of evil. Priests were "emissaries of the man of sin" (the Pope, who, in turn, was an emissary of the devil).[10] The Spaldings had been out for a walk along the riverfront, heard the cathedral bells ringing, and stepped inside for a brief look. Eliza recorded her reaction: "the unpleasant sensations we experienced on witnessing the heartless forms and ceremonies, induced us soon to leave, rejoicing that we had never been left to embrace such delusions." Eliza wasn't much impressed with Saint Louis as a whole. "Arrived at this city last evening—am not pleased with its appearance, particularly the part which is occupied by the French," she wrote. "The buildings are not splendid, many of them are uncouthly constructed, and it has the appearance of a city going to decay."[11]

From Saint Louis the party booked passage on yet another steamboat, the *Chariton*, for a week-long, three-hundred-mile trip to Liberty, Missouri, near present-day Kansas City. This was close to the halfway point between their homes in the East and their final destination in Oregon Country. So far, they had traveled in relative ease on riverboats. Ahead of them lay a tedious slog through eighteen hundred miles of prairie, mountain, and desert. "My mind is free from anxiety respecting the ardous [sic] journey we have in view," Eliza wrote on April 1, 1836, as the boat steamed away from Saint Louis. She found refuge in her faith: "The promises of God are sufficient to calm and console the heart that is stayed on Him." Spalding, meanwhile, convinced the captain of the *Chariton* to reduce the party's fare, from $180 to $100—a sum that included three meals a day for six people for a week.[12]

En route, on the Missouri River just north of Saint Louis, they passed the wreck of the *Siam*, the boat that had carried the Whitmans and their wards from Pittsburgh to Cincinnati. It had hit a snag and sunk. No lives were lost, but Narcissa was sobered by the "melancholy sight." It was a reminder that riverboats, for all their conveniences, were vulnerable to snags, sandbars, fires, explosions, and collisions—some of them caused by the bravado of foolhardy captains. The Whitmans had witnessed one near-collision, as passengers on the *Siam*, when their captain attempted to pass another in a race. His rival "shot into our path before us," Narcissa wrote, and a crash seemed inevitable, "but we passed her unhurt."[13]

The Whitman/Spalding party spent more than three weeks in Liberty—much longer than expected. During that time they acquired the equipment, supplies, and livestock needed both for their trip and for the new homes they intended to establish in the West. The men bought a sturdy farm wagon, a dozen horses, six mules, seventeen cattle, four milk cows, and two calves; life preservers made of India rubber, for a measure of safety when crossing rivers; tools, furniture, clothing, blankets; barrels of flour; and other provisions. Eliza and Narcissa sewed a large conical tent out of "bedticking" (heavy cotton cloth that had been oiled, to make it somewhat water resistant). The tent would be raised with a center pole, the sides fastened down with pegs. The bill for all these supplies came to $3,063.96 (about $70,800 today). They had already spent $2,800 (about $65,000) just getting to Liberty.[14] The secretaries of the American Board of Commissioners for Foreign Missions would not be pleased by the size of these bills when they received them in Boston.

Among the purchases were two sidesaddles for Eliza and Narcissa. Riding astride was a breach of decorum for women of their backgrounds. Sidesaddles were uncomfortable and insecure but protected the riders' sense of propriety. The women rode with both legs positioned on the left side of the horse, the left foot in a single stirrup while the right leg rested on a pommel, the torso twisted to face forward. Eliza, a more tentative rider than Narcissa, ended up being thrown several times when her horse suddenly bolted or jumped to one side.[15]

During the early weeks of the journey, the women (and, at times, the men too) rode in the light wagon that had been a gift from Eliza's father. The wagon, based on a design attributed to a Revolutionary War general named Henry Dearborn, had a flat top and side curtains and could be pulled by one horse. It had no springs, but the passengers sat on baggage and blankets and found it comfortable enough, at least when moving over relatively level ground. Riding in it over rough terrain was a spine-jolting experience. The farm wagon would eventually be abandoned and the Dearborn wagon broken down to a two-wheeled cart. Even so, it would become the first wheeled vehicle to be taken over the Rockies and as far west as Fort Boise, a Hudson's Bay post on the Snake River—a feat many had doubted would be possible.

Before leaving Liberty, the missionary party was joined by a carpenter, William Henry Gray, from Utica, New York, appointed a "lay member" of the Oregon Mission by the American Board; a third Nez Perce youth, whom they called Samuel Temoni; and two young would-be mountain men. One of them is known to history only by his last name, Dulin. The other was Miles Goodyear, a redheaded nineteen-year-old from Connecticut who would later become one of the first white settlers in Utah. Dulin and Goodyear were hired to help drive the livestock to Oregon Country. At times the tent that Narcissa and Eliza had sewn would provide shelter, if not privacy, for all ten of these people.

———✦———

Whitman had made arrangements with the American Fur Company to travel with its annual caravan to the Rocky Mountain rendezvous, to be held that year on a branch of the Green River in Wyoming. The rendezvous was a combination trade fair and bacchanal. Traders, trappers, mountain men, Indians, and hangers-on came together to sell furs, buy supplies, play games, race horses, gamble, fight, drink, and carouse—not a typical environment for the pious. But the missionaries did not believe it would be safe for them to cross through Indian country on the Great Plains without the company's protection. They planned to join the caravan at the Missouri River Indian Agency's trading post at Bellevue, in the southeast corner of what is now Nebraska. Spalding, the three Nez Perces, and the two hired hands left Liberty on April 27 to travel overland to the trading post, 175 miles to the north, with the wagons and livestock. A fur company boat was supposed to pick up Whitman and the women and take them to Bellevue. But when the boat appeared in Liberty, on May 1, the captain refused to stop. Whitman had to hire a wagon and driver and rush to catch up, first with Spalding and then with the caravan.[16]

The ten-person Whitman/Spalding party was reunited in mid-May, but by that point the caravan had already left Bellevue. Thomas Fitzpatrick, its leader, didn't mind having missionaries tag along, but he would not wait for them. The party was already about a week and 120 miles behind the caravan. Among the obstacles they faced was the Platte River, a mile-wide braid of shallow, stagnant pools separated by mudflats and sandbars. Its main channel snaked erratically from bank to bank. The channel was only a few feet deep, but the current was swift and the bottom swampy. It took two days to reach the crossing point, and another two days to get the wagons, baggage, and livestock from the south side of the Platte to the north.

Spalding and Whitman were both physically drained by the effort but the missionaries hurried on, past Bellevue to a Baptist-run mission near a village of Otoe Indians. The need for speed was so great that they even traveled on a Sunday, violating both their deeply held convictions and a key directive from the American Board that they strictly observe the Sabbath as a sacred day of rest. They jettisoned some of their baggage, leaving it behind at the mission. "Though we have now a very limited supply of everything we find that we must leave many things we consider almost indispensable," Spalding wrote to David Greene, secretary of the American Board. "My classical and theological books will nearly all be left. We can take almost nothing in the line of mechanical tools and farming utensils."[17] Rev. John Dunbar, one of the missionaries at the Otoe station, agreed to help them intercept the fur company. The route was fairly level, but it involved crossing two more rivers. After several forced marches, the Whitman/Spalding party finally reached the caravan, at 1:00 a.m. on May 26. "Ourselves and animals very much fatigued," wrote Eliza.[18]

The caravan that year was a particularly large one. Narcissa called it "a moving village."[19] In addition to some seventy men, it included nearly four hundred horses and mules and seven large wagons loaded with supplies, each pulled by a six-mule team. Once under way, the caravan stretched for about a mile. The missionary party brought up the rear: the Spaldings and Whitmans in one wagon, Gray and the baggage in the other, the Indian boys and the hired men on horseback, driving the cattle and other livestock. Everybody followed the same schedule: up at 3:30 a.m.; load the wagons and the packhorses; be on the move by daybreak; stop for dinner at 11:00; start again at 1:00 p.m.; camp at 5:00 p.m.; unload the wagons and animals; prepare, eat, and clean up after the evening meal; picket the horses and mules; and do it all again the next day, seven days a week. The missionaries would not have a Sunday of rest for six weeks.

The trail followed the broad, muddy, meandering Platte across the Nebraska prairies. Daytime temperatures were pleasant and there was plenty of grass for the livestock, but the river bottom-lands were boggy enough to force the company to detour to higher ground at times. Timber was scarce; the only source of fuel for cooking was dried buffalo dung. The travelers' diet now consisted mostly of buffalo meat (supplied by the caravan's hunters), supplemented with milk from the missionaries' cows. (Rev. Asa B. Smith, one of the missionaries who came to Oregon in 1838, observed that "buffalo meat produces very fragrant diarrhea which debilitates the system & for the time renders an individual very uncomfortable."[20]) Most of the flour they had bought in Liberty had been used up; the little that remained was being saved to thicken broth. They all would come to yearn for a taste of bread. Despite the hardships, Narcissa—who kept the most complete of the missionary accounts of the trip—seemed to relish the experience. "I never was so contented and happy before neither have I enjoyed such health for years," she wrote.[21]

In contrast, Eliza, who may have been suffering from tuberculosis as well as the aftereffects of a difficult stillbirth, began to wonder if she would die on the trail. She could not tolerate the buffalo diet and grew weaker as the days and weeks passed. One time, when her horse bolted, her foot caught in her sidesaddle's single stirrup and her body was dragged for several yards over rough ground. She almost drowned while crossing one river channel, when a strong current nearly swept her from the back of her horse. "We are now 2,800 miles from my dear parent's dwelling, expecting in a few days to commence ascending the Rocky Mts," she wrote from Fort William (later Fort Laramie), a fur trading post in present-day Wyoming. "Only He who knows all things, knows whether this debilitated frame will survive the undertaking. His will, not mine, be done." Still, Eliza found time to enjoy the quiet beauty of the landscape. "The majestic sand bluffs and the extensive plains between the bluffs and river, covered with beautiful flowers and roses, presents a delightful scenery to the eye of the traveler," she wrote.[22]

Fort William, at the confluence of the North Platte and Laramie Rivers, was a convenient resting place for fur brigades and, later, for travelers on what became the Oregon Trail. It was established in 1834 by Kentucky-born mountain man William Sublette and his partner, Robert Campbell. The beaver trade was already in decline by then, but the post's location, in the heart of buffalo country, made it the center of a flourishing trade in buffalo skins. The ambitiously named "fort" was only eighty feet wide and one hundred feet long, surrounded by a fifteen-foot-tall palisade. Sioux, Cheyenne, and other Plains Indians camped on the grasslands outside the fort in great numbers during the summer trading season. The only visual record of Fort William, a painting by the American artist Alfred Jacob Miller in 1837, shows it surrounded by teepees, seemingly stretching off for miles.

The caravan arrived at the fort on June 13 and stayed for eight days, a period that included what Eliza described as "the first Sabbath we have spent in quietness and rest since the 8th of May." She noted that it had been several weeks since they had seen a building of any kind; she found it "very pleasant to fix my eyes once more upon a few buildings."[23] The animals were turned loose to graze and regain strength before the long haul over the mountains. All the large wagons, including Whitman's farm wagon, were unloaded. Most of the contents were repacked onto mules and horses; the fur company's leftovers were piled into a two-wheeled cart. The heavy wagons would remain at the fort until the traders returned in the fall, when they would be reloaded with furs and buffalo skins and driven back to Saint Louis. Whitman's experiences the year before had convinced him that Spalding's light wagon could be driven at least as far as the rendezvous, if not farther. When the caravan began moving again, that wagon was in the rear.

The missionaries camped outside the fort but visited frequently. They enjoyed the novelty of sitting on chairs with seats made of buffalo skins, a comfort compared to saddles and wagon seats. One day, they were served "mountain bread"—thick pancakes made of coarse flour and water and fried in buffalo grease. Eating anything made with flour was a treat. The women washed clothes for the first time since leaving Liberty. During this sojourn Narcissa became pregnant. She would fight nausea and increasing discomfort as her pregnancy progressed, but at least it meant an end to the challenges associated with menstruation, including finding the time and privacy to change and wash the rags used to catch menstrual flow.

From Fort William the caravan followed the North Platte River to its confluence with the Sweetwater, near today's Casper, Wyoming. They passed several Pawnee villages. Narcissa and Eliza were the first white women most of these Indians had ever seen. "We, especially, were visited by them both at noon and at night; we ladies were such a curiosity to them," Narcissa wrote. "They would come in and stand around our tent, peep in, and grin in their astonishment to see such looking objects."[24]

It was late June 1836, on the high plains. The soil was thinner, the grass more sparse. "Our Animals have sufered [sic] much for want of grass [and] from forced traveling," Whitman reported.[25] There had been no rain for weeks. The missionaries discovered what it meant to be at the end of a mile-long brigade in dry country. Men in the fur company rotated positions, so that everyone got an equal chance to be at the front and away from the clouds of dust churned up by the animals. But the missionary party was consigned to the rear all the way to the rendezvous.

They found it challenging to keep up during the long climb from the river valleys to South Pass, the lowest (at 7,412 feet elevation) and broadest passageway over the Continental Divide. Spalding's wagon was slower and more cumbersome than the fur company's pack mules and cart. No one was in a celebratory mood on July 4, when they reached the pass. "Crossed a ridge of land today; called the divide, which separates the waters that flow into the Atlantic from those that flow into the Pacific," Eliza wrote in her diary that day.[26] She showed no sign of excitement at having just become one of the first two white women to cross the Rocky Mountains. None of the other missionaries mentioned the milestone or the significance of the date at all. As far as they were concerned, it was just another day of grinding travel.

An entirely fictive version of what happened that day began to circulate decades later, the result of a collaboration between a then elderly Henry Spalding and Rev. Simon J. Humphrey, district secretary of the American Board in Chicago and the editor of a weekly Congregationalist newspaper called *The Advance*. It's hard to say how much of the story sprang wholly from Spalding's imagination and how much was embellished by Humphrey. The gist of it, published in *The Advance* on December 1, 1870, was this: when they reached the summit, the missionaries, "alighting from their horses and kneeling on the other half of the continent, with the Bible in one hand and the American flag in the other, took possession of it as the home of American mothers, and of the Church of Christ."[27]

The invented scene was woven into the Whitman legend that coalesced in 1897, the fiftieth anniversary of the attack on the mission. The *Ladies Home Journal* illustrated it with a drawing that showed Whitman standing in front of his kneeling comrades, one hand holding an American flag in full billow atop a tall pole, a Bible open on the ground in front of him, two buckskin-clad Indian boys looking on. The artist dressed Whitman in a morning coat, with tails, and a cravat. The women looked as if they had just stepped out of church. The drawing was widely reprinted after its initial publication in November 1897 in a *Ladies Home Journal* hagiography titled "When Dr. Whitman Added Three Stars to Our Flag: How Oregon Was Saved for the Union."[28] A variation, first published in *Whitman's Ride through Savage Lands* (1905), had Whitman wearing a white buccaneer shirt, kneeling, arms outstretched while the flag waved from a pole anchored in the ground behind him.[29] The missionaries took neither flag nor flagpole with them to Oregon. Nonetheless, the idea that they had celebrated Independence Day by planting the flag and laying claim to the West in the name of their God, like New World explorers armed with a monarch's banner, persisted for decades.

About two hundred trappers and traders and perhaps a thousand Indians were camped at the Green River when the caravan arrived on July 6, 1836. The presence of two white women created something of a sensation. "Arrived at the Rendezvous this evening, were met by a large party of Nez Perces, men, women and children," Eliza wrote. "The women were not satisfied, short of saluting Mrs. W. and my self with a kiss. All appear happy to see us."[30] The Indians, Whitman reported, were "greatly interested with our females, cattle, and waggon [*sic*]."[31] Narcissa's blond hair attracted particular attention. The reception by "the gazing throng" was "unexpected and affected me very much," she wrote.[32]

The fur company took over a crude shelter that had been erected at the Green River site in 1832 by Capt. Benjamin Bonneville, a French-born Army officer and explorer. The missionaries set up camp to the east of "Fort Bonneville." Most of the trappers and hunters camped to the west. Various bands of Indians stretched out for miles to the south. The two white women were "besieged with visitors, both civilized and savage," according to mountain man (and eventual marshal of Oregon Territory) Joe Meek.[33] Narcissa was not as curious about the Indians as they were about her. She was far more interested in what William Henry Gray caustically called "gentlemen callers," from rough-hewn trappers like Meek to Sir William Drummond Stewart, a Scottish nobleman and adventurer. (Stewart was on the third of his four trips to the rendezvous.) Eliza, in contrast, "showed but little attention to any one except the natives and their wives," Gray wrote.[34] She concentrated on learning the Nez Perce language, the lingua franca among tribes at the gathering, and made much more progress with it than any of her colleagues.

Among the visitors to the missionary camp was Nathaniel Wyeth, the Boston businessman who had led two overland expeditions to Oregon Country in hopes of establishing a fur and fish trading empire. Defeated, he was returning to New England. He agreed to take letters from the missionaries with him, including the first part of what Narcissa called "something of a journal."[35] She did not have a bound diary or journal and wrote instead on individual sheets of thin paper, eight inches wide and thirteen inches long, folded into quarters for mailing. She used a metal pen point, and mixed ink from powder and water as needed. Part of one of the outside sheets was left blank for the address (envelopes had not yet been invented). Postage was paid by the recipient, based on the number of sheets and their weight. To save postage and paper, Narcissa wrote to the very edges of each sheet, with no margins, her handwriting getting smaller and more cramped as she came to the end.

This packet reached Angelica on November 5, 1836—four months after being entrusted to Wyeth.

The missionaries stayed at the rendezvous for a week and a half. At some point they became acquainted with a man identified only as "Hinds, a colored man." He may have been a trapper or a mountain man. In poor health, he may have thought there were advantages to being close to a physician. In any case, he joined the missionary party as a hired hand. Dulin, one of the two young men who had traveled with the group from Missouri, left for parts unknown. "Richard" and "John" were briefly reunited with some of their Nez Perce relatives. The two youths had learned enough English to be useful as interpreters, and Whitman asked that they remain with the missionaries, at least for the rest of the journey.

Samuel Parker, the fiery preacher from Ithaca who was supposed to be waiting for Whitman and the others at the rendezvous and escort them into Oregon, did not show up. Instead, he sent word that he was too worn out to continue and was at Fort Vancouver, waiting to sail on a Hudson's Bay Company ship for Hawaii. He planned to go on from there back to New York on an American merchant ship via Cape Horn—a challenging voyage but still easier than crossing the continent by land. Parker's defection was a bitter disappointment for Whitman. In a letter to the American Board, he complained that Parker had not only failed to meet him at the rendezvous, he had "neglected to write a single letter containing any information concerning the country, company, Indians, prospects, or advice of any kind whatever."[36]

Without Parker the missionaries didn't have a guide for the rest of the journey. They were debating what to do when a small brigade of Hudson's Bay men rode into the rendezvous on July 12. To the missionaries' great relief, the leaders, Thomas McKay and John L. McLeod, graciously offered to escort them at least as far as Fort Walla Walla. "It seems the most marked Providence in our favour, of any we have yet experienced," Henry Spalding wrote.[37] On July 14 the mission party moved to the McKay/McLeod camp, about ten miles to the west. A group of about two hundred Nez Perces and Flatheads came too. They had decided to accompany the brigade to Fort Hall, a trading post on the Snake River near present-day Pocatello. The entire expedition—traders, missionaries, and Indians—set off five days later.

The missionaries now faced the most difficult part of their overland journey: more than eight hundred miles of sun-scorched sagebrush, desert canyons, wild rivers, and mountains. The pace was slow, averaging only twelve or thirteen miles a day. The heat was oppressive, the mosquitoes maddening, the tedium mind-numbing. The men suffered as much, if not more, than the women. Whitman became "so lame with the rheumatism as to be scarcely able to move."[38] Spalding fainted twice from heat and exhaustion. Gray, the carpenter from Utica, was so weak and debilitated that at one point he begged to be left for dead. The trail seemed a vast, gritty oven. They were all heartily sick of the monotonous diet. "Have been living on fresh meat for two months exclusively," Narcissa wrote on July 23. "Am cloyed with it. I do not know how I shall endure this part of the journey." Four days later, they had no fresh meat and were eating dried buffalo jerky instead. "I can scarcely eat it, it appears so filthy, but it will keep us alive, and we ought to be thankful for it," wrote Narcissa, sounding not very thankful at all.[39]

Adding to the travails was the trouble-plagued wagon. It got stuck in creeks, sometimes tipped over on steep trails, and broke down repeatedly. Whitman and Spalding exhausted themselves trying to get it over terrain that no wheels had ever crossed. When one of the axles broke, the women "rejoiced, for we were in hopes they would leave it, and have no more trouble with it," Narcissa wrote, adding: "Our rejoicing was in vain for they are making a cart of the back wheels, this afternoon, and lashing the fore wheels to it—intending to take it through in some shape or other."[40]

They stumbled into Fort Hall on August 3. The post (one of two established by Nathaniel Wyeth) was smaller and more rustic than Fort William, but, as Narcissa commented, "anything that looks like a house makes us glad."[41] Joseph Thing, one of Wyeth's men, welcomed the party with a longed-for taste of bread, along with some turnips and stewed serviceberries. Miles Goodyear, the nineteen-year-old from Connecticut who had helped drive the cattle from Missouri, decamped at this point, partly out of frustration with the wagon. He "was determined, if the Doctor took his wagon any further, to leave the company." In his parting words, Goodyear said he "did not care for missionaries, Hudson's Bay men, nor Indians."[42] Most of the Nez Perce also left, heading north. McKay, McLeod, and the missionary party spent a day and a half at the fort, then moved on, following the Snake River across the deserts of what is now southern Idaho, in the searing heat of August.

The men dragged and pushed the wagon over and around sagebrush that grew in stiff, hard bunches, in some places as tall as "the height of a man's head." In swampy areas along the river, "we were so swarmed with musquetoes [sic] as to be scarcely about to see," Narcissa wrote.[43] It seemed as if the cows would be driven mad by the insects. Eliza's horse stepped into a wasp nest and threw her violently, head first, to the ground. She didn't break any bones but had to be carried in what was left of the wagon for the next few days. In mid-August, at a Snake River crossing near today's Glenn's Ferry, the wagon was completely overturned by strong currents. The two mules that were pulling it were tangled in their harnesses and came close to drowning before they could be cut loose. Everything that had been packed in the wagon was thoroughly soaked. Finally, at

Fort Boise (also called Snake Fort), a Hudson's Bay post on today's Idaho-Oregon border, Whitman and Spalding gave up and stowed the makeshift vehicle at the fort. Thomas J. Farnham, a would-be colonizer who led a group of settlers to Oregon in 1839, saw the remnants when he passed through that year. They consisted of the four wheels, the axle, and not much more.

The party spent three days at Fort Boise, a welcome respite. The women washed clothing; the men repacked. In addition to the cart, they left behind five ailing cattle, hoping to obtain replacements at the next major trading post on their route, Fort Walla Walla. Once again they were able to get fresh game, along with waterfowl and fish and, as they continued west, various kinds of berries. Grazing improved, but the missionaries' mules, horses, and cattle were too worn out to travel very quickly. The party split in two. McLeod and his men, with the Whitmans and Gray, pushed on ahead. The Spaldings and Whitmans' Nez Perce wards followed, with two Indian guides, the pack animals, baggage, and the remaining twelve head of cattle.

Approaching the Grande Ronde Valley and the Blue Mountains beyond, Narcissa was reminded of the hills around her native Steuben County, New York. She noticed familiar-looking trees and flowers and "was not a little delighted." But this pleasant interlude didn't last long. "Before noon," she wrote, "we began to descend one of the most terrible mountains for steepness & length I have yet seen." In some places the descent was almost perpendicular. Shards of broken rock littered the trail, lacerating the horses' hooves. It took most of a day to travel a two-mile, up-and-down course over the Blue Mountains to a spot overlooking the Columbia River Valley. By then it was sunset, but there was enough light to provide distant views of Mount Hood, about three hundred miles to the west, and Mount Saint Helens, to the northwest. It was, Narcissa wrote, "enchanting & quite diverted my mind from the fatigue under which I was labouring."[44] Gray too was charmed by the "sublimely Grand" scene, and "for a moment . . . forgot the toiles [*sic*] of the day."[45]

The Whitmans and Gray arrived at Fort Walla Walla on September 1. The Spaldings came in two days later. They were greeted by Pierre C. Pambrun, chief trader at the fort, and John K. Townsend, a physician and naturalist from Philadelphia. Townsend, who had come to Oregon Country in 1834 with Nathaniel Wyeth, was based at Fort Vancouver but took frequent trips around the region to collect specimens. Whitman had met members of Townsend's family in Philadelphia and brought him a packet of letters—the first news Townsend had received from home in two years. Narcissa would wait even longer than that before receiving any letters from her family. The "*long*, long silence" would make her feel increasingly isolated and despondent.[46]

Townsend thought that the missionaries "appear admirably qualified for the arduous duty to which they have devoted themselves, their minds being fully alive to the mortifications and trials incident to a residence among wild Indians." He observed that "the ladies have borne the journey astonishingly; they look robust and healthy."[47] Gray also commented on how well the women had endured the trip. "Mrs Spaldings health and strength is improved beyond all expectation," he wrote to friends in the East. "Mrs. Whitman has indured [*sic*] the Journey like a heroine."[48] News that the two women had crossed the continent would circulate in the *Missionary Herald* and other publications and help persuade other women to follow.

After a few well-fed days at Fort Walla Walla, the five missionaries were ushered into one of the company's large, thirty-foot-long, flat-bottomed boats, called bateaux, for the last segment of their trip, down the Columbia River to Fort Vancouver. The boats, specially designed for the wild rivers of the Northwest, were equipped with square sails but were powered largely by the muscles of their French

Canadian voyageurs, usually eight to a boat. Pambrun accompanied them. The two Nez Perce boys stayed behind to tend to the livestock. Whitman noted later, in a report to the American Board, that the boys had been "very usefull [sic] to us in driving our cattle" all the way from Missouri to Oregon Country, although the relationship would soon sour.[49]

The missionaries landed at Fort Vancouver on September 12, after a six-day excursion that introduced them to the beauty and terrors of an undammed Columbia. The river, initially "clear as crystal & smooth as a sea of glass," morphed abruptly into a series of wildly frothing rapids, as if it had been "cut up and destroyed by these huge masses of rocks," Narcissa wrote.[50] The boat was carried around the most dangerous portions of the river but sometimes only the passengers were unloaded, while the oarsmen stayed aboard to battle through the rapids. Townsend, who made the same trip a few days earlier, was awed by the skill of the voyageurs: "The middle-men ply their oars; the guides brace themselves against the gunwale of the boat, placing their paddles edgewise down her sides, and away she goes over the curling, foaming, and hissing waters, like a race horse."[51] Narcissa learned later that "many boats have been dashed to pieces at these places, and more than a hundred lives lost."[52]

Fort Vancouver was the headquarters of the Hudson's Bay Company's vast Columbia District. Under the management of Dr. John McLoughlin, the chief factor, it had become a bustling commercial center and supply depot. (In company parlance, business agents and managers were called "factors," a mathematical term reflecting their role in keeping track of money and merchandise.) Fort Vancouver's orchards, fields, and pastures stretched for fifteen miles along the Columbia and five miles inland. Inside the central stockade were some forty buildings, including warehouses, a school, a library, a chapel, a rudimentary hospital, and housing for British officers and company officials. Outside was a multicultural village with inhabitants from more than thirty-five different ethnic and tribal groups, including a large number of Hawaiians who worked for the company. About a thousand head of cattle grazed on nearby pastures, along with sheep, goats, and other livestock. There was a shipyard, a sawmill, a tannery, a dairy, and (to the disapproval of the missionaries) a distillery. All together, up to seven hundred people lived in and around Fort Vancouver in the mid-1830s. Narcissa called it "the New York of the Pacific Ocean."[53] Never having seen New York City, which had a population of three hundred thousand at the time, her enthusiasm can be excused.

It was the custom for traders going down the Columbia by bateaux to stop at the sawmill, a few miles upstream from the fort, to give the men time to shave and dress in cleaner clothes, while a messenger was sent ahead with news that they were on their way. When McLoughlin heard that two American women were in the approaching party, he ordered that they be given a suitable welcome. There were two tall ships at anchor in front of the fort; he asked that the ships be dressed out in all their flags. He himself came out to meet the missionaries at the fort's main gate and usher them into his large white house. The women luxuriated in the experience of sitting on a sofa for the first time in seven months. McLoughlin then took the visitors on a tour of the gardens and other facilities. "What a delightful place this is," Narcissa gushed.[54] Eliza too was impressed, to "find ourselves in the midst of civilization, where the luxuries of life seem to abound."[55]

The American women were surprised to find two English women at the fort. One, the wife of William Capendale—an expert farmer who had been sent from London to take charge of the fort's farm and dairy—had arrived with her husband on the company's ship *Columbia* in May. The other was Jane Beaver, wife of Rev. Herbert Beaver, an Anglican minister who had been hired as a chaplain and schoolteacher. The Beavers had arrived on another of the company's ships, the *Nereide*, just one week before the Whitmans and Spaldings. "This is more than we expected when we left home," Narcissa wrote, "that we should be privileged with the acquaintance and society of two English ladies."[56] The "ladies" were less impressed, both with Fort Vancouver and with the company of the rustic newcomers. The Capendales sailed back to London as soon as they could, departing on the *Columbia* in November. The Beavers remained for another two years, but Jane regarded the missionary women as beneath her and had little to do with them.

The American Board expected Whitman and Spalding to establish one joint mission, with Gray as their assistant. But personality differences helped derail that plan. Whitman was demanding and inflexible; Spalding, self-righteous and quick-tempered; and Gray, universally disliked. In fact, relations among all the members of the board's Oregon Mission—including four couples who arrived as reinforcements in 1838—were contentious. None of them got along. They quarreled about everything from how to load a wagon to how to pray. As writer William Dietrich has pointed out, "the same strong-minded idealism that fired people with Christian zeal made it difficult for them to cooperate."[57] The six couples ended up establishing four missions, hundreds of miles apart.

By the time they reached Fort Vancouver, Whitman and Spalding had made up their minds to establish separate missions. On September 21 the two men and Gray left to survey potential sites. Two Hawaiian laborers and Hinds (the "colored man" who had joined the missionaries at the Green River rendezvous) went with them. Narcissa and Eliza stayed behind. The women spent almost eight weeks at Fort Vancouver while their husbands were gone. They helped out in the school, which had about fifty students, most of them the children of French Canadian fathers and Indian mothers. Narcissa taught singing. Eliza's health improved. Both women shopped in the fort's warehouses, selecting linen, china, blankets, cookware, furniture, and other goods, sending the bills back to the board in Boston. They feasted on the food served at McLoughlin's table, which Narcissa described in lingering detail: coffee or cocoa, salmon and roasted ducks with potatoes for breakfast; soup as a first course at dinner, followed by a succession of entrees; then by pudding or pie; then a melon course; and finally cheese with bread or biscuits and butter—each course served on a clean plate, and all the cooking, serving, and cleaning up done by servants (mostly Hawaiian, Indian, or métis women). The missionary women abstained only from the wine and tried without success to elicit pledges of temperance from "the gentlemen" at the fort.

McLoughlin's wife, Marguerite (a woman of mixed Indian and European heritage), took Narcissa and Eliza horseback riding one day and tried to convince them that they would be safer and more comfortable riding astride, on Indian-style saddles with high backs and fronts, instead of on sidesaddles. The white women demurred. "We have been recommended to use these saddles, as a more easy way of riding," Narcissa wrote, "but we have never seen the necessity of changing our fashion."[58]

As the head of the company's Columbia District from 1824 until 1846, McLoughlin was the most powerful man in the Pacific Northwest. He managed an international trading network; maintained peace among dozens of Indian tribes; and served as de facto governor of a region that stretched from the Rocky Mountains to the Pacific Ocean, as far north as Alaska and south into California. He was a physically imposing figure: six feet four, with broad, muscular shoulders, blue eyes that many described as "steely," and a thick mane of hair that had turned completely white by the time he settled into life at Fort Vancouver, at age forty. Coastal Indians called him Chakchak, meaning White Headed Eagle.

Like many white men in the fur trade, McLoughlin had entered into "country marriages"—first with an Ojibwe woman, who died shortly after giving birth to their fourth child and first son, Joseph; and then, around 1810, to Marguerite, the daughter of a Swiss merchant and a Cree woman. Marguerite had also entered into a "country marriage" with Alexander McKay, a New York–born trader with the North West Company. (Thomas McKay, who helped guide the missionary party from the rendezvous, was their son.) Such marriages—*à la façon du pays*, or "in the manner of the country"— were accepted and even encouraged by both fur companies. The unions could be informal and easily dissolved, as apparently was the case with Marguerite's marriage to Alexander McKay; or enduring, like her second marriage, to McLoughlin, which lasted from around 1810 until his death in 1857.

After McLoughlin became chief factor and the couple moved to Fort Vancouver, in 1824, Marguerite began dressing in the style of a cultured white woman. She had no formal education and could neither read nor write but she spoke three languages: French, English, and her native Cree. She spent her days managing servants, looking after children (she and McLoughlin had four together), and doing needlework, including intricate beading. She was known for her calm and gentle manner. However, her dress and demeanor did not protect her from epithets based on her Indian heritage. When Herbert Beaver disembarked from the *Nereide*, he demanded that the "half-breed women" greeting the ship be moved out of the way so that he and his wife, Jane, could pass safely. Marguerite was one of those women. The other was Amelia Connolly Douglas, the métis wife of James Douglas, second in command at Fort Vancouver. Narcissa was less imperious but still described "Mrs. McLoughlin and Mrs. Douglas" as "natives of the country—half breeds."[59] She spent eleven years in Oregon and never stopped thinking of non-white women as her inferiors.

Narcissa took time during her stay at Fort Vancouver to bring her journal up to date. She had entrusted the first part of it to

Nathaniel Wyeth. The rigors of traveling over the Rockies did not allow her to make detailed daily entries after that, but she kept field notes and used them as the basis for the second half of her travel diary, covering July 18 through November 1, 1836. At Marcus's suggestion, Narcissa made a copy of the diary for his mother. She left both the original and the copy at the fort, in the care of the captain of the *Columbia*, to be delivered to the American Board's mission in Hawaii and forwarded from there to the United States. In the coming years, the missionaries would send mail mostly by the Hudson's Bay "express"—a convoy of fur traders who traveled from Fort Vancouver overland to Montreal twice a year. From there letters could be sent on to the United States. The total delivery time was about six months, compared to at least eighteen months for mail going by ship from Vancouver to Hawaii, around Cape Horn at the tip of South America to London, and across the Atlantic to New York.

Henry Spalding returned to Fort Vancouver in late October with the news that he had chosen a mission site at Lapwai ("Place of Butterflies") in Nez Perce territory on the Clearwater River in Idaho. Whitman had settled on a place about 120 miles southwest of Lapwai, near a Cayuse village at Weyiilet, meaning "Place of Waving Grass" (the suffix "pu," as in "Waiilatpu," meant "people of" that place).[60] It was a pleasant site, next to a branch of the Walla Walla River, but it was miles from good timber. McLoughlin warned Whitman that the Cayuse were less tractable than the Nez Perce. A Nez Perce headman agreed, telling Whitman "the Nez Perces do not have difficulties with the white man as Cayous do" and predicting the missionaries "will see the difference."[61] Whitman ignored the warnings. He, William Henry Gray, the Hawaiians, and Hinds began building an adobe house with an attached lean-to at what they called Waiilatpu, while Spalding went to the fort to retrieve the women. The Cayuse were puzzled to see men putting up a shelter. In Cayuse culture, that was women's work. It was the first of many cultural misunderstandings between the Whitmans and their hosts.

On November 3, 1836, Spalding and the women left Fort Vancouver for lives that would never again have the same degree of comfort and ease they had enjoyed as guests of Chief Factor McLoughlin.

CHAPTER FIVE

EARLY YEARS AT WAIILATPU

At first view the country does not seem adapted for settlement but I am satisfied it will support a great population.

—*Marcus Whitman, March 24, 1838*

Narcissa Whitman and the Spaldings left Fort Vancouver at noon on Thursday, November 3, 1836, traveling upriver in two of the Hudson's Bay Company's bateaux with trader John McLeod and sixteen voyageurs. Narcissa and McLeod sat in one boat, the Spaldings in the other. Packed around them were five tons of supplies and equipment, from china to farm implements to building materials, all bought on credit at Fort Vancouver. The missionaries were almost willfully ignorant of the values, traditions, and expectations of the people they were going to be living with. For example, after Henry Spalding and Marcus Whitman met with a group of Cayuse and Walla Walla headmen while scouting locations for their separate missions, Spalding advised friends in Prattsburg: "Natives very friendly, formerly very dangerous cannibals."[1] The missionaries also underestimated the hardships they would face in simply housing and feeding themselves. But the mood, as they set out, was optimistic. They were confident that they were following God's plan and relieved to be, in Narcissa's words, "so near a fixed location after journeying so long."[2]

It took ten mostly miserable days to get to Fort Walla Walla. It rained almost constantly. The boats had to be rowed ashore, unloaded, and carried around the most impassable parts of the Columbia Gorge, the ninety-mile-long passageway cut through the Cascade Mountains by an untamed river. At calmer stretches the passengers and cargo remained on board with a skeleton crew while some of the voyageurs climbed on shore and used tow ropes to haul the boats upriver. "It is a terrific sight, & a frightful place to be in, to be drawn along in such a narrow channel between such high, craggy, perpendicular bluffs, the men with the rope clambering sometimes upon their hands & knees upon the very edge, so high above us as to appear small, like boys," Narcissa wrote in a letter to her mother.[3] Local Indians were hired to help with both the portages and the ropes. Despite the missionaries' personal objections to use of "the Devil's Weed," they paid the Indians with twists of tobacco, purchased at the fort on Chief Factor McLoughlin's advice. Northwest Indians had come to value Virginia-grown tobacco above almost any other item for trade or gift exchange.

The travelers reached the eastern end of the gorge a week after leaving Fort Vancouver. Behind them lay mossy forests and thick woodlands; ahead, treeless grasslands. The rain continued. Spalding, in a report to the American Board of Commissioners for Foreign Missions, noted the scarcity of firewood. "In this country of no wood, we were of course in danger of being without fire for the night," he wrote. "We were supplied, however, every night, usually from graves or miserable huts of poor natives, for a small piece of tobacco."[4] With his casual remark about the desecration of Indian graves, Spalding underscored a key assumption—widely shared by his fellow missionaries—that native spiritual practices were not worthy of respect or even acknowledgment.

The party arrived at Fort Walla Walla on November 13. Marcus Whitman and William Henry Gray joined them five days later. Marcus told Narcissa the house that he and Gray had been building at Waiilatpu was not yet "a comfortable place" for her. She readily accepted an invitation from Pierre Pambrun, the chief trader, to stay at the fort with him and his family. Marcus returned to Waiilatpu alone. Gray and the Spaldings left for Lapwai with a Nez Perce escort shortly after that.[5] "This dear Sister goes very cheerfully to her location to live in a skin lodge untill [sic] her house is built & this too in the dead of winter," wrote Narcissa, referring to Eliza Spalding, "but she prefers it to remaining here & so should I."[6] In fact, as historian Julie Roy Jeffrey has observed, Narcissa was in no hurry to set up housekeeping "in inconvenient and uncomfortable circumstances."[7] She remained at the fort for another three weeks.

Fort Walla Walla was crude by the standards of Fort Vancouver, but Narcissa enjoyed her time there. She was flattered by the attention that Pambrun and his métis wife, Catherine, gave her. Like Marguerite McLoughlin, Catherine was descended from white men who had married Indian women. Her grandfather was British; her father was of mixed European and Indian heritage; and her mother was Cree and Ojibwe. She and Pambrun had six children at the time of Narcissa's visit (two more would be born later). Both Catherine and her oldest daughter, ten-year-old Maria, spoke some English. Narcissa said it was "a very kind Providence to be situated near one family so interesting & a native female that promises to be so much society for me."[8] Although Narcissa would develop a closer relationship with Catherine than with any other nonwhite women in

Oregon, she never accepted the fact that a "native female" could be her equal, or have anything of value to teach her.

Marcus returned to Walla Walla on December 10 and escorted a heavily pregnant Narcissa to Waiilatpu and the threshold of a half-finished house on the north bank of a bend in a Walla Walla River channel. Aside from a fringe of cottonwoods and willows along the riverbank, the area was treeless. Compared with the rounded hills and dense woodlands of upstate New York, Waiilatpu was an ambush of expanse, filling and intimidating the senses. Wind-whipped grasslands stretched "as far as the eye can reach," Narcissa wrote.[9] The Blue Mountains rose in the southeast, gauzy with distance. The house was an adobe structure, one and a half stories tall, thirty feet wide, and thirty-six feet long. A twelve-foot-wide lean-to, made of split logs fitted into grooved posts and caulked with mud, was attached to one wall. Only the lean-to had been completed by the time Narcissa arrived. There was a chimney and fireplace and a wooden floor, but no windows and only a blanket to cover the door.[10] The couple stayed in the lean-to for several weeks while work continued on the main house.

By early January 1837, doors and windows had been installed and the house partitioned into three rooms: a bedroom for the Whitmans at one end, a kitchen and dining room in the middle, and a small bedroom and pantry at the other end. Like all the buildings that would be constructed at the Whitman Mission, the roof consisted of poles covered with straw topped with six inches of dirt. Narcissa fought a continuing and futile battle against those roofs. They leaked mud during heavy rains and dusted the rooms with silt in drier weather. The family moved into a larger, more elegant house in 1840, but that structure also had a sod roof. Marcus promised to replace it with a board roof, using lumber from a sawmill he planned to construct in the foothills of the Blue Mountains. Seven years passed before the sawmill became a reality. On the eve of the attack in 1847, he had a stockpile of thirteen thousand board feet at the mission and another forty thousand board feet at the mill, awaiting delivery for, among other things, construction of new roofs.[11]

Pierre Pambrun lent the Whitmans a small stove to heat their bedroom and a table for the kitchen. The only other furniture was a rough bedstead and three chairs (two of them made by Marcus, with cottonwood frames and deerskin seats). Narcissa was obviously ambivalent about her situation. In a letter to her parents dated January 2, 1837, she wrote about being "alone, in the thick darkness of heathenism," yet she insisted "I am spending my winter as comfortably as heart could wish."[12] She gave birth in that house to her only child, a daughter, on the evening of March 14, 1837—the day of her own twenty-ninth birthday. Named Alice Clarissa after her two grandmothers, the child was the first born of American parents in what is now Washington State.

It was apparently an easy delivery. Narcissa wrote that she was "sick" (i.e., in labor) for only about two hours. Catherine Pambrun and her daughter Maria came to help. It must have been strange for Catherine to see a man—Marcus Whitman—attending the birth. In her culture only women assisted with a delivery. After the birth the baby would have been dried off, wrapped in rabbit fur, nursed, and placed in a cradleboard lined with moss.[13] Narcissa was amused to see Catherine and Marcus fumbling with Euro-American-style clothing for her newborn. "It would have made you smile to see them work over the little creature," she wrote to her mother. "Mrs P never saw one dressed before as we dress them having been accostomed [sic] to dress her own in the native stile [sic]."[14]

The Mission House was located about a mile west of a small Cayuse winter village. Most of the fifty or so occupants had been away on the annual fall hunt when the Whitmans moved in, but they had returned in time to greet the arrival of Alice Clarissa. "The Little Stranger is visited daily by the Chiefs & principal men in camp & the women throng the house continually waiting an opportunity to see her," Narcissa reported to her parents. The Indians seemed intrigued by the baby's fair skin and light brown hair; apparently none of them had ever seen a Caucasian infant before. "Her whole appearance is so new to them. Her complexion her size & dress & all excite a deal of wonder," Narcissa wrote.[15] One curiosity, she added, was the fact that her child was not confined to a cradleboard. The Indians "think it very strange that she should sleep with me without being tied up, so that I should not kill her."[16]

Among the visitors who came to see the baby was Tiloukaikt, a leader of the Walla Walla band of Cayuse, one of three major bands during the 1830s. The other two bands were centered on the Umatilla River—one on the headwaters in the Blue Mountains, the other downstream, near present-day Pendleton, Oregon. In her first mention of this headman, Narcissa called him "Tee-low-kike, a kind, friendly Indian." He told her Alice Clarissa was a "Cayuse *te-mi*" (girl), because she had been born on Cayuse land. Narcissa had the impression that "the whole tribe are highly pleased because we allow her to be called a Cayuse Girl."[17]

Tiloukaikt showed an early interest in adopting what Narcissa called "the manners and customs of civilized life."[18] He began cultivating a plot of land under Marcus Whitman's direction, regularly participated in religious services led by the missionaries, and sent three of his children to school at the mission. Narcissa gave them all Christian names. She named the oldest "David," after one of her childhood friends, and the other two "Edward" and "Jane," after two of her siblings. But this was during a honeymoon period. Tiloukaikt later became one of the Whitmans' primary critics and eventual foes.

Arriving at a time when fresh food was scarce, the Whitmans supplemented their diet that first winter by killing and eating nine horses, bought from the Indians at a cost of $6 total, paid mostly in tobacco. They didn't butcher any of the cattle they had driven west from Missouri until 1841, after the small herd had increased to a sustainable level. Whitman tried to buy more cattle from John McLoughlin at Fort Vancouver, saying it was cheaper to raise them for free on the open grasslands than buy horsemeat from the Indians, but McLoughlin refused to sell. More than thirty Indian horses were slaughtered to feed the mission's residents and visitors during the first four years.

Whitman began preparing fields for planting as soon as the snow melted, in late February. It was grueling, bone-cracking work to cut through the thick mantle of sod and the stirrup-high grass that gave Waiilatpu its name. He had one plow for his own use but only fifteen rudimentary hoes to offer would-be farmers among the Cayuse. Still, Whitman was encouraged by the fact that Tiloukaikt, his sons, and several other families were willing to experiment with American-style agriculture. "I think there can be no doubt of their rediness [sic] to adopt cultivation," he exulted (prematurely, it would turn out), "and when they have plenty of food they will be little disposed to wander."[19] He begged the American Board to send him at least fifty more plows and three hundred hoes. "If we had them," he explained, "it would not be long before we should see [Indians] located arround [sic] us, with houses, fields, gardens, hogs, and cows."[20]

Convincing Indians to adopt a settled, agrarian lifestyle was a key agenda item for all Protestant missionaries in Oregon Country. People who moved from place to place as the seasons and food sources changed could not be exposed to "the benefit of constant instruction" in missionary schools and churches. "This field is emphatically white for the harvest," Whitman said, referring to the harvesting of souls, but first the Indians would have to be "attracted and retained by the plough and hoe."[21] Spalding put it more bluntly: "No savage has ever become christianized upon the wing."[22]

Whitman selected Waiilatpu as a location partly because of its potential for agriculture. "We have far more good land for cultivation here," he told the American Board, "than at any other place on the uper [*sic*] Columbia."[23] The site included good soil, lots of sunshine, and a long growing season. What it lacked was abundant rainfall. The Walla Walla Valley averages only about eighteen inches of rain a year. There was plenty of water, though, flowing out of the snowfields in the Blue Mountains and into the tributaries of the Walla Walla River. Whitman dug irrigation ditches to move water from the channel behind his house to his ever-expanding fields. However, easy access to the water proved to be a mixed blessing. The stream regularly rose high enough with spring snowmelt to overflow its banks and flood the cellar in the house. The cellar was lined with adobe bricks, made of mud and straw. The bricks absorbed so much water that at one point Whitman feared they would collapse and the house "would fall upon us."[24] He stubbornly repaired the damage, year after year, until finally giving up and building a new, larger house on higher ground in 1840.

All timber for the mission had to be hauled on horse-drawn sleds from the Blue Mountains, fifteen miles away. It would have been easier to build in the Cayuse style, making use of materials close at hand. John Townsend, the Philadelphia-born naturalist who came to Oregon Country with Nathaniel Wyeth in the early 1830s, remarked on the snug construction of the tule lodges in a Cayuse village on the Umatilla River that he visited in July 1836. Townsend had stayed in the headman's lodge. "The house is really a very comfortable one," he wrote. It was about sixty feet long, fifteen feet wide, well ventilated in summer, weather-tight in winter.[25] But the Whitmans would have been horrified at the idea of living in such a "heathen" dwelling. Instead, they sought to re-create the familiar. Their house looked like one that could have been built anywhere in western New York during frontier times.

The Whitmans worked tirelessly to create the scaffolding for the life they wanted: to build and maintain what they considered suitable shelter; to grow, harvest, and preserve the kind of food they wanted to eat; and to provide the amenities they valued, from woven cloth for their garments to venetian blinds for their windows. They had little help. Three of the four hired hands who had been with them on the Great Plains left before they reached Oregon. The fourth, his name recorded only as "Hinds, a colored man," died of what Whitman called "dropsy" (meaning edema, or swelling of the soft tissues, possibly due to congestive heart failure) while working on the lean-to at Waiilatpu. Hinds was the first person to be buried in the mission cemetery.[26] The Whitmans tried to hire Indians as laborers, but none of the Cayuse and only a few of the neighboring Walla Wallas were willing; only slaves did the kind of work the missionaries wanted done. Their most dependable laborers were Hawaiians recruited from the multicultural workforce at Fort Vancouver, but none of them stayed very long. Narcissa usually had one or two young métis girls to help with household chores, but she complained that they needed constant supervision. She found it frustrating that so few of the native and mixed-race people who would work for them spoke English. "You have no idea how difficult it is to realize any benefit from those who do not understand you," she wrote.[27]

The language barrier was a constant challenge. Whitman confessed he had only a limited command of Nez Perce, the primary language spoken by the Cayuse, after four years in Oregon. Narcissa, by her own account, was never able to "do much more than stammer" in it.[28] Whitman had hoped that the two Nez Perce boys that he had taken east with him would learn enough English to serve as interpreters, but one of the boys, "John," returned to his Nez Perce homeland in November 1836, and the other, "Richard," quarreled with Whitman and left Waiilatpu six months later. Whitman said he was "expeled"; Spalding said he had run away.[29] For the most part, the Whitmans relied on Chinook Jargon to communicate with Indians. They learned the words and phrases that an employer would use in directing the labor of a simple-minded servant: make a fire; chop this wood; cook this food; plow this field, dig this ditch.[30] To explain basic concepts of Christianity, they used language like this, from a lesson created by a Methodist missionary in the Willamette Valley in 1838:

> Your heart good? (*Mican tum-tum cloosh?*) Your heart no good (*Mican tum-tum wake cloosh*). By-and-by you die (*Alaka mican ma-ma lose*). Your heart good you go to God (*Mican tum-tum cloosh mican clatamay Sakalatie*). God make very good your heart (*Sakalatie mamoke hiyas cloosh mican tum-tum*).[31]

After two years in Oregon, Whitman proudly reported to the American Board of Commissioners for Foreign Missions that "the heaviest part of our establishment is made." He had forty acres under cultivation and was producing enough corn, wheat, and potatoes to send Spalding some of the surplus. Whitman's cattle and horses had wintered as well on grassland as if they had been stabled and fed corn and oats in the East. He and Narcissa were raising chickens, turkeys, and hogs and were expecting to have a few sheep soon, imported from Hawaii. "We have no want of Provisions for ourselves and Seed for the Indians," he wrote.[32]

However, there was less evidence of progress with Indians. Whitman couched that part of his report in vague terms. "Several" families were cultivating small plots of land. From fifteen to twenty children were coming to the mission to attend school, at least during the winter. "Many" had acquired "good proficiency" in reading, writing, and speaking English, in classes Narcissa taught in her kitchen. "Some" parents had expressed an interest in having their children go to school year-round. The Indians were apparently "much pleased" with the hymns the missionaries taught them to sing, in Sunday services held in a chief's lodge in the nearby village because the Whitmans' house was too small to accommodate everyone who wanted to come.[33]

The Cayuse had already adopted some elements of Euro-American culture by the time the Whitmans arrived. A few wore articles of European clothing and raised cattle as well as horses. Many prayed twice a day—a practice introduced by French Canadian fur traders working for the Hudson's Bay Company. But their cultural borrowing was limited, and they showed no interest in jettisoning their entire way of life. They planted only those crops—such as potatoes, corn, beans, and melons—that required relatively little tending and did not interfere with hunting, fishing, or root- and berry-gathering cycles. They continued to spend months away from the mission. They were also selective in responding to the Whitmans' brand of Christianity. They enjoyed chanting along with hymns and prayers (sacred chants had long been part of Cayuse spiritual practice). But to the degree that they understood what the Whitmans had to say about damnation and the evils of idolatry, polygamy, original sin, and other aspects of Calvinistic doctrine, they rejected it. "Some feel almost to blame us for telling them about eternal realities," Narcissa wrote. "One said it was good when they knew nothing but to hunt, eat, drink and sleep; now it was bad."[34]

In a letter to the American Board in March 1838, Whitman acknowledged that he and Narcissa were spending more time on "secular affairs" than desirable for missionaries whose professed purpose was to "be the humble instruments of good to the bodies and souls of the benighted Indians." He blamed the lack of help. If they had more "associates and labourers," he explained, they could spend more time learning the language; if they had better command of the language, they could be more effective in transforming the spiritual and physical lives of Indians.[35] Two months later, he sent a more urgent plea to the board. "We are now at an important crisis, and need men and means to carry out what has been so auspiciously begun," he wrote. The "crisis" came into focus with the appearance of Jason Lee, head of the Methodist mission in the Willamette Valley, who stopped by Waiilatpu and then Lapwai while traveling east with plans to convey a shipload of Methodists to Oregon. The Methodist Mission Board had already sent two small groups of missionaries and laypeople, about twenty in all, to reinforce the Willamette mission and establish a satellite station at The Dalles. Lee hoped to add maybe two hundred more. He had been promised at least $40,000 (nearly $1 million today) to finance it. Whitman and Spalding were stunned by the breadth of Lee's ambitions. Deeply envious and more than a little wistful, they hurriedly composed an appeal to their board, asking that they "not be left unsupported while our Methodist Brethren devise so liberal things."[36]

Nearly every letter that Whitman and Spalding had sent to the American Board in the previous two years had included a generic request for more help. Now they went into detail, at length. They asked that thirty ordained ministers, thirty farmers, thirty schoolteachers, ten physicians, and ten mechanics (including blacksmiths), with their wives—a total of two hundred twenty men and women—be sent out "with the least possible delay." The Oregon Mission needed "several tons of iron and steel, a sufficient quantity of balls, 2,000 gun flints, 50 gross Indian awls, 100 dozen knives, blankets, crockery, tinware, two cook stoves, six box stoves. . . ." The list went on and on: four pit saws, two crosscuts with handles, augers, axes, adzes. They wanted "five hundred yards of striped or checked cotton for shirts to be made by native girls." Also, "books, slates, pencils, ink-powder, ink stands, & paper suitable and sufficient for two English schools of 50 scholars each." And brass kettles, glass tumblers, teacups and saucers, eight two-quart pitchers, four washbowls. Not to be omitted: one dozen chamber pots with covers, because it could get cold at Waiilatpu and Lapwai in the winter; and "12 palm leaf hats," because summers were hot; six pairs of men's shoes, an equal number of women's shoes, and how about six large cowbells as well as "maps & charts, etc." It seemed as if the two men were adding to the list as soon as things came to mind, expecting the people in Boston to sort it out. They were in a rush to finish their letter to the board, because Lee had agreed to deliver their message and was ready to depart. Spalding wrote the cover letter, but they both signed it. It included this warning: "You can no longer suffer this great harvest field to remain unoccupied by laborers without inflicting an incalculable injury upon these immortal souls & inciting the fearful displeasure of Heaven."[37]

David Greene, secretary of the board, must have been incredulous and possibly apoplectic when he received this letter and the multipage list accompanying it. The board was overextended, with 360 missionaries and laypeople at 69 locations around the world, and underfinanced, consistently spending more than it was taking in through donations. It had been accumulating ever larger annual deficits even before a banking crisis in 1837 triggered a major depression in the United States and left the board "much embarrassed for want of funds."[38] Greene had not been pleased by the latest bill he had received from the Hudson's Bay Company for purchases made by the Oregon missionaries. He received that bill, for more than $2,000, on July 5, 1837. The very next day, he fired off a letter to Whitman and Spalding, ordering them to slash their spending to $1,000 a year, total, for both stations. "Your mission must be sustained hereafter at a less comparative expense than it has been hitherto, or the Committee will feel obliged to discontinue it," he warned.[39] The two messages—the grandiose hopes for expansion from the West and the warning to cut back from Boston—crossed each other in transit. When Whitman and Spalding sat down with their pens to scratch out their wish list, Lee's voice ringing in their ears, the American Board had already dispatched the only additional group of missionaries that it would ever send to Oregon.

William Henry Gray had returned east on his own in the fall of 1837. After spending time in Ithaca with the Rev. Samuel Parker and briefly attending medical school, Gray convinced the board to send him back to Oregon with reinforcements. Three newly married couples who were already in the pipeline for assignment to overseas missions agreed to go with him. The party traveled overland with the American Fur Company's caravan and arrived in Waiilatpu at the end of August 1838. Greene received the appeal from Oregon for 220 missionaries and laypeople and boatloads of supplies a month later. His wry response was measured: "I would say that your expectations are too high for the means of the Board or for the spirit of a Christian community."[40]

⁓

The new arrivals had little in common besides evangelistic zeal. Three of the men were Congregational ministers. Elkanah Walker, named after a figure in the Old Testament, was a tall, awkward, thirty-three-year-old former farmer from Maine. His wife, Mary Richardson, twenty-seven, was an acerbic, strong-minded woman who had applied on her own to become a missionary before she met Elkanah. Like Narcissa Prentiss, she had been rejected because she was single. Cushing Eells, twenty-eight, born and raised in western Massachusetts, had paid his way through college and seminary by working as a schoolteacher. He was married to Myra Fairbanks Eells, five years his senior, the daughter of a church deacon in Holden, Massachusetts. Twenty-nine-year-old Asa B. Smith of Vermont, a graduate of Middlebury College and Yale Divinity School, was a man of firm convictions and little patience for divergent opinions. His wife, Sarah, twenty-five, traced her ancestors back to the *Mayflower*. Cornelius Rogers, an unmarried twenty-two-year-old, was an acolyte of Rev. Lyman Beecher, the prominent abolitionist minister in Cincinnati. Inspired by the reception the three couples had received when they visited Beecher's church, en route to Oregon, Rogers signed on too.

Gray had impulsively joined the Whitman/Spalding expedition as a carpenter and mechanic in 1836, and just as impulsively returned to his hometown in Fairfield, New York, a year later. He wanted to find a wife, promote the Oregon Mission, and become a full-fledged missionary with a station of his own. He enrolled in medical school (the same one Whitman had attended) but dropped out after three months. To Whitman's extreme annoyance, Gray appropriated the title of "Doctor" anyway. He met his future wife, Mary Augusta Dix, at a church social in Ithaca. He courted her by promising that "thousands will immediately feel your influence and tens of thousands must in time, and unnumbered souls may bless the house in which you did decide to devote your life to the Salvation of 6,277,000 natives on our own continent."[41] They were married on February 25, 1838, eleven days after being introduced, and left for Oregon the next day, joining the three other couples and Cornelius Rogers in Saint Louis in mid-March.

By the time the "reinforcements" reached Waiilatpu, almost six months later, they were all thoroughly sick of each other. "We have a strange company of Missionaries," Mary Walker confided in her diary. "Scarcely one who is not intolerable on some account."[42] The same sense of moral certainty that had drawn them to missionary work seemed to apply to their personal relationships as well, making it hard for them to tolerate what they viewed as shortcomings in others. None of them showed much Christian forbearance for one another.

The seven male members of the American Board's newly expanded Oregon Mission conducted their first business meeting on September 1, 1838. The women were not allowed to participate. The main issue was who was to go where. The men decided that Walker and Eells would establish a new station near Spokane Falls, where the Spokane Indians had given Spalding and Gray what seemed a cordial reception a year earlier. Smith would stay with Whitman. Rogers was to help Spalding at Lapwai. Nobody wanted Gray. Finally, Spalding agreed to take him.

Two days later, the six wives crowded into a room by themselves and organized the Columbia Maternal Association, the first American women's club in the Northwest. Only Narcissa and Eliza were mothers at the time, but two of the other women were pregnant, and they all expected that motherhood would be their primary role in life. Isolated in what they considered a "heathen land," far from family and friends, the women turned to each other for help in "the right performance of our Maternal duties."[43] Such groups, sponsored by evangelical Protestant churches, were common in western New York and New England. By creating an association of their own, the women hoped to connect not only with each other but with the worlds they had left behind. The charter members were never able to meet as a group, in person, again, but they held the equivalent of virtual meetings twice a month, sometimes in the company of one or two other women but often on their own. They set aside an hour on the second and fourth Wednesdays of the month when they would think of each other, read selected texts, and pray for the strength to be mothers in the wilderness.

The Spaldings soon returned to Lapwai, accompanied by Rogers and the Grays. The remaining four couples bickered their way through a long winter in very close quarters at the Whitman Mission.

The only housing consisted of the original Mission House, a total of fifteen hundred square feet, partitioned into five small rooms. Twelve people had been sharing this space before the newcomers arrived: the Whitmans and their toddler daughter; Charles Compo (the French Canadian trapper who had served as an interpreter for Samuel Parker), his Nez Perce wife, and their eighteen-month-old son; four Hawaiian servants; a teenage métis girl; and a young half-Hawaiian, half-Indian boy. The addition of six other adults, one of whom— Mary Walker—was nearly full-term pregnant, seemed to bring out the worst in everyone. Petty grievances flared into major ones under the stress of overcrowding and incompatible personalities. Elkanah Walker chewed tobacco, much to Narcissa's disgust. Myra Eells resented the time Narcissa spent writing. The Walkers used wine for medicinal purposes, and all the newcomers drank wine with communion, offending the teetotaling Whitmans. Asa Smith was "a hog at table."[44] The Smiths were shocked that Mary Walker gave birth to a son exactly nine months and two days after her marriage—a demonstration, they thought, of unseemly carnality.

Myra Eells's use of snuff drove Mary Walker to distraction. Cushing Eells objected to Mary Walker's habit of staying up late. She, in turn, thought he was "very uninteresting and unsocial."[45] Narcissa was alternately peremptory and withdrawn. None of the women felt that the others were doing their share of the household chores. Marcus groused that the board had sent three clergymen as reinforcements when what he needed were people who could work with their hands. Before the winter was over, Smith declared that he would rather leave the Oregon Mission than have any further association with Marcus Whitman. Sarah Smith irritated nearly everyone by weeping almost constantly. "How do you think I have lived with such folks right in my kitchen for the whole winter?" Narcissa asked, in a letter to her sister Jane.[46]

OREGON COUNTRY, 1840s

1 Fort Walla Walla
2 Waiilatpu
3 Pašx̣á
4 Saint Anne's Mission
5 Pendleton
6 The Dalles/Methodist Wascopam Mission
7 Fort Vancouver
8 Oregon City
9 Methodist Mission, Willamette Valley
10 Astoria
11 Tshimakain/Walker, Eells Mission
12 Lapwai/Spalding Mission
13 Kamiah
14 Fort Boise
15 "Cayuse Sisters"

● Landmarks   ◇ Modern-day cities

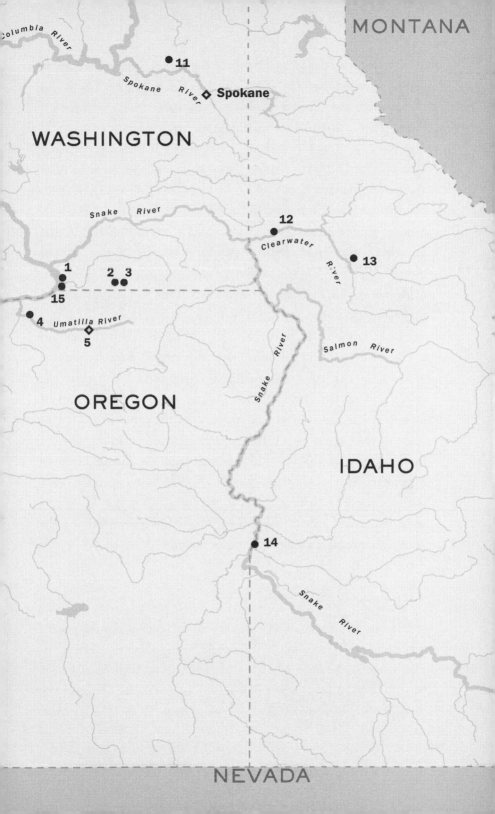

The Smiths moved into a separate structure, hurriedly built of adobe, in early December 1838, just days before Mary Walker's son, Cyrus, was born. Mary was unable to nurse successfully; her attempts brought her such pain that she felt as if she had "two broken breasts."[47] Narcissa, who was still nursing her own child, two-year-old Alice Clarissa, nursed Mary's son for a few weeks but then weaned Alice and stopped feeding Cyrus. She told Mary that if Cyrus got hungry enough, he would somehow get milk from his mother's breasts. A hungry, wailing infant could only have added to the tensions in that household. Mary tried a rudimentary breast pump; she tried artificial nipples. She finally gave up altogether and, over Narcissa's objections, fed Cyrus cow's milk from a bottle. The conflict permanently soured the relationship between the two women.

In early March 1839 the Walkers and the Eells left to establish a new mission at Tshimakain ("Place of Springs"), near present-day Spokane, about 160 miles north of Waiilatpu. The Smiths left at the end of April for a station of their own, at Kamiah, about 60 miles southeast of Lapwai. Members of American Board's Oregon Mission thus ended up on four widely separated stations. One of the consequences was that Whitman had even less time to devote to missionary work at Waiilatpu. He was often called away to the other stations, on business or medical matters (including the delivery of some two dozen American missionary babies over a period of eight years), leaving Narcissa alone and overwhelmed at home.

Neither of the Whitmans ever mastered the language of the people they were trying to convert, but their young daughter seemed to pick it up easily. Alice Clarissa was babbling in both English and Nez Perce when she was just eighteen months old. The Indians were "very much pleased to think she is going to speak their language so readily," Narcissa told her family. "They appear to love her much."[48] By age two the child was speaking both languages "quite fluently," Narcissa bragged.[49] The little girl loved to sing and seemed as interested in the Indians as they were in her. She might have served as a conduit, to help her parents and their hosts recognize the humanity in each other. But around 2:30 p.m. on June 23, 1839, a Sunday, while Marcus and Narcissa were reading and a teenage métis servant was preparing supper, Alice Clarissa took two cups down to the river behind the Mission House to get some water, tumbled in, and drowned. An Indian found her body, lodged against some brush. She was two years, three months, and nine days old.

The Walkers had been visiting the Spaldings at Lapwai and were on their way back to Tshimakain when a messenger reached them with news of the death. If Mary Walker felt much sympathy, she didn't share it with her diary. "We had travelled about 40 miles in an opposite direction & did not deem it expedient to return" for the funeral, she wrote.[50] The same messenger contacted the Spaldings. Henry Spalding had cracked some ribs in a recent fall and was not able to travel by horseback, but he, Eliza, and their toddler daughter set off by canoe for the Whitman Mission. They arrived on the afternoon of June 27. Spalding conducted the funeral later that day.

Narcissa had been a doting and anxious mother. Lacking friends, separated from her family, with a husband who was often away from the mission for weeks at a time, her daughter was "the joy and comfort" of her "lonely situation."[51] She hardly let the child out of her arms until Alice Clarissa was almost a year old. She slept with her until just a week before the drowning, when the toddler asked for a bed of her own. Narcissa reluctantly agreed but put the bed right next to her own, so that she could reach out and touch her at any time.

Narcissa sat with her dead child for four days, only agreeing to a burial after the Spaldings arrived and the body had begun to decompose. "She did not begin to change in her appearance much for the three first days," she wrote in an anguished letter to her parents. "This proved to be a great comfort to me, for so long as she looked natural and was so sweet and I could caress her, I could not bear to have her out of my sight; but when she began to melt away like wax and her visage changed I wished then to put her in so safe, quiet and desirable a resting place as the grave—to see her no more until the morning of the resurrection."[52] The child was buried in a spot north of the house, in a shroud Narcissa made from a gray dress that she had brought with her over the mountains.

The death had at least a temporary mellowing influence on the members of the Oregon Mission. Tensions between Whitman and Spalding, in particular, eased. In an October 15, 1840, letter to David Greene at the American Board, Whitman said that he had been on the verge of leaving the mission because of the strained relationship with Spalding. However, "the Providence of God arrested me in my deliberate determination to do so, by taking away our dear child in so sudden a manner by drowning. Since that time many appearances have changed and I have not seen it my duty to leave."[53]

Narcissa drew her grief around her like a shield. She sank into an almost suicidal depression, manifested by frequent bouts of illness, sometimes staying in her room for days at a time. She sent tortured letters to her friends and family. Perhaps God was punishing her for loving Alice Clarissa too much? Had it been a mistake to let her daughter have so much contact with Indians? Just a month before the drowning, a visiting missionary from Hawaii had warned the Whitmans about "the evils" of allowing the child to learn Nez Perce.[54] Eventually Narcissa decided that "the Lord saw fit to take her from us" because she could not devote herself to the duties of a missionary without neglecting her daughter and thereby exposing her "to the contaminating influence of heathenism."[55] She made a few desultory attempts to continue teaching Indian students, but soon gave it up. "I am tired of living at this poor dying rate," she told the wife of a Methodist missionary at The Dalles. "To be a missionary in name and to do so little or nothing for the benefit of heathen souls, is heart-sickening." Narcissa professed a wish to "do more for their good" but meanwhile walled herself off from Indians as completely as she could.[56]

She found some diversion by taking in foster children, beginning with Helen Mar Meek, the two-year-old daughter of mountain man Joe Meek and a Nez Perce woman. Meek brought the child to the mission in the fall of 1840 and asked the Whitmans to raise and educate her. A year later, mountain man Jim Bridger sent his mixed-race daughter, Mary Ann, then six, to the mission. The grandmother of a third child, the son of a Walla Walla mother and a Spanish father, left him with the Whitmans in 1842, when he was about three. Narcissa gave him the name David Malin, after a minister she had known in Prattsburg. Finally, in 1844 the Whitmans adopted seven orphans whose emigrant parents, Henry and Naomi Sager, had died on the Oregon Trail. Narcissa kept all the children away from the Cayuse and did not allow any of them to speak a word of Nez Perce.

There was plenty of room for the growing family. In June 1840, a year after Alice Clarissa drowned, the Whitmans moved into a large, T-shaped adobe building, three times the size of the original house and located farther from the riverbank. It was an imposing structure, with smoothly plastered, whitewashed exterior walls, surrounded by a high picket fence. The doors, window frames, and shutters were painted a bright green; the interior walls and ceilings were white; the woodwork was a light slate gray; and the floors and pantry shelves were yellow. The kitchen had a huge hearth, thirteen feet long and eight and a half feet wide. A metal cookstove, installed in 1842, supplemented the cooking that was done over the open hearth. There were five other fireplaces, including one in the Whitmans' private parlor and bedroom. The building included a spacious living room, a 1,760-square-foot schoolroom, servants' quarters, a pantry, storerooms, a washroom, and two privies. All the children slept in a large, open loft on the second floor, reached by stairs from the living room.[57]

Indians were permitted to enter this house through only one door and to be in only one room, originally called Indian Hall. Later, that room would be turned over to emigrants, and Indians would be barred from the Mission House entirely. "They are so filthy they make a great deal of cleaning wherever they go," Narcissa complained in a letter to her mother. "We must clean after them, for we have come to elevate them and not to suffer ourselves to sink down to their standard."[58] She never learned to speak the language of the Cayuse, but she made her contempt for them clear. The fencing, the shutters, and the locked doors were physical manifestations of the emotional distance between the Whitmans and the people they had once hoped to "save."

CHAPTER SIX:
MUTUAL
DISILLUSIONMENT

He demanded of me what I had ever paid him for the land.
I answered him "Nothing," and that I never would give him
anything. He then made use of the word "Shame," which is
used in Chinook the same as in English.

—*Marcus Whitman to David Greene, November 11, 1841*

Relations between the Whitmans and the Cayuse deteriorated quickly after the death of Alice Clarissa. Cayuse leaders—including Tiloukaikt, the "kind, friendly Indian" who had christened the child a "Cayuse *te-mi*"—confronted Marcus Whitman on several occasions, demanding that he either pay them for occupying their land or leave. Meanwhile, the missionaries resumed their internal sniping. In 1842 the American Board of Commissioners for Foreign Missions—exasperated by an incessant stream of complaining letters from the four scattered outposts of the Oregon Mission—recalled Henry Spalding and ordered Whitman to leave Waiilatpu and join

129

"Til-au-kite, or The Man in the Act of Alighting," by Paul Kane. The artist visited Cayuse leader Tiloukaikt in his lodge near the Whitman Mission in July 1847 and produced this sketch. The drawing depicts an older man, with a somewhat weary and pensive look, quite unlike the nearly naked, menacing figure in Kane's painting of "Tilli-koit," (page 184) based on the sketch but completed years later. *Stark Museum of Art, Orange, Texas; 31.78.59.*

the group at Tshimakain (near present-day Spokane). Whitman made a dangerous midwinter journey back to Boston, hoping to persuade board members to change their minds. He returned a year later with the first large wagon train on the Oregon Trail. From that point on, the Whitmans maintained only a pretense of ministering to Indians and focused instead on promoting the colonization of Oregon Country by American settlers.

Some of the tension between the missionaries and the Cayuse could be traced back to promises made by the Rev. Samuel Parker, the Bible-thumping Ithaca preacher who convinced the American Board to send him and Whitman on a reconnaissance mission to Oregon in 1835. The two traveled with the American Fur Company to the rendezvous in Wyoming and then parted ways, Whitman returning east to recruit other missionaries, Parker continuing west "to ascertain by personal observation the condition and characters of the Indian tribes, and the facilities for introducing the gospel among them."[1] A fussy, imperious man in his late fifties, Parker spent the winter of 1835–36 at Fort Vancouver as a guest of chief factor John McLoughlin, head of the Hudson's Bay Company's vast Columbia District. McLoughlin's motives were not entirely altruistic. Befriending American missionaries was one way to defuse criticism of the company's hard-nosed efforts to undercut its American competitors in the fur business.

In April 1836, Parker met with three leaders of the Walla Walla Cayuse band—Umtippe (sometimes recorded as Hiyumtipin), an elder; his brother, Waptashtakmahl (also known as Feathercap); and Tiloukaikt—at the place where the Whitmans ultimately built their mission. Parker was accompanied by Pierre Pambrun, head trader at Fort Walla Walla, and John Toupin, the fort's French Canadian interpreter. According to Toupin, Parker told the headmen: "I come to select a place for a mission but I do not intend to take your lands for nothing," explaining that "a big ship" would arrive every year, loaded with goods that would be given—not sold—to the Indians in return for the use of the land. Parker then traveled north to the Lapwai area, where he made the same promises to the Nez Perce. "Next spring there will come a missionary to establish himself here and take a piece of land," Parker reportedly said, "but he will not take it for nothing; you shall be paid every year; this is the American fashion."[2]

Rather than meeting Whitman and his companions at the rendezvous that summer, as planned, Parker abruptly ended his "exploring tour" and returned to Fort Vancouver. He sailed from there to New York via Hawaii and was back in Ithaca by May 1837. He left no useful information for Whitman or Spalding; they had to search for mission sites on their own. His never-fulfilled promise of annual payments to the Indians became a source of growing discord as the years went on.

Fundamental cultural differences contributed to the increasing friction between the missionaries and their hosts. The Cayuse customarily had free access to each other's lodges; the Whitmans put up fences and locked their doors to keep the Indians out. Narcissa, in particular, fought to retain the standards of privacy she had enjoyed in her middle-class New York home. Barriers to free entry offended Indian ideas about community. The Cayuse refused to give up the seasonal mobility that anchored their traditional way of life. "Their being absent so much of the time is exceedingly trying to us," Narcissa complained.[3]

Gift-giving was an essential part of social and political interaction in Cayuse life; the missionaries regarded the practice as extortion. The Whitmans had scarcely settled in at Waiilatpu when Umtippe called on them, for what he probably supposed would be an exchange of gifts. Narcissa expressed outrage. "A few days ago he took it into his head to require pay for teaching us the language," she wrote to her parents. "He is a mortal beggar as all Indians are." The letter was dated January 2, 1837. She had been living among Indians for less than a month.[4]

Cayuse men scoffed when they saw Whitman and his hired hands building houses at the mission. Constructing shelters was a task for women in Indian society. The way Whitman treated his wife disturbed some Indians too. Tiloukaikt told him he was setting a bad example by allowing Narcissa to travel with him on social calls and deferring to her in public. The missionaries, for their part, thought Indian men treated their women like slaves. Polygamy was an established part of Plateau culture. Having multiple wives indicated a man's high status and added to the family's economic security, since women gathered much of the food. To the missionaries, polygamy was a sign of moral depravity, along with gambling, horse racing, and many other aspects of traditional Cayuse life.[5]

As religious evangelists, the missionaries tried to impose a rigid, restrictive belief system on people who were essentially religious synthesizers. The Indians were willing to graft new ideas onto old beliefs, but not to abandon old beliefs altogether. The missionaries insisted that they shrug off all the remnants of their old spiritual lives and be reborn into entirely new ones, based on baffling Calvinistic concepts of original sin and predestination. Whitman tried to tell the Cayuse that they were "lost, ruined & condemned" and prayer alone would not save them.[6] It was not enough to simply go to church, lead good lives, and pray every day. They could avoid the horrors of hell only by recognizing that they were essentially wicked, doomed by the fall of Adam; accepting their guilt, and offering their souls to Christ for complete regeneration. Narcissa summarized their reaction in a letter to her father: "They feel so bad, disappointed, and some of them angry. . . . Some threaten to whip him [Marcus] and to destroy our crops, and for a long time their cattle were turned onto our potato field every night to see if they could not compel him to change his course of instruction with them."[7]

There were many conflicts over the issue of property. From the Indian perspective the houses, tools, livestock, crops, even the clothing worn by the missionaries represented great wealth, and those who possessed great wealth were obliged to share it with those who had less. Historian Larry Cebula has written that white ideas about the ownership of crops would have been foreign to people "accustomed to helping themselves to the bounties of the earth."[8] The Whitmans, however, considered themselves mere stewards of property that was actually owned by the American Board; they balked at giving any of it away and sometimes went to drastic lengths to prevent Indians from "stealing" anything, including food. In one notorious instance in 1841, William Henry Gray (who had returned to Waiilatpu to help build more housing at the mission complex) injected tartar emetic into some ripe watermelons and placed them in a field as bait. A few Indians ate the melons and were sickened. Gray joked about it. Archibald McKinlay, chief trader at Fort Walla Walla that year, said later that "the melon affair" was a turning point in Cayuse attitudes toward Whitman. "After that," McKinlay wrote, "they began to suspect he was a dangerous medicine man."[9] Although it was Gray who poisoned the melons, Whitman got the blame. Whitman himself was known to put out meat laced with strychnine or arsenic to poison wolves to protect his livestock, especially his sheep. He supposedly warned the Indians not to eat the meat, but the warnings alone could have contributed to the impression that he had lethal forces at his command. And on at least one occasion, according to one of Whitman's employees, several Indians sampled the poisoned meat and nearly died.[10]

Whitman's status as a medicine man, or *te-wat*, was a recurring issue. In his initial meeting with Cayuse leaders, Samuel Parker described Whitman as "a sorcerer of great power" who would be coming soon to Cayuse country. The comment was intended to awe the Indians. It ended up becoming, in Whitman's words, "a cause of much anxiety to me."[11] In Plateau culture, a *te-wat* was recognized as having supernatural powers that could be used to cure the ill or, in certain circumstances, to kill. It was considered acceptable, even mandatory, to take the life of a *te-wat* whose patients died, on the grounds that his (or her) power to heal had somehow been corrupted.[12] Whitman was well aware of Cayuse attitudes toward healers who failed to heal. He and Narcissa had been living at Waiilatpu for less than six months when Umtippe brought his wife to the mission for treatment of what Whitman diagnosed as "inflammation of the lungs" (possibly pneumonia). Umtippe warned Whitman that if his wife died, he would kill him. "It has been, and still is the case with them, when one dies in your care they will hold you responsible for his life, and you are in great danger of being killed," Narcissa wrote shortly afterward.[13]

Umtippe's wife recovered, possibly despite (rather than because of) Whitman's treatment. His medical arsenal consisted chiefly of calomel, a purgative that would have contributed to dehydration and made most sick people sicker; tincture of iodine, taken internally as a cure-all for everything from bronchitis to gangrene; a mercury-based compound called "blue mass" or "blue pills"; and bleeding. Still, Indians often came to Whitman, demanding medicine or asking to be bled—practices they apparently associated with white man's power. Narcissa occasionally dispensed pills when Marcus was away from the mission, giving her something of the aura of a *te-wat* as well. Both Whitmans would find themselves in danger a few years later, when a measles epidemic struck the Walla Walla Valley. While most of the whites in their care then recovered, they couldn't keep Indians from dying.

The Cayuse and their Nez Perce relatives confronted Whitman and his colleagues on several occasions in the early 1840s, clearly expressing the feeling that they were not reaping the rewards, spiritual or material, that they had expected when they invited missionaries into their communities. On one occasion a group of Nez Perces angrily told missionary Asa Smith to pay for the use of the land at his mission at Kamiah or leave. Indians living near Spalding's station at Lapwai destroyed the dam used to power the waterwheel at his newly completed sawmill, and destroyed it again after he rebuilt it. A Nez Perce leader known as Old James stood up during a Sunday service at Lapwai to say the missionaries were making the people miserable and ruining their lives, instead of helping to make what had been good lives better.

Whitman was the target of the most overt acts of hostility. He detailed some of them in a 5,055-word letter to the American Board in 1841. In one incident a Cayuse named Tilkanaiks deliberately turned some of his horses into the cornfield at Waiilatpu. When Whitman protested, the Indian "demanded of me what I had ever given him for the land. I answered 'Nothing,' and that I never would give him anything. He then made use of the word 'Shame,' which is used in Chinook the same as in English." Then Tilkanaiks punched Whitman, twice, hard, on the chest. A few days later, several Cayuses forced their way into the main Mission House, broke windows, and smashed the kitchen door. One yanked Whitman's collar, tore his clothes, and hit him in the mouth with his fist.

Another time, Tiloukaikt approached Whitman and tugged on the missionary's ears, first one, then the other—perhaps a gesture meaning that Whitman must open his ears and listen. Not happy with the response, Tiloukaikt pulled the hat from Whitman's head and threw it into the mud. Whitman, in turn-the-other-cheek mode, put the dripping hat back on his head. They went through this routine three times. Whitman insisted there would be no concessions. The missionaries would not pay for land or timber; they would not allow the Indians to enter the Mission House through any door and go into any room they wanted; and they would not stop expanding the mission. Archibald McKinlay sent his interpreter to calm things down. Waptashtakmahl (Feathercap), one of the leaders who had met with Samuel Parker years earlier, indicated that it was customary to settle arguments by distributing gifts, as a goodwill gesture. Whitman, in a remarkable display of arrogance and intransigence, said he wouldn't give away a single awl or pin.[14]

Whitman blamed the Indians' "agitation" on Catholics. Two Catholic priests—François N. Blanchet and Modeste Demers, both Jesuits from Quebec—had arrived at Fort Walla Walla in 1838. They celebrated mass; blessed the marriage of Pierre Pambrun and his métis wife, Catherine; baptized three of their children; and met with Walla Walla and Cayuse tribal members before going on to Fort Vancouver. Demers returned in the summer of 1839, proselytizing and baptizing Indians throughout the region. To the Whitmans, "Papist" priests represented a threat secondary only to paganism itself. "The conflict has begun—what trials await us we know not," wrote Narcissa.[15]

The French Canadian Catholics were markedly more successful in converting Indians than their American Protestant counterparts. The priests had been invited to Oregon by the Hudson's Bay Company (many of whose employees and executives were Catholic) and thus benefited from association with an organization the Indians knew and respected. Also, as single men, they were more mobile than missionaries with families. They could accompany Indians on their seasonal rounds, which gave them more time to learn native languages and customs. This approach meant that the priests became "culturally steeped, like Catholic teabags" and may account for their ability to repackage Catholicism in ways that appealed to Indians.[16] Perhaps above all, they won converts by being willing to baptize anyone who wanted baptism. The Protestant missionaries, in contrast, withheld baptism until potential converts demonstrated proof of complete conversion and rebirth—"an entire change of heart."[17] In the eleven-year tenure of the Whitman Mission, not a single local Indian was ever deemed worthy of baptism.

A useful tool for the Catholics in the battle for Indian souls was a visual aid that Blanchet devised to illustrate the steps to salvation. His "Catholic ladder" consisted of lines and symbols carved onto a long, narrow board, originally called a Sahale stick ("stick from heaven" in Chinook Jargon). It depicted Protestantism as a withered branch of Christianity, falling into the flames of hell. In response, Henry Spalding designed and his wife Eliza drew and painted a Protestant ladder, showing Martin Luther leading the way to heaven and the Pope as the Antichrist, roasting in hell. Each version implied that damnation awaited converts to the other's faith.

Oregon Country became a landscape of competition. The interdenominational rivalry between Catholics and Protestants was mirrored in the rivalry between the United States and Great Britain over the northwest boundary between the United States and British-owned Canada. The Americans wanted the border set at the forty-ninth parallel; Great Britain wanted it to be drawn farther south, along the Columbia River. The two nations had signed a treaty of joint occupation in 1818 and amended it in 1827 but did not finally settle the border dispute until 1846. Neither country acknowledged that the land was already occupied by peoples whose ancestors had lived there for thousands of years. "While the missionaries vied for their souls, the U.S. and Britain vied for land," one historian commented.[18] Meanwhile, the Hudson's Bay Company competed with American companies for furs and other resources extracted from the land. As Confederated Tribes scholar and member Roberta Conner put it in 2009: "There's a resource competition going on, there's a land competition going on, there's a philosophical or theological competition going on, and we're just in the middle of all of it."[19]

The grim truce that the American Board's missionaries had cobbled together after Alice Clarissa's death soon unraveled. Long, bickering letters from Oregon piled up on the desk of board secretary David Greene in Boston. The complaints ranged from the petty (a dispute over a milk cow) to the poisonous (overlapping accusations of mismanagement, incompetence, lying, and theft). Whitman said either he or Spalding had to go. William Henry Gray threatened to leave if he could not have a mission of his own. In one particularly venomous series of rants, Asa Smith claimed Spalding was insane. He accused Spalding of deliberately exaggerating the number of Indians in the Northwest and their interest in Christianity to gain support from unsuspecting church groups in the East, urged the board to recall both Spalding and Gray, and suggested that it close down the entire operation and sell everything to the Methodists.

By 1842 the American Board had had enough. It ordered Spalding to return home, advised Smith and Gray to do the same, and told Whitman to close his mission at Waiilatpu and move, with Cornelius Rogers, north to the station at Tshimakain. David Greene wrote that the board was "deeply grieved" by "the divisions and contradictions, the want of confidence in each other and the want of fraternal intercourse." It was evident "that your company cannot live and labor together, and that the mission must either be abandoned, or new men must be sent in to the field to take your places." The missionaries were setting a bad example for traders and others in the region through their internecine quarreling, and the board was embarrassed by their behavior.[20]

When Greene wrote those words, in February 1842, missionaries Smith and Rogers had already resigned and Gray was preparing to leave as well. The remaining members of the Oregon Mission had pledged comity and brotherhood and sent letters to that effect to Boston. Under the best of circumstances it took six months for correspondence from one coast to reach the other, and an equal amount of time for a reply to be received. News of the ceasefire reached Greene two months after he had sent out the orders to break up the mission. He dashed off another letter, telling Whitman and Spalding to carry on as usual. By the time that letter reached Oregon, Whitman was on his way to Boston to persuade the board to rescind an order it had already rescinded.

Whitman had received Greene's initial directive on September 14, 1842, when Elijah White, a former Methodist missionary, showed up at Waiilatpu and handed it to him. White, a medical doctor from New York with an unflinching sense of self-importance, had been kicked out of the Methodist mission in the Willamette Valley in 1841. He returned east by ship and ended up in Washington, DC, where he somehow convinced the War Department to appoint him as "sub-Indian agent for Oregon," even though the federal government had no legal authority to do anything in Oregon. White arrived at Waiilatpu as part of the first substantial group of emigrants to cross the Rockies, about 125 men, women, and children, bound for the Willamette Valley. In addition to the instructions from the American Board, White brought news that a Missouri senator had introduced a bill offering every settler who made it to Oregon the right to claim a whole section of land, 640 acres, free and clear. The offer was made, of course, without the knowledge or approval of any of the indigenous inhabitants of the land. The bill never passed, but it dangled like a beacon in front of land-hungry would-be emigrants.

Whitman called an emergency meeting of his remaining associates. They agreed that he should go to Boston as quickly as possible and plead for a second chance to maintain the stations at Waiilatpu and Lapwai. He left on October 3, 1842, accompanied by Asa L. Lovejoy, a Massachusetts-born lawyer who had just arrived in Oregon (with Elijah White's party); an Indian guide; and a dog named Trapper. Whitman was in such a hurry that he forgot to pack his comb, pencil, journal, and compass.[21] The three men pushed eastward, through snowstorms and icy rivers, to Fort Hall, then cut south, taking a thousand-mile detour to the Santa Fe Trail for fear of alleged "Indian trouble." At one point, out of food, they ate the dog. They averaged a then-record-setting sixty miles a day for 150 days, despite being immobilized by occasional blizzards and refusing to travel on Sundays.

Narcissa, back at Waiilatpu, lasted less than a week on her own. In a lengthy, disjointed letter to her husband, she claimed that an Indian had tried to break into her bedroom three nights after Marcus left. She said she had been asleep when someone shoved against her door and tried to unlatch it, and only her hysterical screams had driven off the assailant and "delivered me from the hand of a savage man." Afterward, she insisted that one of the Hawaiian hired hands move his bedding into the kitchen, to be closer to her room if needed.[22] There is no evidence to corroborate Narcissa's account of what happened that night. Biographer Julie Roy Jeffrey has pointed out that Narcissa was always anxious about sleeping alone; she could have imagined or dreamed the whole thing.[23] None of her fellow whites in Oregon Country, however, ever doubted that she had been the target of an attempted rape.

Real or imagined, the incident gave Narcissa an excuse to leave the mission. She sent word to Archibald McKinlay at Fort Walla Walla. He came himself to take her to the fort in a wagon. She traveled most of the twenty-five miles lying down in a trundle bed in the back, prostrated, it would seem, by remembered terror. Her three young Euro-Indian wards—Mary Ann Bridger, seven; Helen Mar Meek, four; and David Malin, perhaps four—came along too. Spalding arranged to have William Geiger, another newly arrived emigrant, live at the Whitman Mission and take care of the property. Narcissa, less content with the rustic accommodations at Fort Walla Walla than she had once been, gratefully accepted an invitation to move in with the Methodist missionaries at The Dalles. She and the two young girls, traveling in a Hudson's Bay boat, arrived there on October 29, 1842. She left the boy at Fort Walla Walla. Except for a brief visit in May 1843, Narcissa did not return to Waiilatpu during the entire year that Marcus was gone.

Within weeks of Marcus Whitman's departure for Boston, rumors began to circulate among the Cayuse about the purpose of his trip. Some said he had gone east to get soldiers who would force the Indians off the land and enslave them; others said he had gone to get poison to kill them all. The Cayuse had heard stories from Iroquois and Algonquian people about lives lost to disease and land lost to greed when Americans came into their ancestral lands. A Delaware Indian known as Tom Hill or Delaware Tom warned the Nez Perce, who warned the Cayuse, that the missionaries would bring in many more whites who would take land and not pay for it.[24] "They have heard that you have gone home and are coming back next fall with fifty men to fight them," Narcissa reported in a letter to her husband, sent to him in care of David Greene in Boston.[25] The rumors fed on each other, in a petri dish of suspicion and distrust.

William Geiger, the caretaker at Waiilatpu, sent alarming reports about "the excitement" to Narcissa at the Methodist mission. He said some of the young Cayuse were talking about going to war against "the Bostons" (a term for Americans) and were held back only by the counsel of older men. Frissons of panic spread from the missionaries at The Dalles to Oregon City, the center of white settlement in the Willamette Valley, and to Elijah White, newly ensconced there as the dubiously commissioned "sub-Indian agent." Oregon City, near the falls of the Willamette River, was a hamlet of perhaps seventy people. Nervous residents demanded that White either fortify the town to fend off an attack or gather a militia and march inland to subdue the restive Cayuse by force. "If words would not answer," Narcissa wrote to Mary Walker, at the American Board's mission at Tshimakain, the plan was to "make powder and balls do it."[16]

Elijah White arrived at the Whitman Mission in late May 1843 for a council with the Cayuse and Walla Walla. He had held a similar meeting with the Nez Perce at Lapwai five months earlier. White's objective in both cases was twofold: to impose "laws" protecting missionaries and other white people; and to convince the Indians to adopt a system of leadership that would make it easier for whites to deal with them. Joining him at Waiilatpu were a reluctant Narcissa, two of her Methodist hosts, and Henry Spalding, who traveled down from Lapwai with a large party of Nez Perces. Two Christianized Nez Perce leaders, known to whites as Ellis and Lawyer, served as the main interpreters.

An estimated three hundred Cayuse and Walla Walla men showed up to hear what Elijah White had to say. He began by asking them to accept the "Laws of the Nez Perces," so-called because they had been nominally adopted by the Nez Perce during the council at Lapwai. Spalding, who had probably written most of the "laws" himself, had printed them in an eight-page booklet. The list ran to eleven. The interpreters read them out loud. Article 1: "Whoever willfully takes life shall be hung." Article 2: "Whoever burns a dwelling house shall be hung." Most of the rest were aimed at curbing behavior the missionaries found annoying. Article 5 prohibited anyone from entering a dwelling without permission from the occupant. Article 6 made minor theft (valued at less than one beaver pelt) punishable by twenty-five lashes; the penalty for major theft was fifty lashes. Article 8 stipulated: "If anyone enter a field, and injure the crops, or throw down the fence, so that cattle or horses go in and do damage, he shall pay all damages, and receive 25 lashes for every offense." Under Article 9 only those who "travel or live among the game" could have dogs, and if a dog killed any domestic animal, the owner would have to pay damages and kill the dog. (Spalding was obsessive about keeping Indian dogs away from his sheep.) Article 11 required: "If an Indian break these laws, he shall be punished by his chiefs; if a white man break them, he shall be reported to the agent, and be punished at his instance."[27] The difference in wording was subtle but significant. Punishment for any violation of the rules by white people would be at the discretion of Elijah White or his successor as "agent."

Clues about the Indians' reactions to this presentation can be found in an account by Rev. Gustavus Hines, one of the two Methodist missionaries who witnessed it. According to Hines, the first comments came from PeoPeoMoxMox, a prominent Walla Walla leader (also known as Yellow Bird), who asked: "Where are these laws from? Are they from God or from the earth? I would think you might say, they were from God. But I think they are from the earth, because, from what I know of white men, they do not honor these laws." A Cayuse identified as "the Prince" said the laws reminded him of all the unfulfilled promises made to him and his fathers. White people had been coming into the country for a long time, he said, always promising to do good, "but they had all passed by and left no blessing behind them." Tauitau (also spelled Tawatoy), a headman from a large Cayuse band on the Umatilla River, "appeared quite angry, and disposed to quarrel." But there were others who spoke in favor of accepting the laws, and after two days of discussion, the headmen essentially shrugged and apparently agreed.[28]

Elijah White's other objective was to get the Cayuse and Walla Walla to adopt a centralized power structure, with a "principal chief" at the top; below him, a network of "subordinate chiefs," representing individual villages; and below them, "officers" who would enforce commands coming from the top—like a corporate flow chart.[29] It was a completely foreign concept to Plateau peoples. The Nez Perce, for example, were less a "tribe" than a collection of roughly forty autonomous bands, connected by language and culture but each with its own system of leadership. The Cayuse were divided into at least nine bands (some sources say as many as nineteen). Membership was fluid and leadership diffuse, situational, and limited. It was unfathomable to give one person authority over everyone. Still, Elijah White insisted that the Indians pick a "chief." The Cayuse finally seemed to consent to the selection of Five Crows, Tauitau's older half-brother. With that, White gave the Indians an ox, and Narcissa contributed a hog. The animals were butchered and everyone—about six hundred men, women, and children—sat down for a feast. Ellis, the Nez Perce "chief," passed around a pipe to close the ceremonies. Then the Indians and the white people went their separate ways. "In the evening all was still," Hines wrote, "and, walking out to the camping ground where the fires were still blazing, I found but one solitary old Indian, who was boiling up the feet of the ox for his next day's supplies."[30]

The conference might have seemed a pointless exercise. White had no authority to impose any "laws." There were no "chiefs" who could enforce them. As historian Elliott West has noted, several days of discussion with a white man were not going to overturn "a social order seasoned for centuries."[31] But there would be consequences. Two years later, PeoPeoMoxMox sought justice under the "Laws of the Nez Perces" for the death of his eldest son, christened Elijah Hedding by the Methodist missionaries who had educated him. The young man spoke English, professed Christianity, and was admired by both whites and Indians. He was shot and killed by a white man in a dispute over a mule during a cattle-buying trip to California. White, purveyor of the "laws" that PeoPeoMoxMox tried to invoke, expressed sympathy for the death of "this educated and accomplished young chief" but said he could do nothing to punish the perpetrator. He called on Ellis, the designated Nez Perce "high chief," to smooth things over but concluded, with some prescience: "There might be much difficulty in settling the affair."[32] The degree to which he was right is discussed in more detail in Chapter 7.

Narcissa left Waiilatpu the day after the council ended. In letters to her family and friends, she said Elijah White, acting as a medical doctor, had insisted she go to Fort Vancouver and put herself under the care of Dr. Forbes Barclay, "an eminent physician" newly arrived from Scotland. She shrouded the guilt she might have felt for not staying at the mission by writing at length about her various ailments: stomach pains, bowel pains, headaches, rheumatic pains, fatigue, kidney problems, failing eyesight, a persistent pain in her side, "prolapses," even "a beating tumour which is liable to burst and extinguish life at any moment."[33] Depression may have accounted for much of her poor health. Or perhaps, as her biographer suggests, she simply "used invalidism as a means of escaping from some of the difficulties of her situation"—like many women of her class in the mid-nineteenth century.[34]

Narcissa spent a pleasant two months at Fort Vancouver. Barclay told her that the source of her problems was an "enlargement" of her right ovary. He prescribed iodine (taken internally, a popular medical shot in the dark at the time), rest, and light recreation. Feeling "very much improved by his kind attentions," Narcissa left Fort Vancouver in July 1843 for a sojourn with the Methodists at their main mission station on the Willamette River near present-day Salem.[35] She took a side trip with Jason Lee, head of the Methodist operations in Oregon, to Astoria (then called Fort George), to enjoy "the benefit of a sea breeze" and say goodbye to a group of Americans set to sail back to New York on a Hudson's Bay Company ship. She also visited a nearby Methodist satellite station at Clatsop. "My beloved parents may think it strange that I should wander about the country so much when my dear husband is absent," she wrote, in one of several self-justifying letters home. "It serves to occupy my mind . . . and besides this, journeying is beneficial to my health."[36]

Back in the Willamette Valley, Narcissa enjoyed what she would later tell her father were some of the happiest moments in her life. The highlight was a four-day camp meeting—the kind of emotion-laden revival she had loved while growing up in Prattsburg. It was "a precious season" that "filled me with joy inexpressible." She was in the midst of a second "protracted meeting" at Willamette Falls when word came that her husband had returned and would be waiting for her at The Dalles.[37] Her ambivalence was unmistakable: relief, on the one hand, that he had survived a hazardous journey; and dread, on the other hand, because it meant she would be going back to "dwell among the heathen" in a "dreary land of heathenish darkness."[38] She had been living with white people for more than a year, "free from any distracting cares of my family and the station." There had been no Indians peeking into her windows, no endless cycle of chores awaiting her.[39]

Narcissa had begged her sister Jane to come west with Marcus on his return trip and was bitterly disappointed to find that she had not. Whitman had brought only one family member with him: his thirteen-year-old nephew, Perrin. With an obviously heavy heart, Narcissa left the Willamette for The Dalles in late September 1843 for a reunion with her husband and her foster children. From there, "I turned my face with my husband toward this dark spot [Waiilatpu] and dark, indeed, it seemed to me when compared with the scenes, social and religious, which I had so recently been enjoying with so much zest."[40]

Whitman had stumbled into Boston six months earlier, ragged, stinky, frostbitten, and not particularly welcome. David Greene scolded him for leaving his station, gave him some money for new clothes, and told him to come back after he had cleaned up. It turned out that the American Board's Prudential Committee had reversed itself once again and reimposed its original order to shut down the missions at Waiilatpu and Lapwai. That decision was made largely on the basis of finances: facing a deficit of $80,000 in 1843, the American Board was in no mood to finance activities that seemed fruitless. A more presentable Whitman made his case to the committee on April 4, 1843. He argued that Waiilatpu was a strategic rest stop and supply station for travelers to Oregon and that "Papists" (Catholics) would take it over if the Protestants abandoned it. Also, he and Spalding could "do more for the civilization and social improvement" of the Indians if they did not have to spend so much time working to feed, clothe, and house themselves and their families. After several days of deliberation, the committee reversed itself once again and agreed that Whitman and Spalding could continue their operations. It also gave Whitman permission to essentially sublease mission property to "a small company of intelligent and pious laymen," who could take over the farming at both stations, manage the livestock, operate the mills and the shops, and relieve the missionaries of the "great amount of manual labor which is now necessary for their subsistence"—but only if it could be done without any expense to the American Board.[41]

Whitman spent about six weeks in the East. En route to Boston, he had stopped in Washington, DC, where he met with James Porter, the new secretary of war. He later sent Porter a proposed bill that would have established a line of military posts stretching to Oregon, each surrounded by a farming community to provide food for travelers, with a blacksmith shop to repair wagons and reshoe horses, and other businesses catering to emigrants. He also envisioned a pony express for mail service to all these new communities in the West. In New York City, Whitman had an interview with Horace Greeley, the influential editor of the *New York Tribune*, who called him "the roughest man we have seen this many a day," but also "a man fitted to be a chief in rearing a moral empire among the wild men of the wilderness."[42] Whitman visited members of his family and Narcissa's, spoke in a number of churches, raised a little money, and tirelessly evangelized for the settlement of Oregon by the righteous. He was in Massachusetts and New York during a period of increasingly intense debate about slavery, but he made no mention of it in any of his surviving correspondence. As he prepared for his return journey, he sent a letter to one of Narcissa's brothers. "It is now decided in my mind that Oregon will be occupied by American citizens," he wrote. "Those who go only open the way for more."[43]

He arranged to take his nephew, Perrin (the son of Whitman's recently widowed brother, Samuel) back to Oregon with him. By mid-May 1843 the two of them were in Saint Louis, where they joined a wagon train organized by Peter H. Burnett, a Missouri lawyer with a pile of debts and dreams of escaping them in Oregon.[44] The train included one hundred twenty wagons, at least eight hundred and possibly as many as one thousand emigrants, and from three thousand to five thousand horses, mules, oxen, and cattle. It was so large that the assemblage soon split into two. Jesse Applegate, another Missourian, led the second, slower group. Although Whitman was not involved in organizing this wagon train, he played a key role in its success by convincing its leaders that the wagons could be driven all the way to Oregon.

The first of the wagons rolled into the Whitman Mission in late September 1843. The watching Cayuse must have been stunned.

Charles Wilkes, commander of the United States Exploring Expedition, estimated that there were only about eleven hundred Indians in the entire Walla Walla Valley when he led a naval squadron to the region in 1842. The number of emigrants on the trail the next year was equal to 80 to 90 percent of that population. To borrow an analogy from historian Elliott West, for people in Boston the equivalent would have been more than seventy-five thousand western Indians marching through that city on their way to settle in Cape Cod.[45]

Most of the emigrants quickly moved on to the Willamette Valley, but when Marcus returned to the Whitman Mission with Narcissa in early November 1843, the complex was crammed with people. The only unoccupied room in the large Mission House was the dining room. A couple from Illinois and their newborn infant had settled into the Whitmans' bedroom; a family of seven and a bachelor were packed into the one-time "Indian Hall"; a couple with four young children had claimed a room off the kitchen; and a French Canadian man was sleeping in the kitchen. All together, there were twenty-six people in the Mission House and another twelve in a one-and-a-half-story dwelling that would soon become known as the Emigrant House. One man was bedded down in the blacksmith shop. The evening meal on Narcissa's first day back was a dramatic reminder of the relative comfort she had left behind. It consisted of cornmeal mush with a little milk, potatoes, and tea. The newcomers had bought or stolen and eaten nearly everything else.

A trickle of emigrants (13 in 1840) became a stream (24 in 1841), then a river (112 in 1842), and then a flood. Discouraged by his lack of progress in converting Indians, Whitman found a new mission. "I have no doubt our greatest work is to be to aid the white settlement of this country," he wrote to Narcissa's parents. "The Indians have in no case obeyed the command to multiply and replenish the earth, and they cannot stand in the way of others doing so."[46]

CHAPTER SEVEN

EXPLOSION OF GRIEF
AND VIOLENCE

The Indians are roused a good deal at seeing so
many emigrants.

—*Narcissa Whitman to her sister Clarissa, May 20, 1844*

The Cayuse watched with increasing alarm and resentment as more
and more whites moved through their territory, using up scarce
firewood, killing game without permission, and depleting grasses
needed for Indian horses and cattle. Between 1843 and 1847
nearly ten thousand settlers traveled overland to Oregon Country
in rut-making wagon trains. Most bypassed the Whitman Mission
after 1844, using a more direct route to the Willamette Valley, but
hundreds still detoured to rest and recover at Waiilatpu. More out-
buildings were added to the mission complex, more fields fenced
in. The Whitmans retreated from missionary work to focus almost
exclusively on supporting the emigrants. Cayuse leaders warned
Marcus Whitman that he was, in effect, violating his lease. "His

expressed purpose for being with the Cayuse was to teach them about the Christian religion," Antone Minthorn, former chairman of the Confederated Tribes of the Umatilla Indian Reservation, wrote in a tribal history. "But he brought more people, developed more land, and brought sickness that killed many Cayuse."[1]

Whitman ignored the warnings. He had come to believe that American colonization of Oregon Country was inevitable, even divinely ordained. Like the biblical Canaanites, the Indians had ignored the dictates of the Lord and would have to forfeit their lands. "I am fully convinced that when a people refuse or neglect to fill the designs of Providence, they ought not to complain at the results," he wrote in a letter to Narcissa's parents, "and it is equally useless for Christians to be anxious on their account."[2] In other words, the Indians were doomed and Christians shouldn't worry about it.

Whitman was delighted when mountain men Robert Newell and Joe Meek showed up at Waiilatpu in September 1840 with three mostly intact wagons—the first ones to be driven over the Blue Mountains and into the Walla Walla Valley. The two men, accompanied by their Indian wives and children and two other trappers, had used mules to haul the wagons to the Whitman Mission from Fort Hall, some 450 miles to the east, over steep, rocky terrain. They arrived "in a rather rough and reduced state," Newell wrote, "quite sorry that we had undertaken the job." Whitman insisted they would never regret it. "You have broken the ice," he reportedly told Newell, "and when others see that wagons have passed, they, too, will pass, and in a few years the valley will be full of our people."[3]

Whitman was proud of his role in encouraging "our people" to settle in Oregon Country. He boasted that he had "eminently aided the Government," first by bringing two white women over the Rocky Mountains in 1836, paving the way for many others to follow; and then by guiding the first major wagon train through the Blue Mountains and into the Walla Walla Valley in 1843, using the rudimentary road that Newell and Meek had carved out earlier.[4] The subsequent influx of Americans tilted the boundary dispute with Great Britain in favor of the United States in 1846. Whitman took credit for that too. "By means of the establishment of the wagon road," he wrote, "the present acquired rights of U. States by her Citizens hung."[5]

Midwestern farmers, battered by financial panics in 1837 and 1841, packed up and headed west in growing numbers. Missouri senator Lewis Linn sponsored a bill in 1841 granting free land in Oregon to anyone who could travel across the Rockies to claim it. The bill never passed—Great Britain and the United States were still arguing over the boundary then—but it raised hopes that similar legislation would soon be adopted. Newspapers from New England to the Midwest sang the glories of Oregon. "There is the place to build anew the Temple of Democracy," the *Cleveland Plain Dealer* declared. The editor of the *Boston Daily Evening Transcript* called Oregon "the pioneer's land of promise." The *Ohio Statesman* claimed that "Oregon fever is raging in almost every part of the Union."[6]

Among the estimated fifteen hundred Americans who left their homes and set out for Oregon in 1844 were seven children who would arrive at Waiilatpu as orphans. Their father, Henry Sager, a restless man, had moved his family from Ohio to Indiana to eastern Missouri and then to western Missouri before deciding to try his luck in Oregon. Their mother, Naomi, pregnant with a seventh child, was probably not happy about yet another move—the family's third in four years. She gave birth while they were on the trail, somewhere in Kansas. It was a difficult delivery, and Naomi never fully recovered. Henry died, probably of typhoid, on the Green River in Wyoming in August. Naomi died a month later, in southern Idaho. A middle-aged German known as "Dr. Dagon," aided by women on the train, took charge of the children: John, age thirteen; Francis (also known as Frank), twelve; Catherine, nine; Elizabeth, seven;

Matilda, five; Hannah Louise, three; and the baby, four months old. Several women who had infants of their own took turns serving as wet nurses for the baby.

Wagon train captain William Shaw escorted the six older orphans to the Whitman Mission on November 6, 1844. One of the women brought the baby a few days later. The Whitmans had mixed feelings about becoming foster parents to such a large brood. Marcus wanted the boys but not the girls, especially not the baby. Narcissa wanted the girls, especially the baby, "as a charm to bind the rest to me."[7] In the end the Whitmans agreed to take all the Sager children, at least for a while. Catherine, the oldest girl, described the scene when the children finally met their new guardians. Two worn-out oxen pulled the remnants of the family's wagon, reduced to a two-wheeled cart, into the yard in front of the Mission House. John, sitting on the cart, wept bitterly. Francis stood next to him, his arm on a wheel, sobbing. The girls, bare-headed and bare-footed, huddled together, "looking first at the boys and then at the house, dreading we knew not what." They were dirty, ragged, malnourished, and sunburned. When Narcissa, dressed in dark calico and a gingham sunbonnet, smiled at them, "we thought she was the prettiest woman we had ever seen."[8]

Narcissa gave up all pretense about being a missionary to Indians after the Sager children's arrival. She had not been actively engaged in such work for several years, but evidently felt some guilt about that, judging from her many efforts to rationalize it in letters to her family and friends. Her health was too "feeble"; the challenges of "getting a living" made it impossible to do much for "the benefit of heathen souls"; taking care of "weary, way-worn" emigrants was as important—if not more so—than anything else she and Marcus could be doing.[9] "When my health failed, I was obliged to withhold my efforts for the natives," she told her mother. But now, "the Lord has filled my hands with other labors."[10]

The seven new foster children became the focus of Narcissa's life. She was particularly devoted to the baby, named Rosanna at birth but renamed Henrietta Naomi, to honor the child's parents, at the request of her siblings. It's easy to imagine that Narcissa saw, in the white infant, a replacement for the daughter she had lost five years earlier. In any case, she forged closer bonds with the Sager orphans than with any of the three métis children already in her care. Helen Mar Meek had been just two years old when her father, Joe Meek, brought her to the mission in 1840; Jim Bridger's daughter, Mary Ann, was six when she arrived in 1841; and the young boy Narcissa had named David Malin (after a neighbor and minister in Prattsburg) was about three in early 1842 when his Indian grandmother asked the Whitmans to take him in. Narcissa's letters indicate that she never felt the same emotional connection with her brown-skinned wards as with their white counterparts.

Life for all the children at the Whitman Mission was regimented and austere. In addition to "family worship" every morning and evening, there were prayer meetings on Wednesdays, children's prayer meetings on Thursdays, Bible class on Saturdays, and "Sabbath school" and church on Sundays. Every day the children were given verses of scripture to memorize. Because cleanliness was next to godliness, daily baths in the river were mandatory throughout most of the year and at least weekly in a tub in the house during the winter. "We had certain things to do at a certain hour," Matilda recalled, describing her foster parents as "very particular in our being very regular in all our habits of eating and sleeping." The girls did household chores; the boys helped with the livestock. They all had garden plots to tend to.[11]

The Whitmans did not celebrate Christmas, which they considered a pagan holiday. Narcissa disapproved of giving children sweets. The girls adapted fairly easily, the boys less so. Francis Sager ran away to The Dalles after less than a year. Marcus coaxed him back by promising to help him and his brother acquire cattle and horses that they could raise and eventually use as a stake to establish their own homesteads.

The addition of the Sagers brought to twenty-six the number of school-age children at the mission in the fall of 1844. To educate them, the Whitmans hired Alanson Hinman, a newly arrived emigrant from upstate New York. Narcissa described him as "a good and faithful disciplinarian."[12] Catherine Sager remembered Hinman as "a small-souled tyrant of a man [who] took delight in torturing helpless children."[13] He was the first in a series of teachers hired each year to take charge of the mission school, which by then was open only to white and a few métis students (including the offspring of Hudson's Bay Company employees). Marcus had decided that Indian children could be properly educated only in residential schools, away from their parents, to minimize if not eliminate the influence of traditional cultures. He planned to open such a school "as soon as the relations of the country" were "stable."[14] He was not able to realize this vision, but in 1879 a Civil War veteran named Richard Henry Pratt opened the Carlisle Indian Industrial School, in Carlisle, Pennsylvania. The school's motto—"Kill the Indian, Save the Man"—reflected principles that Whitman had embraced thirty-five years earlier: that the only way to "save" Indians was to strip away all traces of their native language, religion, identity, and way of life and force them to assimilate into white culture.

Over time, the mission at Waiilatpu became increasingly mercantile in nature. "Situated as we are, necessity compels us to become supplyers [*sic*] to Immigrants and we may as well make the best of it we can," Whitman wrote to David Greene at the American Board of Commissioners for Foreign Missions.[15] He came to rely on emigrants as a source of both income and labor. He sold them wheat, corn, potatoes, and other provisions. If they could not pay in cash, Whitman accepted cattle or oxen in trade. He then sold the livestock to Indians. Some emigrants complained about his prices (a dollar a bushel for grain, 40 cents a bushel for potatoes), but Whitman said he was only trying to cover his expenses. He extended credit to those who had nothing to offer in trade, although he expected repayment once the emigrants had established themselves in the Willamette Valley. He took steps to collect by placing a legal notice in one of the first issues of the *Oregon Spectator*, published in Oregon City, warning "all persons indebted to Dr. M. Whitman" to settle their debts within three months or face legal action.[16]

An improved wagon road, developed in 1844, skirted the Whitman Mission by about thirty miles to the south. Whitman worried that the decrease in direct traffic would leave him with produce and grain he could not sell and bills he could not pay. To compensate, he began hauling supplies to the Umatilla River, where he could intercept wagon trains on the new route. The sales there disappointed him, but he also used the trips to recruit carpenters, blacksmiths, millwrights, and others with special skills to come and work for him at Waiilatpu. Whitman had ambitious plans. He wanted to create a center of white settlement that would rival Oregon City, with farms, churches, schools, even a college. "He wanted to see the country settled," wrote Henry K. W. Perkins, a Methodist missionary at The Dalles, who knew Whitman well. "The beautiful valley of the Walla Walla he wanted to see teeming with a busy, bustling white population. Where were scattered a few Indian huts, he wanted to see thrifty farm houses." Instead of vast herds of Indian horses on the rich grassland of Cayuse country, he "wanted to see grazing the cow, the ox, and the sheep of a happy Yankee community."[17]

When the New York–based Methodist Mission Board (an arm of the Methodist Missionary Society) offered to sell its property at

The Dalles in 1847, Whitman urged his board to buy it. He had been interested in the station for years, primarily because of its strategic location on the Columbia. The board finally agreed, somewhat reluctantly, and Whitman went to Oregon City in August to complete the transaction. A down payment of $69.75 on a total purchase price of $721 gave him control of the property. "This I think now is to be our best station," he wrote to David Greene. "It will be here we must have two Schools. One for the children of the Mission. And a boarding school for the natives."[18] Whitman installed his nephew Perrin, then age seventeen, and Alanson Hinman, the former schoolteacher at the Whitman Mission, as caretakers of the property.

Greene, unhappy about Whitman's growing interest in commerce, often chastised him for paying too much attention to "temporal" affairs—for becoming more businessman than missionary. Whitman, sensitive to the criticism, wondered "where the line of duty lies" between "diligence in business" and "fervency in spirit in the service of the Lord." Was it not his duty to "lay the foundation for the speedy settlement of the country"? To "found & sustain institutions [of] learning & religion"?[19] Besides, the American Board had repeatedly pressured its missionaries in Oregon to become self-sufficient; if Whitman didn't make money by selling supplies to emigrants, he would have to "draw upon the Board" to pay his bills.[20] Whitman also insisted he was making progress with the Indians. "A vast change has already been wrought among them," he declared to Greene. "There are but few who have not cattle, a number have sheep and nearly all have plantations, more or less."[21] It was a dubious claim. Perhaps a third of the Indian families living near Waiilatpu tended crops, but only intermittently, in ways that didn't interfere with seasonal food-gathering cycles. Those Indian families who cultivated land maintained only small plots of a quarter acre to three acres—hardly enough for conversion to an agrarian lifestyle.

There was even less evidence of the missionaries' impact on Cayuse spirituality. Whitman still conducted services for Indians every Sunday, but he conceded that attendance had declined. He blamed inroads by "Papists." A number of influential Cayuses had converted to Catholicism, and one, the headman Tauitau, had donated land and a building for use as a Catholic mission near his village on the Umatilla River. In one early attempt to quantify the results of his evangelistic efforts, Whitman counted "two to four hundred" attending Sunday services and "twenty to fifty" at weekday meetings.[22] In later years, tellingly, his references to spiritual activities involving Indians were usually brief and vague, with no headcounts. Greene continued to caution Whitman about his priorities. "I fear you do not labor as much for the salvation of the Indians as Christ claims of you," he wrote on October 22, 1847—about five weeks before the attack that put an end to the Whitman Mission.[23]

Cayuse attitudes toward the Whitmans during the last few years of the mission, at least as revealed in the Whitmans' letters, alternated between overt hostility and grudging tolerance. Historian Julie Roy Jeffrey attributes the pattern to "factional struggles and shifts in power and influence" among various Cayuse leaders.[24] Some saw value in the presence of the missionaries; others saw malevolence; and some vacillated, moving first to one side and then the other. When the prevailing sentiment seemed supportive or at least neutral, Whitman hoped the change was permanent. When tension flared again, he talked about leaving but took no concrete steps to do so.

Whitman continued to be dogged by Indian doubts about his status as a medicine man, or *te-wat*. In 1844 he was accused of causing two deaths. One was a young man who died of what Whitman diagnosed as "apoplexy." The other, more problematic for Whitman, was Waptashtakmahl (Feathercap), one of the headmen who had welcomed Rev. Samuel Parker to Cayuse country years earlier. Parker had claimed that Whitman was "a sorcerer of great power." As discussed in Chapter 6, Plateau Indians credited *te-wats* with spiritual powers that could be used to cure or, at times, to kill. Healers whose patients died could be suspected of misusing or failing to control their powers and be put to death themselves. After his father died, Waptashtakmahl's son angrily accused Whitman of causing the death and threatened to kill him in retaliation. Both Marcus and Narcissa were troubled enough by the encounter to wonder whether it had become too dangerous for them to stay at Waiilatpu.[25]

A series of confrontations about other issues in 1845 gave Whitman even more reason to consider relocating to the Willamette Valley. He twice came close to blows with Tomahas, a subchief in the band headed by Tiloukaikt. Whitman wanted the Indians to pay him for grinding corn and wheat at the mission's gristmill (he expected payment of one horse in return for grinding enough grain to fill twenty sacks).[26] Tomahas demanded that Indians have free access to the mill, since it was on their land. Catherine Sager remembered seeing Whitman stumble into the mission house after being threatened by Tomahas for a second time, "exhausted in body and vexed in spirit," saying if the Indians wanted him to go, "he would gladly leave as he was tried almost beyond endurance."[27] But Tiloukaikt apparently smoothed things over, and Whitman carried on as usual.

A more serious issue flared up later that year when a delegation of Cayuse, Walla Walla, and Nez Perce headmen met with Whitman, Henry Spalding, and a few other whites at Waiilatpu to demand retribution for the murder of Elijah Hedding, the eighteen-year-old son of Walla Walla chief PeoPeoMoxMox. Hedding had been educated and trained as a preacher at the Methodist mission school and seemed destined to assume a place in leadership circles on the Plateau. But in 1844, while taking part in a joint Cayuse and Walla

Walla expedition to trade horses and furs for cattle in California, he was fatally shot by an American during a quarrel at Sutter's Fort. His enraged and grief-stricken father appealed to Elijah White, the putative "sub-Indian agent" in Oregon City, asking that White punish the perpetrator, in keeping with the "Laws" that he had convinced the Indians to adopt in 1843. White said he was sorry but could do nothing. Since Hedding had been "a leader in religious worship and learning," as Whitman put it, some Indians proposed to avenge his loss by killing an American of equal status, and "Mr. Spalding or myself" were deemed suitable candidates.[28] After lengthy discussion of this and other grievances, the headmen agreed to take no action against the missionaries but warned that they would no longer accept responsibility for whatever their young men might do.

Anger about the death of Elijah Hedding surfaced again six months later during a tense exchange between Whitman and Tauitau (also known as Young Chief). Tauitau and his half-brother, Five Crows, were headmen of the Cayuse band on the lower Umatilla, near today's Pendleton. Tauitau had initially been friendly to the Whitmans and for a while maintained a winter lodge near Waiilatpu. He later converted to Catholicism. After he and his son accepted baptism by Father François N. Blanchet at Fort Walla Walla in 1838, Whitman took to calling Tauitau "the Papist," and their relationship soured.

In late November 1845, Tauitau and a Nez Perce ally visited Whitman to unload a long list of festering complaints, beginning with the unavenged death of Elijah Hedding (one of Tauitau's nephews) and the loss of horses and other property that the Indians had been forced to leave behind at Sutter's Fort. Tauitau said he would never again send children to a mission school. He accused Whitman in particular and Americans in general of planning to seize the Indians' land, even if they had to use poison and disease to get it. He also said he was always wary when offered food by white people for fear it had been poisoned. Whitman denied that he was trying to steal land or poison Indians, but Tauitau said he would hold Whitman responsible for such deeds, either directly or through "conniving." Whitman was so frightened by this confrontation that his hand shook as he wrote about it in a letter to his colleagues, Elkanah Walker and Cushing Eells, at Tshimakain. He didn't think that Tauitau himself would do him harm but worried "such language to me would remove all restraint from the reckless, and I would have no assurance but that I might be killed on the most slight or sudden occasion."[29]

Whitman told Tauitau he would leave by the next spring if Cayuse headmen agreed he should go. He told Walker and Eells that he would keep the mission property in readiness for a quick departure if needed. But Tauitau returned to the Umatilla, a semblance of calm returned to Waiilatpu, and there was no more talk, for the moment, of abandoning the mission.

It's hard to know why Whitman, in the face of so many warnings about the precariousness of his position, did not leave. Perhaps it was simply hubris that kept him at Waiilatpu, or reluctance to admit defeat, or the conviction that despite any threats from Indians he and his wife were under the protection of God. Perhaps the element of competition with the Catholics clouded his judgment. Both Marcus and Narcissa regarded their mission as a vital bulwark against the spread of "Papism" and were loath to see it "fall into the hands of Catholics."[30] Still, Whitman often confessed ambivalence about whether to stay or go. "I would like to be discharged could I feel as sure I was wright [sic] in leaving as I was in coming among the Indians," he wrote to David Greene in the spring of 1847. He said he was thinking about filing a claim to land in the Willamette Valley, "to be ready in case of retirement."[31]

More than four thousand people traveled overland to Oregon Country in 1847, the largest emigration yet. Whitman nearly ran short of food to sell them. Winter had come early and lingered long, cutting into his crop yields. At Whitman's request, Henry Spalding brought seventeen packhorses loaded with wheat and corn to Waiilatpu to restock the storehouses. Whitman was worried that too many pitiable travelers with few resources would detour to the mission. "The first passers never give us any trouble," he commented. "The weak teams and needy persons come last, as also generally the sick. But we cannot move ourselves out of the way and must meet the trial the best we can."[32] It was Narcissa who noticed that the influx also made the Cayuse anxious. "The Indians are amazed at the overwhelming numbers of Americans coming into the country," she wrote to her parents in the summer of 1847. "They seem not to know what to make of it."[33]

The arrival of the wagon trains that year coincided with a virulent epidemic of measles among the Indians. The source of the outbreak is not clear. Anthropologist Robert Boyd, among others, traces it to a Cayuse–Walla Walla expedition that had just returned from an extended trip to the Sacramento Valley. About thirty of the two hundred men, women, and children who went to California died of measles while on the journey home. It is possible that survivors carried the virus back with them, initiating a chain of transmission that continued for months.[34] However, members of at least one and possibly three emigrant families were sick with measles when they arrived at the mission in September. Any one of them could have been the unwitting vector that brought a highly contagious disease to a population with no acquired immunities to fight it and already weakened by a hard winter.

Euro-Americans, after millennia of exposure, rarely died after contracting measles. In contrast, mortality rates among indigenous people were distressingly high. Traditional treatments, in which the sick sat in a sweathouse as long as possible and then plunged into an icy river, didn't help. Measles is characterized by a raging fever and in severe cases can be followed by pneumonia, dysentery, or encephalitis. Patients with fever can become dehydrated in a sweathouse; a dive into cold water could send a body into shock. Marcus Whitman's treatments were equally counterproductive—he relied on calomel, cayenne pepper, and bleeding—but his white patients tended to recover while his Indian patients did not. The epidemic took a terrible toll on Cayuse families. According to William McBean, chief trader at Fort Walla Walla, about thirty Indians in Tiloukaikt's band on the Walla Walla River died within two months, mostly children, "one after another."[35] Measles also killed Cayuses in the two Umatilla River bands. A Cayuse messenger reportedly told a large gathering of Nez Perce at Lapwai in early December that a total of 197 Cayuses had died—a number that, if correct, means the tribe lost more than a third of its estimated five hundred members during the epidemic. Among the victims, it was said, was the wife of Tomahas, the subchief who had quarreled with Whitman about the gristmill.[36]

On November 22, when Henry Spalding brought his daughter Eliza to Waiilatpu to attend school for the winter, he found lodges filled with sick and dying Indians, "some in the midst of measles, others in the last stages of dysentery," with "no suitable means to alleviate their inconceivable sufferings." Disease was "sweeping them off—one, three, and five in a day."[37] At least a dozen children (including three of the Whitmans' wards) and several young adults at the mission also had measles, but so far there had been only one death among them. Six-year-old Sylvia Jane Osborn, daughter of a carpenter working at the mission, died on November 24. Narcissa invited a Cayuse into the house to see the body, hoping the sight of a dead white child would ease the Indians' "growing distrust" of the missionaries.[38] It did not.

The epidemic revived old suspicions that Whitman was using poison to kill Indians in order to take their land and give it to white settlers, just as he had poisoned wolves to protect his sheep and cattle, and just as his onetime missionary colleague, William Henry Gray, had poisoned melons to keep Indians from eating them. Joe Lewis, an English-speaking métis of Delaware heritage who arrived at the Whitman Mission in the fall of 1847, took on the role of provocateur. Whitman had hired Lewis as a laborer but soon fired him, calling him a "worthless vagabond."[39] For weeks afterward, Lewis floated from one Cayuse lodge to another, fanning flames of hostility toward the missionaries. He claimed to have overheard the Whitmans and Spalding discussing plans to kill all the Cayuse, and Nez Perce too, by giving them poisoned medicine. If the Cayuse did not kill the missionaries soon, Lewis warned, they would all be dead before spring.[40]

Even so, many Cayuses resisted the call for violence. No headmen from the Umatilla River bands supported it. Camaspelo, leader of the band at the headwaters, later said he had been approached by a messenger from Tiloukaikt's band who told him that an attack was being planned and asked for his support. "I pointed to my sick child, and told him my heart was there, and not on murder," Camaspelo said.[41] Tauitau, putting aside his earlier disagreements with Whitman, took a neutral position. Tiloukaikt himself apparently sanctioned the attack only because some of the young men in his band—possibly hoping to earn status as warriors—goaded him into it.

Marcus Whitman was an exhausted, harried man during those last few cold, damp days in November 1847. His mission had become, in effect, a settlement of Euro-Americans, and he was the overworked governor. More than seventy people were crammed into the complex. Some were sick and needed his medical care. Endless other responsibilities demanded his time: there were repairs to oversee, workers to instruct, provisions to be doled out, letters to write. He spent long hours on horseback, visiting Indian villages, trying to treat the sick, sometimes helping to bury the dead.

On November 27, a Saturday, a messenger asked Whitman to come to Tauitau's village, about twenty-five miles southwest of Waiilatpu, because of illness there. Spalding accompanied him. The pair left at sundown—about 4:00 p.m. at that time of year—and rode all night, arriving at dawn. They stopped first at the lodge of Stickus, one of the missionaries' earliest and most loyal allies. Spalding, injured in a fall from his horse, stayed there while Whitman went on to do what he could for the sick. Before returning to Stickus, Whitman called on Bishop Augustin M. A. Blanchet (brother of Father François N. Blanchet) and Father Jean B. A. Brouillet at their newly established Saint Anne's Mission near Tauitau's village. To Brouillet, Whitman appeared "much agitated."[42] Given Whitman's deep antipathy toward Catholics, he might have been more distressed over the presence of the priests than by any other concerns. Declining an invitation to stay for dinner, Whitman returned to Stickus's lodge. There, according to Spalding, Stickus bluntly told Whitman that some Cayuses were planning to kill him. Visibly shaken, Whitman left alone for the long ride back to Waiilatpu. Spalding probably owed his life to the injury that kept him with Stickus that night.

Whitman reached the mission around midnight. Catherine Sager said she heard him tell Narcissa what Stickus had said. Narcissa did not come down for breakfast the next morning. One of the girls took her a plate of food and saw her weeping. The tray was later found in Narcissa's room, the food untouched. After frying a steak for his breakfast, Marcus assisted with the burial of yet another Indian child, one of three who would die of measles that day, Monday, November 29. He wondered why only the immediate relatives and no other Indians attended.

The first shots were fired shortly after the midday meal. Two Indians pushed their way into the kitchen, asking for medicine. When Whitman turned to get it, one man sliced into his head with a hatchet. The other shot seventeen-year-old John Sager, who was in the kitchen winding twine for brooms, and then cut his throat. Several survivors swore later that the two assailants were Tiloukaikt and Tomahas. Outside, about a dozen Indians dropped the blankets they had been using to hide weapons. By the end of the day, nine "Bostons" were dead: Marcus and Narcissa Whitman, five other men, and two teenage boys. Two more men were shot and killed the next day. A week later, two other men, both young and recovering from what might have been measles, died in a final bloody assault at the Whitman Mission.

Three American men at the mission when the attack began managed to escape. Peter D. Hall, a carpenter from Illinois, staggered into Fort Walla Walla shortly after dawn on November 30, "half naked and covered with blood."[43] William McBean, the Hudson's Bay Company official then in charge of the fort, immediately dispatched a messenger, pleading for help from Fort Vancouver. McBean may well have hesitated about offering refuge to Hall. With only a handful of men to defend his post from an Indian attack, McBean did not want to seem overly friendly to Americans. But he claimed later that Hall was too afraid to stay at the fort and wanted to go on to the Willamette Valley. He said he gave Hall food, clothing, and other supplies and saw him safely on his way.[44] Hall was never heard from again. In the crossfire of recriminations after the attack, some said McBean had callously turned him away out of cowardice.

Another escapee, Josiah Osborn, showed up at Fort Walla Walla on December 2, carrying his three-year-old son and begging for help in rescuing his wife and two other children. When the attack began, the family had hidden under some floorboards in what had once been the "Indian Hall." They cowered there until late that first night, when it was clear that the Indians had left the mission complex unguarded. The family crawled out and started walking the twenty-five miles west to the fort. Osborn's wife, Margaret, was weak from the effects of a recent stillbirth. When she collapsed along the route, Osborn left her hidden in some willows on the edge of the river with their seven-year-old daughter and two-year-old son. Although apparently still wary of antagonizing the Cayuse, McBean provided a guide to help Osborn find the rest of his family and then let the reunited family stay at Fort Walla Walla. The third escapee, William Canfield, reached safety at Lapwai on his own.

Father Brouillet was baptizing the sick in Tiloukaikt's main village at Pašx̣á ("Place of Balsamroot Sunflower," about three miles east of Waiilatpu) when he heard about the attack, on November 30. He and an interpreter arrived at the Whitman Mission early the next morning, the first outsiders on the scene. They found ten bodies, scattered here and there, and Indians in control of the mission. Some of the emigrant women were sewing shrouds to encase the bodies for burial, since there were no carpenters who could build coffins. Joseph Stanfield, a French Canadian and one of Whitman's hired hands (spared because he was not a "Boston"), was digging a mass grave. Brouillet helped bury the dead, offered what comfort he could to the survivors, and returned to the Umatilla. Like McBean, he took pains to maintain an air of neutrality. Brouillet worried that if he showed "too marked an interest" in helping the Americans, "it would only have endangered their lives and mine."[45]

Two of the Whitmans' wards—Hannah Louise Sager and Helen Mar Meek—died of measles shortly after the attack. The Indians held forty-five other people, mostly women and children, as hostages for a month. The women sewed shirts, knitted socks, and cooked for their captors (who made them taste the food first, to show that it hadn't been poisoned). Archaeologists who excavated the site in the 1940s found evidence of an "orgy of feasting by the Indians," including floors littered with animal bones in the Mission House.[46] Among the captives were the two families that had been living at the sawmill in the Blue Mountains. Indians brought them to the mission and put the men to work at the gristmill. Their lives may have been spared because they claimed to be Englishmen, not "Bostons"—although it's also possible that by that point, the Indians just wanted their labor.

Three prominent Cayuse men each took a young white woman as a "bride," a fact that would inflame the citizens of Oregon City when it became known. In some ways, however, the arrangements offered the women a degree of protection. Lorinda Bewley, twenty-one, claimed by Five Crows, acknowledged that he had shielded her from "a general abuse by the Indians."[47] She said that about a week after the initial attack, while Tiloukaikt was away, a warrior named Tamsucky dragged her into the mission yard and raped her. When Tiloukaikt returned, two days later, he sent her to the lodge of Five Crows on the Umatilla, some twenty-five miles away. She said she begged Tiloukaikt to let her stay with the other women, but he told her she would be safer with Five Crows. She did not sugarcoat what happened after that. She was allowed to spend her days with Father Brouillet and the other priests at the nearby Saint Anne's Mission, but most nights Five Crows "compelled me to go to his lodge and be subject to him during the night."[48] Still, she thought "he was disposed to pity me, and not to abuse me."[49]

After Lorinda Bewley was taken away, Tiloukaikt held a council in the hostages' quarters at Waiilatpu. Speaking through two layers of translation (from Nez Perce to French and then to English), he said the young women would be better off as wives of chiefs who could protect them, rather than be "dragged around by worthless fellows, who would beat and abuse them."[50] According to Catherine Sager, the decision was left to the women. Two of them eventually agreed to accept Indian "husbands." Sixteen-year-old Susan Kimball went off with a brother of Tomahas, known to whites as Frank Eskaloom (or Escaloom), identified later by some of the survivors as the man who shot Narcissa Whitman. Tiloukaikt's eldest son—one of the first students in the school the Whitmans established in the early, ambitious years of their mission, and given the name "Edward" in honor of Narcissa's favorite brother—claimed Mary Smith, age fifteen.[51] Mary's father, one of the men from the sawmill, reportedly urged her to yield, saying it would protect both of them.[52] Father Brouillet and his fellow priests "entreated" the Indians to give up their white wives, but they were still fearful for their own safety and felt powerless to intervene.[53]

The principal men from all three Cayuse bands gathered at Saint Anne's for a council hosted by Bishop Blanchet and Father Brouillet on December 20. Each headman spoke in turn. Tiloukaikt was the most voluble. In a two-hour speech he talked about the history of the Cayuse people from the time of first contact with whites, the death of Elijah Hedding, the unkept promises of the missionaries, the unwanted intrusions by the emigrants, and the grief of those whose families had been shredded by disease. He finished by saying he hoped the Americans would forget "what had been recently done, that now they [the Cayuse and the Americans] were even."[54] Blanchet forwarded their translated statements to George Abernethy, newly appointed provisional governor at Oregon City. The headmen asked that the Americans not go to war; that they "forget the lately committed murders as the Cayuses will forget the murder of the son of the great chief of Walla Walla"; and that the Americans "not travel any more through their country, as their young men might do them harm."[55]

The headmen promised to free the hostages as soon as terms could be arranged. The delicate job of negotiating the release fell to Peter Skene Ogden, a seasoned explorer, trader, and diplomat, and, since 1846, one of two joint administrators of Fort Vancouver. Although the United States now claimed sovereignty over the region, the Hudson's Bay Company was still the recognized authority in Oregon Country, with resources and experience that the provisional government in Oregon City lacked. Ogden had spent decades developing relationships with Plateau tribes. He spoke several native languages, including Nez Perce, and had been married for many years to a woman of Spokane and Flathead heritage. He was probably better equipped than anyone else to serve as a mediator between the Cayuse and the Americans.

Ogden was at Fort Vancouver when he received news of the attack. He left the next day, with sixteen men and three boatloads of trade goods. When he arrived at Fort Walla Walla, he convened a council with Cayuse, Nez Perce, and Walla Walla headmen and others, many of whom he knew. The Catholic priests also attended. Five Crows, notably, did not. Ogden began by scolding the Cayuse leaders for failing to control their young men and the young men for not listening to their elders. He offered blankets, shirts, guns, ammunition, tobacco, handkerchiefs, and knives in return for the safe delivery of all the captives within six days. He asked the Nez Perce delegates to bring the Spalding family (Henry and Eliza and their three youngest children) and any Americans with them at Lapwai to the fort, offering a ransom for them as well. Ogden thought it best for the Spaldings to leave the region given "the present excited, and irritable state of the Indian population."[56]

Tiloukaikt said he would release the captives to Ogden because Ogden "was old, and his hair was white, and he had known him a long time."[57] The beleaguered headman faced opposition from those who feared that giving up the hostages would eliminate their strongest defense against reprisals. Neither Tiloukaikt's son, Edward, nor Five Crows wanted to relinquish their white wives. But after a tense week of waiting, the Cayuse brought all their captives to Fort Walla Walla. The Spalding party arrived on January 1, 1848. The next day, Ogden loaded sixty-one men, women, and children (including the Osborn family of five) into Hudson's Bay Company boats for the trip downriver to the security of the garrisoned settlement in Oregon City.[58]

David Malin, the métis boy the Whitmans had taken in five years earlier, remained at the fort. Abandoned by his parents and brought to the mission at age three, the mission family was the only one he had ever really known. "I am more and more pleased with my little boy every day," Narcissa once wrote about him. "He is so mild and quiet, and so happy in his new situation that I have not had the least regret that I took him in."[59] Matilda Sager noticed David as the boat she was in pulled away from shore. "The last look I had of him," she wrote, "was when we rowed away from Fort Walla Walla, leaving him standing on the bank of the river, crying as though his heart were breaking."[60]

CHAPTER EIGHT

AFTERMATH

For the barbarian murderers and violators: let them be
pursued with unrelenting hatred . . . let them be hunted
as beasts of prey; let their name and race be blotted
from the face of the earth, and the places that once knew
them, know them no more forever.

—Oregon Spectator, *January 20, 1848*

To most non-Indians, then and for many decades afterward, what
happened at the Whitman Mission on November 29, 1847, was a
massacre. William McBean, chief trader at Fort Walla Walla, the first
outsider to hear about the attack, called it "a horrid massacre" in a letter to his superiors at Fort Vancouver.[1] It took a week for the news to
reach Oregon City, capital of a provisional government established by
settlers in the Willamette Valley. Governor George Abernethy immediately called for a volunteer militia to avenge "the horrible massacre
committed by the Cayuse Indians on the residents at [W]aiilatpu."[2]
Oregon City's bimonthly *Oregon Spectator*, then the only newspaper
in the Northwest, filled its pages with incendiary reports about "the

Marcus Whitman placidly reads a book in front of a fire, seemingly unaware of the alarmed women and shrieking children behind him, in this engraving titled "The Assassination of Marcus Whitman," by Nathaniel Orr. *Originally published in Frances Fuller Victor's* The River of the West, *1871.*

Massacre at Waiilatpu," including one that declared "that dreadful event" was "one of the most atrocious which darkens the annals of Indian crime."[3] Virtually no non-Indian source—politician, bureaucrat, publisher, or private individual—described the attack on the mission as anything other than a massacre (usually a "brutal" one, as if there were any other kind).

Less than a decade after that attack, a militia of 175 Americans opened fire with little or no warning on a gathering of Cayuse and Walla Walla families camped at a camas harvesting site twenty-five miles southeast of the Whitman Mission. Members of the militia killed sixty men, women, and children in what Americans called the Battle of the Grande Ronde.[4] In those days, when Indians killed whites, it was a "massacre"; it was a "battle" when whites killed Indians.

It's a loaded word, "massacre." It implies unprovoked, indiscriminate slaughter of the innocent. Antone Minthorn, former chair of the Confederated Tribes of the Umatilla Indian Reservation, has pointed out that its use "prejudges and freezes the event in time." It ignores the context, including in this case "the hundreds of people who died in the epidemic that Whitman could not cure" as well as the "*tewatat* 'medicine doctor tradition,' which calls for the life of the healer to be taken if he fails to cure the sick."[5] The violence was brutal but not random; the Whitmans and the male "Bostons" at the mission were the only targets. Narcissa may have been targeted because she sometimes took on the role of physician, dispensing medicines when Marcus was away, as he frequently was. What Minthorn prefers to call "the Whitman incident" can be seen today as an act of retribution—a response to multiple aggravations that built up over time. It was, in the words of anthropologist Theodore Stern, a "final desperate stroke," driven by an "overwhelming sense of hopelessness in the face of the crushing flow of overland migrations, capped by an epidemic disease and the interpretation that linked Marcus Whitman as agent to both."[6]

Cayuse leaders made several efforts to explain the rationale for the attack and avoid a full-out war with the Americans, using Catholic priests and Hudson's Bay Company officials as intermediaries. Relatively few Cayuses (fewer than twenty, according to most accounts, all from Tiloukaikt's band in the Walla Walla Valley) had participated in the killings. Headmen from the Umatilla River bands worried (with cause, it turned out) that whites would retaliate against the entire tribe. At their request, Bishop Augustin A. M. Blanchet, head of the Catholic mission on the Umatilla, sent a personal message to Governor Abernethy, urging him not to send troops but to come instead in person to negotiate a settlement with the Cayuse. Blanchet described "the tragedy of the 29th" as the result of "a moment of despair" driven by "an anxious desire for self-preservation." The Indians hoped "to have the past forgotten," he wrote, "and to live in peace, as before."[7]

The likelihood that further bloodshed could be avoided vanished when the freed hostages arrived in Oregon City in early January 1848. Sensationalized accounts from some of the survivors about murder, mutilation, and forced marriages inflamed the settlers. They clamored for revenge, particularly in response to reports that some of the young women had suffered what Henry Spalding called a "fate more terrible than death itself."[8] The editor of the *Oregon Spectator* said the women had been subjected to such "outrage and insult" that "our mind recoils with horror" and "our pen refuses—we dare not chronicle the terrible story of their wrongs."[9] Wild rumors circulated: that the Indians had participated in demonic "scalp dances"; cut the hearts out of some of their victims and displayed them on sticks; and chopped up bodies and rolled the pieces in the mud. Marcus Whitman's nephew, Perrin, who helped rebury the dead in March 1848, later insisted that Indians had not mutilated the bodies. "Indians are the most superstitious people in the world about touching the dead," he said in an 1898 interview, and would not have "molested" the bodies for any reason.[10] In the heat of the moment, however, even the most dubious stories went unchallenged, feeding a toxic stew of hysteria and fear.

The provisional legislature quickly passed and the governor signed a bill authorizing a volunteer militia "for the purpose of punishing the Indians, to what tribe or tribes soever [*sic*] they may belong, who may have aided or abetted in the massacre of Dr. Marcus Whitman, his wife, and others, at Waiilatpu."[11] The bill basically gave carte blanche to anyone to go hunt Indians. Abernethy appointed Cornelius Gilliam as the commanding officer. A Baptist preacher who came to Oregon with his extended family in 1844, Gilliam had fought against Indians in the Black Hawk War in Illinois and the Seminole War in Florida in the 1830s. Contemporaries described him as bad-tempered, impetuous, and not terribly bright, but he had more military experience than any other candidate.[12]

The legislature also made it illegal for anyone to "barter, sell, give, make or repair for any Indian any kind of firearms or other munitions of war."[13] James Douglas, codirector of Hudson's Bay Company operations in the Northwest, strongly objected to the measure. In a January 4, 1848, letter to Abernethy, he called it harsh, ill-advised, and "fraught with danger to the country," because the Indians would regard it as "an act of unjustifiable cruelty" and react with anger. Indians had become reliant on guns for hunting, he noted, and would face starvation without them. The ban would thus hurt the innocent along with the guilty. Douglas did not defy the Americans openly, but he privately told the company's traders to use their discretion in deciding whether or not to comply with the new law.[14]

Gilliam and a militia of about 230 "Oregon Volunteers" left for the Walla Walla Valley in mid-January.[15] It was a slapdash operation from the beginning. The men were to be paid $1.50 a day and be supplied with food, shelter, and ammunition (they had to provide their own horses and guns), but the provisional government had no taxing authority to raise the money. James Douglas politely declined a legislative finance committee's request to arrange a loan of up to $100,000 from the Hudson's Bay Company. Having tried to avert war, company officials would not now take sides. Douglas softened the rejection by giving the committee a personal loan of $1,000. An appeal to settlers raised another $4,000 or so, which was enough to finance a few months of operations. As time passed, however, food and other supplies became scarce, the promised pay either shrank or never arrived, and the volunteers' enthusiasm for fighting Indians flagged.

Gilliam found only deserted village sites as he and his troops marched east. Frustrated, he took 130 of his best mounted men and rode ahead, searching for Indians. In late January they came upon a village of Western Columbia Sahaptins ("River Indians") on the

Deschutes River, near its confluence with the Columbia, about a hundred miles east of Oregon City. The group included Tenino, Celilo, and Tygh Valley peoples—none of whom had had anything to do with the Whitman killings. Gilliam ordered an attack. He claimed later that his men killed or wounded twenty to thirty warriors, a number that probably reflects braggadocio more than reality. After the last of the Indians fled, the troops looted the village, taking away about $300 worth of goods, forty horses, and four head of cattle. They burned everything else, including large quantities of dried salmon, robbing the Indians of a vital source of food for the winter. Gilliam turned the property and livestock over to the paymaster, to be "appropriated to the pay of the Regiment."[16]

When the Cayuse heard about the raid on the Deschutes village, they retaliated by returning to the Whitman Mission and destroying as much of it as they could. They piled parts of wagons in the Mission House and set fire to them. The fire burned through wooden supports for the heavy sod roof; the roof collapsed, covering the area below with four to six inches of dirt. That proved to be a gift to the archaeologists who excavated the site a century later. By protecting the area from the tramping and souvenir hunting of soldiers and others who came on the scene afterward, the blanket of earth preserved many artifacts and remnants of life during the missionary era.

Oregon's provisional government did not entirely ignore the Cayuse headmen's request to send a few "great men" to negotiate a truce. In late January 1848, Abernethy appointed a peace commission headed by Joel Palmer, an emigrant from Indiana, newly named superintendent of Indian affairs. The other two commissioners were Robert Newell, the ex-trapper who had helped bring the first wagons to Oregon and then settled in the Willamette Valley; and Virginian

Henry A. G. Lee, who had served on a US Army exploring expedition to the Northwest in 1843. The three men joined Gilliam's main force at The Dalles in late February and traveled with the militia to Waiilatpu for a council with the Indians. Their relations with Gilliam were tense from the beginning. The commissioners had two objectives: persuade the Cayuse to surrender those responsible for the attack and secure the neutrality of the other Plateau tribes. Gilliam simply wanted to fight Indians.

The commissioners and the militiamen found a gruesome scene when they arrived at Waiilatpu. Wolves and other scavengers had dug into the shallow, mass grave where most of the dead had been buried, devoured parts of the corpses, and scattered bones around the premises. Soldiers gathered up the bodies and reburied them. They covered the new grave with an upturned wagon bed and piled several feet of dirt on top of that. They rebuilt and fortified part of the mission and dubbed it Fort Waters, in honor of Gilliam's deputy, James Waters.

According to Robert Newell, soldiers also found what they thought was some of Narcissa's hair. "The hair of Mrs. Whitman was brot [sic] in," he wrote in his journal. "I have saved Some of it."[17] He didn't say what condition the hair was in, but it couldn't have been good. Rain had fallen steadily throughout the month of November 1847, and the mission grounds were muddy on the day of the attack.[18] Most of the bodies, including Narcissa's, had lain outdoors for two days before they were wrapped in thin cotton shrouds and buried for the first time. Wolves began tearing into the common grave within days.[19] By the time the soldiers and the commissioners got there, the bodies had been left to the animals and the elements for four months. Still, Newell believed he had some of Narcissa's hair, and he planned to save it.

It was not uncommon in the nineteenth century for people to cut hair from the dead as mementos. It was even more customary to give locks of hair as gifts to family members and close friends. But samples of what purports to be Narcissa Whitman's hair have become almost as common as alleged pieces of the true cross. There are at least ten in various repositories around the country, from a curl displayed in the house in Prattsburg, New York, where she was born, to six separate samples in a collection at Whitman College, near the site of her death. None are muddy or bloody. They range in color from honey blond to faded straw to dark brown. Two are said to have been hair Narcissa herself gave to friends. The others were supposedly gathered by soldiers and others at the mission site. They did not begin to appear in public collections until the 1890s, when the fiftieth anniversary of the attack brought renewed attention to victims of the "Whitman Massacre." No matter how tenuous the connection to the real-life Narcissa, the strands of hair served as sacred relics—potent embodiments of a woman whose death at the hands of the people she had wanted to "save" made her an instant martyr.

About 250 Indians (mostly Nez Perces, with a few Cayuses and Walla Wallas) rode in to Waiilatpu for a peace council that began on March 7, 1848. The pipe was passed until, according to a report by the commissioners, "our hearts were all good and our eyes watery."[20] Then a translator read a letter from Governor Abernethy demanding the surrender of those who had killed people at the mission and those who had forced women into marriage. Abernethy warned that any Indians who protected the outlaws would be considered enemies of the Americans and punished. Robert Newell, married to a Nez Perce woman and acquainted with many of the headmen present, reiterated the message. If the Cayuse did not turn in "the murderers," he declared, they would lose everything but a name: "the 'Bloody Cayuses.' They will never lose that."[21]

Among those who spoke in response was an elder known to whites as Joseph, father of the better-known Chief Joseph, who would gain fame as a leader during the Nez Perce War of 1877.

Joseph the elder was a half-brother of Five Crows, the Cayuse head-man who had only reluctantly given up the hostage he had claimed as a wife after the Whitman killings. Ten days earlier, Five Crows had been wounded in a skirmish with Gilliam's forces at Sand Hollow, south of the Umatilla River.[22] Joseph was in a delicate position, torn between family loyalty and a desire to avoid conflict. "I speak for all the Cayuses present and all my people," he said, according to a transcript of the proceedings. "I do not want my children engaged in this war, although my brother is wounded."[23]

The only Cayuse headman to speak was Camaspelo, leader of the neutral band centered at the headwaters of the Umatilla. Reportedly saying, "My people seem to have two hearts," he wanted the Americans to know that the Cayuse had been deeply divided about the Whitmans. After repeating an earlier statement, that he had been asked to approve plans for the attack and had refused, Camaspelo vowed he would not "protect or defend the murderers."[24] Tauitau, the influential headman on the main stem of the Umatilla, did not attend the council but sent word that he too would remain neutral in any conflict with the Americans. The council ended with an exchange of hopeful words but no real progress toward a settlement. The discouraged commissioners returned to Oregon City.

Gilliam, impatient, went back out on the hunt. Having heard that Tiloukaikt and his band were fleeing north into Palus (Palouse) territory, Gilliam and his militia chased after them.[25] On the morning of March 14 they seized several hundred horses and cattle at the mouth of the Tucannon River, assuming the animals belonged to Tiloukaikt's band. Within hours, Gilliam's militia was under attack by an estimated four hundred Indians, mostly Palus, angry because the livestock belonged to them, not to the Cayuse. The outnumbered "Oregon Volunteers" hastily retreated and eventually released the animals. Two days later—weary, dispirited, and hungry—they straggled into Fort Waters.[26] The increasingly dismal conditions and plummeting morale prompted the officers to leave only a token force at Fort Waters and move most of the troops to the former Methodist mission at The Dalles, now being called Fort Wascopam. En route to The Dalles on March 20, 1848, Gilliam knocked over a loaded shotgun while pulling a rope out of a wagon and accidentally shot and killed himself.[27]

Gilliam's deputy, James Waters, took command of what had become less a military force than a state-sanctioned mob. One of his officers passed out orders to arrest any Indian who looked "suspicious."[28] In mid-May, Waters led about 120 men into Nez Perce territory, "in pursuit of our enemies." Finding no Cayuse, they shot three Nez Perce men who resisted the soldiers' efforts to steal their livestock.[29] "It's a very sad thing that after we killed the Whitmans it sort of becomes open season on Indians," Roberta Conner, director of the Tamástslikt Cultural Institute, said in a 2009 interview. "Everybody paid. All kinds of people paid for our Whitman killings."[30]

Meanwhile, mountain man Joe Meek was on his way to Washington, DC, bringing news of the attack to the federal government along with demands for protection for Americans in Oregon. Like Robert Newell, Meek had settled in the Willamette Valley and become active in civic affairs. He claimed a personal motivation for seeking federal intervention: his nine-year-old daughter, Helen (who had lived with the Whitmans since she was a toddler), had died of measles shortly after the attack, and Meek held the Indians responsible. Meek and three companions left Oregon City in January 1848 and arrived in Washington, DC, in three months, a record at the time. He introduced himself as "envoy extraordinary and minister plenipotentiary from the republic of Oregon to the court of the United States."[31] He met with President James K. Polk (who was married to Meek's second cousin) and other dignitaries and lobbied hard for passage of a long-delayed bill to make Oregon an official territory of the United States. The measure had been stalled in Congress for two years by a debate over whether slavery would be permitted in the new territory. A bill excluding slavery finally passed, by a narrow margin, in August 1848. Polk appointed the first slate of territorial officers, including Joseph Lane, a Mexican War veteran and Indiana legislator, as governor general and superintendent of Indian affairs. Joe Meek, rewarded with the title US marshal for the Territory of Oregon, escorted Lane to his new posting.

Shortly after reaching Oregon City in March 1849, Governor Lane opened negotiations with tribal leaders for the surrender of "those concerned in that horrible massacre." He offered peace and friendship if the guilty were given up. If not, he promised the Cayuse a war "which would lead to their total destruction," because "we could not discriminate between the innocent and guilty."[32] Still, the Cayuse held out. They faced new pressures that fall, when the first federal troops arrived in Oregon—631 mounted riflemen, dispatched from Fort Leavenworth in Kansas. Roughly 20 percent of the soldiers soon deserted, heading for gold fields in California, but the rest gave Lane new leverage to end what had become known as the Cayuse War. By that point the Cayuse had endured nearly two years of harassment by volunteer militias. They had found limited support from some traditional allies, including the Umatilla, but the Walla Walla, Nez Perce, and the powerful Yakama held back.[33] Tiloukaikt's band had been forced into hiding in the Blue Mountains. Disease and hunger had weakened the tribe as a whole. In November 1849, Governor Lane sent a message to Tauitau, acknowledged leader of the neutral bands on the Umatilla, and to Nez Perce headmen at Lapwai. He again threatened wholesale war if "the guilty" were not taken, "dead or alive." He made it clear there was no longer a place for neutrality.[34]

Paul Kane completed this painting (reproduced here in black and white), titled "Tilli-koit," in 1856, after he had learned that Tiloukaikt and Tomahas, both of whom he had sketched during his 1847 visit to the Whitman Mission, were among the five Cayuses who had been hanged in connection with the attack. In both cases, the finished paintings depict men who are younger and more "savage" than the figures in the original sketches. *Used with permission of the Royal Ontario Museum © ROM; 912.1.74.*

Finally, in April 1850, Tauitau arranged the surrender of five Cayuses. Among them was Tiloukaikt, the "kind, friendly Indian" who had welcomed the Whitmans' infant daughter as a "Cayuse girl." Tiloukaikt had played a complex role in the story of the Whitman Mission. He had sent three of his children to school at the mission; been among the first of his people to experiment with western-style agriculture; and often served as a moderating influence in relations between the Whitmans and less accommodating members of his band. Theodore Stern, a noted scholar and anthropologist, concluded that Tiloukaikt had given only reluctant consent to the attack, pushed into it by young warriors, including his own son, "Edward" (the Christianized name Narcissa had given him). Tiloukaikt was, Stern wrote, "a man swept along, desperately striving to regain his footing, and his leadership, in waters too swift and deep for him."[35] Catherine Sager said she felt sorry for Tiloukaikt, seeing him move around the mission complex during the month that the survivors were held as hostages, looking like "a heartbroken conscience-stricken man."[36]

It is difficult to know how the Cayuse made the decision to turn in those five men. There was some speculation, at the time and afterward, that they simply gave up five volunteers in order to appease the whites and end the persecution. According to one oft-cited account, when a guard asked Tiloukaikt why he had surrendered, he replied: "Did not your missionaries teach us that Christ died to save his people? So die we to save our people."[37] For his part, Governor Lane seemed unconcerned about whether any of the prisoners had participated in the killings or whether any of the actual attackers had gone free. "The punishment of these Indians," he told the Territorial Legislature, "will remove the barrier to a peace with the Cayuse, and have a good effect upon all the tribes."[38]

A grand jury in Oregon City indicted the prisoners on charges of murder on May 13, 1850, in one of the first formal judicial proceedings held in the new territory. The jury issued a total of nineteen "true bills," but only one went to trial: indictment number eleven, alleging that "Telakite, Tomahas otherwise called the Murderer, Clokomas, Isiaasheluckas and Kiamasumkin, with certain other Indians whose names are to the Jurors unknown, with force and arms in and upon one Marcus Whitman, the said Whitman not then and there being an Indian, did make an assault," resulting in "several mortal wounds, of which said mortal wounds, he the said Marcus Whitman then and there died."[39]

The names of all five defendants were spelled in various ways in the trial record, but the court clerk had particular trouble with Tiloukaikt. The variations included "Telakite" (in the indictment); "Teloquit" and "Teloquoit" (in a defense motion challenging the court's jurisdiction); "Telekite" and "Telokite" (in a motion for a new trial); and "Tilikite" (in an appeal). The spelling on the indictment prevailed, and the case was filed as *United States v. Telakite et al.* The presiding judge was Orville C. Pratt—at that time the only federal judge in Oregon Territory. He appointed Kintzing Pritchette, the territorial secretary, as lead defense counsel, to be assisted by two military officers. Pritchette, a lawyer from Pennsylvania, was the only member of the defense team who had any legal training. The prisoners were held in a makeshift jail on Abernethy Island, at the foot of Willamette Falls. Joe Meek served as their jailer, bailiff, and eventual executioner.

Oregon City at that time was a frontier town of about seven hundred. For lack of a courthouse, the four-day trial took place in a tavern. The prisoners, taken from the jail in chains, remained chained throughout the proceedings. Two men interpreted for them, one from English to Chinook Jargon, the other from Chinook Jargon to Nez Perce. The defense filed a handwritten motion on the opening day, May 21, 1850, arguing that the court lacked jurisdiction because the killings had occurred on Cayuse land and therefore the accused were subject to the "laws and usage of said Cayuse nation," not the laws of the United States.[40] The judge denied that motion and several others and ordered the trial to proceed. The prosecutor called four witnesses, all survivors of the attack. Only two testified to having seen any of the defendants engage in violence. An emigrant who had been at the mission for only a few months said she had seen "Telokite" hit Whitman in the head with a hatchet, three times, in the yard outside the Mission House. Whitman was actually assaulted in his kitchen. Elizabeth Sager, age ten at the time of the attack, said she saw Isiaasheluckas shoot and kill Lucian "Luke"

Saunders, the schoolteacher. Elizabeth was in the schoolroom when Saunders was killed, and it's doubtful she would have had a view of what was going on outside.

The defense did not challenge the testimony of either witness. Instead, its case centered on the argument that the Cayuses had acted within the boundaries of tribal law.[41] John McLoughlin, former chief factor at Fort Vancouver, swore he had warned Whitman that under Cayuse law medicine men whose patients died could be killed in retribution. Stickus, one of Whitman's most loyal Cayuse allies, and Henry Spalding, Whitman's fellow missionary, both said that Whitman knew he faced danger because of his inability to combat the lethal effects of measles on the Cayuse.[42] Ronald Lansing, an Oregon law professor and author of a book about the trial, concluded that the defendants in effect "confessed to the killing but said the killing was fitting and proper."[43]

The jury of twelve white men deliberated for one hour and fifteen minutes on the morning of May 24 before returning the expected verdict: guilty. The defense immediately filed several motions on appeal; all were denied. Judge Pratt reconvened the court in the late afternoon and pronounced his sentence. He ordered the prisoners to be confined until 2:00 p.m. on Monday, June 3, 1850, when Marshal Joe Meek would take them to a gallows erected in Oregon City, "and there by him be hung by the neck, until you are dead."[44]

In a final repudiation of the Protestant missionaries, the prisoners refused to meet with Henry Spalding, who offered to pray with them while they awaited execution. Instead, they not only welcomed visits from Bishop Blanchet and another priest, they accepted baptism and admission to the Catholic Church with new names: Andrew, Peter, John, Paul, and James. The priests accompanied the prisoners to the scaffold, where a large crowd had gathered to watch. Tiloukaikt (newly christened as Andrew) begged to be shot, like a man, instead of hanged, like a dog. "Hanging, however, was the requirement of the law, and hang they did," the *Oregon Spectator* reported. Marshal Meek fixed the ropes and sprang the trapdoors. Eyewitnesses said three of the men died quickly, but two others struggled, one for at least fifteen minutes.[45] They were buried on the outskirts of Oregon City, in unmarked graves.

Any hope the Cayuse may have had to resume their old way of life quickly faded. By 1850 about eight thousand Americans were living in what was then called Oregon Territory, compared to perhaps 150 Americans a decade earlier, and thousands more were on their way. The Oregon Donation Land Act of 1850 gave married couples the right to claim a section of land (640 acres), free. To accelerate the process of colonization, Anson Dart, superintendent of Indian affairs for the territory, recommended that Congress buy the Cayuse/Walla Walla homelands and open them up for settlement. Dart claimed that the two tribes were "nearly extinct," with only 126 and 130 tribal members, respectively.[46] Other sources at the time reported much higher figures. Undercounting the Indian population was a way of reinforcing the argument that their lands should be turned over to whites. The pressure increased in 1853 when much of Oregon Territory was sliced off to create Washington Territory. The new territory's first governor and superintendent of Indian affairs, Isaac I. Stevens, a thirty-five-year-old engineer and Mexican War veteran, was a determined champion of the nation's Manifest Destiny. Stevens promptly set about organizing a series of treaty councils to divest the region's Indians of title to most of their ancestral lands and move them to reservations, making way for white settlers.

In May and June 1855, Stevens and Joel Palmer, who had replaced Dart as Oregon Territory's superintendent of Indian affairs, met with representatives of the Cayuse, Umatilla, Walla Walla, Nez Perce, and

Yakama at Mill Creek, on what is now the Whitman College campus in Walla Walla. Estimates of the number of Indians attending range from eighteen hundred to five thousand. None of the Cayuse wanted to surrender title to their lands. Headmen from the Umatilla bands, who had tried an appeasement policy five years earlier by arranging the surrender of "the Cayuse Five," now led the opposition to the whites' demands. Tauitau had died in 1853. His nephew and protégé, Weyatenatemany (also spelled Weatenatimenin), had succeeded him as the new Young Chief, recognized by whites as the main spokesman for the Cayuse. "The earth says, God has placed me here," Young Chief said, according to his translator. "The earth says that God tells me to take care of the Indians on this earth."[47] Palmer told the Indians they could not prevent the whites from coming, any more than they could stop the wind from blowing or the rain from falling. "Like the grasshoppers on the plains, some years there will be more come than others, you cannot stop them," he said.[48] Palmer urged the Indians to select a reservation where they could live in peace, while there was still time.

Stevens originally proposed creating just two reservations for all the Plateau peoples. The larger one would encompass most of the existing Nez Perce country. The Cayuse, Walla Walla, and Umatilla bands would be moved there, sharing the land with the Nez Perce. The Yakama and several smaller tribes would be settled on a reservation between the Columbia and Yakima Rivers. All the other land—tens of millions of acres—would be "the Great Father's for his white children."[49] The Nez Perce, represented by a spokesman known to whites as Lawyer, argued for acceptance of the offer. Young Chief reacted with scorn. If Lawyer could see any sense in what Stevens had planned, Young Chief said, then "I am blind and ignorant."[50]

The Indians' refusal to accept the initial terms forced Stevens and Palmer to offer a smallish third reservation, in the Umatilla Valley, for the Cayuse and their Walla Walla and Umatilla neighbors. The tribal spokesmen reluctantly agreed. In a treaty signed on June 9, 1855, they ceded 6.4 million acres to the United States, in return for 510,000 acres to live on, the promise of a cash payment of $150,000, and the right to hunt, fish, gather, and pasture livestock at all the usual and accustomed places, on and off the reservation. Congress did not ratify the treaty until March 8, 1859. In the intervening years, non-Indian miners and settlers moved in to exploit resources for which the tribes had not yet been compensated.[51] When the reservation was actually surveyed, it totaled approximately 245,000 acres—roughly half the land set aside by treaty. Thinking of the tribes' traditional homelands as a huge outstretched hand, what they had left was the tip of a pinky finger.

The reservation shrank even more in subsequent years. In 1874 the Oregon state legislature asked the federal government to terminate the reservation and move the Indians somewhere else because they weren't putting the land to good use—that is, they were hunting, fishing, and grazing horses instead of farming. "We favor their removal as it is a burning shame to keep this fine body of land for a few worthless Indians," the *East Oregonian* (Pendleton's newspaper) editorialized in December 1877.[52] A decade later, Congress passed the Dawes Act, which authorized the division of reservations into allotments for individual tribe members and the sale of any "surplus" land to non-Indians. By the early 1930s only about 160,000 acres of the Confederated Tribes of the Umatilla Indian Reservation remained in Indian hands.

The Cayuse lost not only land but a voice in the narrative that would be told in dominant forums during the coming decades. The self-congratulatory history of the Northwest, as curated by whites, had little room for Cayuse perspectives about the Whitmans, the reasons for the attack on their mission, or the legacy of vengeance.

CHAPTER NINE

CANONIZATION

I like the story of Whitman. If it isn't true, it ought to be.

—*President Warren G. Harding, July 3, 1923*

More is imagined than known about what Marcus or Narcissa Whitman looked like. Neither was ever photographed or painted. That did not deter Chicago newspaperman Oliver W. Nixon from including black-and-white photographs of "Dr. Marcus Whitman at the time of his marriage" and "Mrs. Narcissa Prentice [*sic*] Whitman" in early editions of his 1895 book, *How Marcus Whitman Saved Oregon: A True Romance of Patriotic Heroism, Christian Devotion and Final Martyrdom*. The "Whitman" in the photo is a clean-shaven man with mutton-chop sideburns, a high forehead, and a strong jaw. He wears a dark suit, a vest, and the clerical collar favored by Presbyterian and Congregational clergymen in the late nineteenth century. "Mrs. Whitman" has a longish face, hair parted in the middle and pulled back tight, thin lips, and a mouth as straight as the edge of a prayer book. She is clad in a Salvation Army–like uniform, with severe tailoring and a high neck.[1]

Purported photographs of "Dr. Marcus Whitman at the time of his marriage" and "Narcissa Prentice [sic] Whitman" were published in Oliver Nixon's How Marcus Whitman Saved Oregon (1895). Nixon later admitted that the man in the photo was a Chicago minister; he never identified the woman. There are no known photographs of either of the Whitmans.

Nixon, the author of several treacly tributes to Marcus Whitman, later conceded that the man in the photo was Rev. Marcus Whitman Montgomery, a Chicago preacher whose only relationship to the missionary was a partially shared name. Nixon never identified the woman. In subsequent editions the photo of the man was retouched to eliminate the ministerial collar. A new caption identified Montgomery as the subject while claiming that he "resembled Dr. Whitman very closely." The photo of the woman was replaced by a portrait of someone much prettier, with a heart-shaped face, an upturned mouth, large, widely spaced eyes, and a softer hairstyle and dress. Nixon said the illustration was "drawn under the supervision of a gentleman familiar with [Narcissa's] appearance" and was "considered a good likeness" of her.[2]

Entirely different purported images of the Whitmans surfaced in the 1970s (reproduced in Chapter 3). They were based on two small, rough pencil sketches by Canadian artist Paul Kane, who visited the Whitman Mission in July 1847, midway through a two-year odyssey to document Indian life in the Pacific Northwest. One drawing is a profile of a man with a long, pointed nose, a prominent chin, and the suggestion of a vandyke beard. He wears what appears to be a buckskin jacket, fringed at the shoulder, and a bucket-type hat with a narrow, sloping brim. The other sketch depicts a woman sitting at a table outdoors, one arm bent at the elbow, hand on her cheek. Her hair is loosely coiled above her ears. The sleeves of her low-necked, billowy dress are pushed up to the elbows. Her expression is dreamy and serene.

Kane never identified the subjects or dated the sketches, but in 1968, Ross Woodbridge, a Whitman enthusiast from Pittsford, New York, decided they were Marcus and Narcissa Whitman, not some random white people Kane encountered either at the mission or elsewhere during his extensive travels.[3] There is no evidence that Whitman ever possessed a buckskin jacket. Indeed, he associated the material with "heathen" culture. Matilda Sager, one of the Whitmans' adopted children, swore that Narcissa was "severe both in dress and the way she dressed her hair," always wore a sunbonnet outdoors, and "never had her bare neck exposed."[4] Nonetheless, Woodbridge convinced historian Clifford Drury that the people in the sketches were the "real" Whitmans. Drury, in turn, commissioned idealized, full-color paintings based on the drawings for his 1973 book, *Marcus and Narcissa Whitman and the Opening of Old Oregon*.

Whatever they really looked like, Narcissa became more beautiful and saintlier and Marcus more manly and heroic in published accounts as the years passed. In the 1920s, Honore Willsie Morrow, a novelist who specialized in historical fiction, created a template for many subsequent writers by envisioning a Narcissa who was "tall and beautiful, of noble proportions and bearing," with long-lashed blue eyes, "chiseled" features, and shining, golden hair.[5] Drury called Narcissa "a woman of both physical and spiritual beauty."[6] To Arch Merrill, the "Poet Laureate of Upstate New York" in the 1950s, Narcissa was "a comely, vivacious girl with golden hair, a village belle."[7] Eliza Spalding was often cut out of the script, while Narcissa was cast as the "golden-haired, hymn-singing beauty" who was the "first woman to cross the continent."[8] If Eliza did appear in the story, it was usually as a foil—"as dark and scrawny as Narcissa was golden and buxom."[9]

Marcus Whitman, meanwhile, was enveloped in a carapace of myth as the man who had "saved Oregon for the Flag." That story—a claim that Whitman had rushed to the nation's capital in the winter of 1842–43 to prevent the American government from trading the country to Great Britain for a worthless "cod fishery" off Newfoundland—emerged in the 1860s and gained traction in the 1880s.[10] Whitman himself bragged that Oregon "might have slept forever" in the hands of the British or, possibly worse, "Jesuit Papists," had he not "superintended" the first major wagon train to Oregon in 1843, an action that laid "the foundation for the speedy settlement of the country."[11] In fact, there was no likelihood at all, in the era of Manifest Destiny, that the United States would cede control of Oregon to the British or anyone else. Although Whitman was an ardent advocate of American colonialism, he rode east to save his mission, not Oregon. His goal, as shown earlier, was to persuade the American Board of Commissioners for Foreign Missions to rescind an order to shut down his operations at Waiilatpu. The wagon train Whitman joined on his return trip was organized and underway by the time he caught up with it.

Historians began debunking the Whitman-saved-Oregon myth in the early 1900s, but it lived on in newspaper and magazine articles, in historical fiction, and in speeches by politicians, including one delivered by President Warren G. Harding on July 3, 1923. Harding was midway through a two-month railroad tour of the West when he visited the tiny town of Meacham, in northeastern Oregon, to help commemorate the eightieth anniversary of the opening of the Oregon Trail. Rumors had begun circulating about scandals within his administration. Harding would die of a heart attack in San Francisco just one month later. But the mood in Meacham was buoyant. More than twenty thousand people had gathered for an event organized by boosters in nearby communities to promote auto tourism along the newly designated Oregon Trail Highway. The attractions included a historical pageant, featuring "pioneers" in covered wagons; and an "Indian Village," set up by members of the Confederated Tribes of the Cayuse, Umatilla, and Walla Walla.

At one point, Harding walked over to the village for a "pow-wow." He was greeted by a man called Sumpkin, identified in press accounts as "chief of the Cayuses and spokesman for all of the Indians." Sumpkin used his audience with the president to protest the federal government's treatment of Indians in Oregon. Speaking through an interpreter, he said the government was not meeting its treaty obligations. The Indians had not been able to "adjust their troubles" with the resident Indian agent. A reporter deemed it "a long address."[12] Harding responded with platitudes about friendship and peace and the need for mutual understanding. "If we had only understood each other from the beginning," he said. "If the Indian had known of the purposes of the nation and the nation had understood the Indian, we need never have had any warfare between the races." He deflected Sumpkin's complaints by telling him to take them up with the superintendent of Indian affairs in Washington. The *New York Times* described this as a charming encounter between "the old redskin warrior" and "the Great White Father."[13] The dismissive tone was typical of non-Indian reactions when Indians tried to claim federally guaranteed rights in the 1920s.

The organizers had expected Harding to speak about pioneers and patriotism in general terms. Instead, the president focused on Marcus Whitman, "the pioneer missionary hero of the vast, unsettled, unexplored Oregon country." Harding repeated as fact the old and entirely fanciful claim that Whitman—"a man among men"—had met President John Tyler in the White House in 1843 and persuaded him not to "barter away" Oregon. "Never in the history of the world has there been a finer example of civilization following Christianity," he added. He was apparently oblivious to the irony of canonizing Whitman before an audience that included people whose ongoing hardships in the midst of "Christian civilization" began with Whitman's arrival in their homeland.[14] Interviewed after his speech, Harding said he was "mindful" that the story he had just recited was "a subject of controversy," but he liked it anyway. "Whether it is correct or not it is an inspiration and should be handed down from generation to generation," he said.[15]

Stories about the Whitmans as heroic, almost saintly agents of civilization were widely disseminated among non-Indians and rarely challenged for more than a century after their deaths, a fact that reveals more about contemporary social and political conditions than it does about the missionaries themselves and the lives they actually led. In the 1890s, a period of rapid industrialization and unsettling social change, the Whitmans represented an idealized past, marked by Protestant virtue and pioneer spunk. When the Great Depression made greed unfashionable in the 1930s, white Americans honored the missionaries as selfless individuals who went west to harvest

Indian souls, unlike the fur traders, miners, and others who sought only profits and power. During the Cold War tensions of the 1950s, the Whitmans were emblems of Christendom, standing against the advance of godless Communism. Not until the 1970s did the Whitman legend begin to crumble, as new perspectives on the history of the West began to emerge and long-ignored voices began to be heard.

There was a sense, in the 1890s, that America's best days might be behind it. The "frontier era"—US expansion into new areas of North America—had come to an end. Venerated early settlers were dying off. The country was in the grip of a major depression. Agricultural communities like Walla Walla were particularly hard-hit. The selling price of wheat, the region's primary crop, fell from $1.11 a bushel in 1877 to 47 cents in 1895, while shipping costs (controlled by railroad monopolies) remained high. The supply of credit dried up, affecting farmers and the local businesses dependent on them. The industrial revolution was accelerating the pace of cultural change. As historian Peter Boag observed, the rocky transition from "the traditions of the nineteenth century to the uncertainties of the twentieth" created a cultural crisis. The idea that American life was more heroic and virtuous in the past fed a market for nostalgia. One result, especially in the region once known as Oregon Country, was a "fixation on, embellishment of, and memorialization" of the pioneer generation.[16] In these circumstances the Whitmans, already portrayed in many forums as martyrs, were sure candidates for glorification.

In 1891 the Oregon State Legislature commissioned a history of "the heroic deeds of those brave men and noble women" who "saved this state to the United States." That same year, the Oregon Pioneer Association began publishing installments of Narcissa Whitman's travel diary and many of her surviving letters, bringing renewed attention to the missionaries. Oliver Nixon's book, *How Marcus Whitman Saved Oregon*, came out in 1895. The *Ladies Home Journal*

From left, Catherine Sager Pringle, Elizabeth Sager Helm, and Matilda Sager Delaney, photographed in Walla Walla in November 1897, during the fiftieth-anniversary commemoration of the attack. The last of the surviving "Sager orphans" (brought to the Whitman Mission as children in 1844), each of the women wrote memoirs about their years with the Whitmans, the attack, and its aftermath. *Whitman College and Northwest Archives, Sager Family Collection, Box 2, Folder 82.*

took the story to a mainstream audience two years later with an article titled "When Dr. Whitman Added Three Stars to Our Flag." (Oregon became a state in 1859, followed by Washington in 1889 and Idaho in 1890.[17]) Newspapers around the country picked up the tale about the daring cross-continental ride and the missionary who, with his self-sacrificing wife, had met a martyr's death.

Whitman College president Stephen B. Penrose played a key role in elevating the school's namesake to the status of national hero. When he began his forty-year tenure as president of Whitman, in 1894, the college was in financial crisis and its survival in doubt. It was skipping payments on a $12,000 mortgage, owed $3,000 to its underpaid faculty, its major donor had threatened to withdraw a $50,000 gift, and enrollment had dwindled to fewer than forty students. A member of a prominent Philadelphia family, Penrose realized that the story of a missionary who secured a western empire for the United States would resonate with the kind of philanthropists he had known in the East. He wrote a Whitman-saved-Oregon pamphlet titled "The Romance of a College," printed hundreds of copies, prepared a speech based on its major points, and set off on a nationwide fund-raising tour. "The patriotic people of the United States have to say whether the only monument of a national hero shall be allowed to perish from the earth," he declared.[18] Penrose's campaign was successful enough, according to a history of the college by G. Thomas Edwards, that although Marcus Whitman did not "save Oregon," the Whitman myth ended up saving the school.[19]

As the fiftieth anniversary of the Cayuse attack approached, in early 1897, Penrose worked with a Portland-based group to revive a long-dormant campaign for a permanent memorial to the Whitmans on the grounds of the former mission. They planned to build a new vault and place a marble tombstone on the common grave where most of the victims had been buried; install a twenty-seven-foot-tall obelisk and pedestal on the hill overlooking the gravesite; and dedicate the new tomb and the "Whitman Shaft" with two days of commemoration, beginning on November 29, the anniversary day. The new tomb could not be constructed without temporarily disinterring the bones in the "Great Grave." Catherine Sager Pringle and Elizabeth Sager Helm, then in their sixties and the oldest of the surviving Sager orphans, objected to plans to open the grave, which held the remains of their two brothers, but they were overruled. Penrose himself supervised the excavation.[20]

Only five skulls and a few bones were found. Two Walla Walla doctors who examined the remains identified one skull as Marcus Whitman's because its size allegedly indicated "superior mental development." A gold filling in one molar was consistent with knowledge that Whitman had a tooth filled in Saint Louis in 1843. Also, the doctors declared, "the seats of muscular adjustment show a strong, well developed man." Just one skull was clearly female, they said, and thus belonged to Narcissa, the only woman killed in the attack. Moreover, they claimed, those two skulls (and none of the others) had been "cut in two" with a surgical saw—presumably belonging to Whitman—in an act of postmortem mutilation.[21] One doctor speculated that Indians had hacked into the skulls in the belief that "when a great man or woman died, if the head was opened the spirit of the departed would enter the body of the operator," in a sort of transmigration. The doctors gave their report to Penrose and to the *Spokesman-Review* (Spokane), which published it under the sensational headline "Skulls Cut In Two."[22]

Catherine Sager Pringle was among the few who questioned the forensic abilities of the Walla Walla doctors. In a lengthy letter to the *Spokesman-Review*, she said she had seen wolves dig into the grave and drag away parts of the bodies, including the bodies of the Whitmans. "Where the bones of Dr. Whitman and many of his associates are, God only knows," she wrote. She thought the skull with the gold filling was probably that of Lucian Saunders, the lawyer Whitman had recruited to teach school at the mission. As an educated man from the East, Saunders was as likely as Whitman to have such a filling. She also wondered whether "the learned doctors" could really identify a skull by gender. The skull they said was Narcissa's might instead have belonged to one of Catherine's teenage brothers.

She also challenged the assertion that Indians had sawed into the skulls. "As I saw the corpses before burial," Catherine wrote, "I know there were no such wounds as described." If the Indians had wanted to open the Whitmans' heads to release spirits or some such, they would have used tomahawks or knives, not something as unfamiliar as a surgical saw. Besides, she concluded, "the Cayuses were superstitious about the dead and would never have picked up one of those skulls to saw it."[23] Perrin Whitman, Marcus's nephew, agreed that the dead bodies had not been mutilated.[24] Photos of the alleged Whitman skulls, filed away in the Whitman College archives, clearly show they were intact—not literally "cut in two."[25] But ghoulish stories about "severed skulls" appeared in newspapers around the country, reinforcing an image of the Whitmans as victims of ruthless barbarians.

The tombstone and the obelisk were still at a marble quarry in Vermont on the eve of the anniversary, but the commemoration proceeded as planned. Rev. Leavitt H. Hallock, a trustee of Whitman College, delivered the opening oration in the Walla Walla Opera House. The *Walla Walla Union* reprinted it—all 7,437 words—confident that it would "be read with delight by numerous readers throughout the United States, if not in every English speaking quarter of the World." One wonders how many listeners had nodded off by the time Hallock reached his crescendo, in which he compared Whitman to George Washington and Abraham Lincoln and asked why Paul Revere's ride was so revered when it had lasted but a scant hour while Whitman had spent half a year traveling to Washington to save Oregon.[26]

A special excursion train took at least two thousand people from Walla Walla to the gravesite the next day, a drizzly Tuesday. Eight survivors of the attack, including the three remaining Sager sisters, attended. Afterward, "hundreds crowded around the aged survivors, eagerly listening to their graphic recitals of the thrilling and bloody events of '47."[27] Later that day, President Penrose presided over a lengthy program in the Opera House. Dignitaries spoke, bands played, the Whitman College choir sang. Perrin Whitman, unable to attend, sent his grandson, who gave Penrose a lock of what he said was Narcissa's hair. The *Seattle Post-Intelligencer* summed up the proceedings with this headline: "Whitman's Grave No Longer Unkept / Vast Throngs Do Honor to His Memory / Entire Northwest Represented in Gathering of Pioneers at Waiilatpu, Where the Missionary Band Was Butchered Fifty Years Ago."[28]

When the obelisk and grave marker finally arrived, at the end of January 1898, Penrose conducted a brief dedication ceremony for a handful of onlookers.[29] Three of the thirteen names carved into the new marble tombstone were misspelled; one victim was remembered only by his last name, and another was not included on the list at all. The last name on the list, "Jacob D. Hall," referred to Peter D. Hall, who escaped from Waiilatpu on the first day of the attack, probably was not killed by Indians, and definitely was not buried in the "Great Grave." Today, all the names on the tombstone are weathered and barely legible.

The next large-scale effort to memorialize the Whitmans came in 1936, the centennial of their arrival in the Northwest. Planning began a full year earlier, when the Walla Walla Chamber of Commerce established a nonprofit corporation to commemorate the anniversary with a multipart extravaganza, including a historical pageant with a cast of thousands. The goal was to raise money to turn the former mission into a national monument administered by the National Park Service. The owners of a thirty-seven-acre farm adjacent to the eight-acre site of the "Great Grave" and the "Whitman Shaft" had offered to sell it for $10,000. Walla Walla's business leaders believed a national monument, located just seven miles west of town, would attract tourists and boost the local economy. At the least, they expected the centennial celebration to bring in some money and serve as a distraction from the grim realities of the Great Depression. The theme would be "One Hundred Years of Progress."

The festivities, spread out over four days, began on August 13, 1936. The Whitmans did not establish their mission until late December, but winter in the Walla Walla Valley was not a good time to throw a big party with main attractions that would be staged outdoors. The official program (cost: 25 cents) featured a photo of a perky cowgirl in a short skirt, black cowboy boots, and a white hat, pointing west toward an image, superimposed on the background, of a long wagon train snaking its way through hilly scrubland. The centennial drew an estimated ten thousand visitors to Walla Walla. Activities included daily parades, with marching bands, oxen-drawn wagons, floats featuring parasol-toting "pioneer mothers," and hundreds of horses with costumed riders. The entire business district was transformed with false fronts into a pioneer town. Hotel, retail, and even office workers dressed in pioneer garb. Vendors sold souvenir posters, postcards, pins, and medallions.

Narcissa Whitman, hailed as the woman who "established the first home in what is now the state of Washington" and "gave birth to the region's first baby," was the star of an afternoon devoted to the "pioneer mothers." (Nonwhite homes and babies did not figure into the narrative.[30]) Clifford Drury, who had just published the first of his many books about the Whitmans and the Spaldings, eulogized her. Members of the Spokane Monday Musical Club sang excerpts from an opera about her (*Narcissa*, music and libretto written in 1912). A full-length portrait of Narcissa as a beautiful blond, taken from its usual spot in a Whitman College women's residence hall named in her honor, was displayed in an amphitheater before an admiring crowd.[31]

The pageant, a spectacle called *Wagons West!* (admission: $1, plus 5 cents tax), presented the Whitmans as "heroic Christian soldiers and martyrs in the cause of humanity."[32] Stephen Penrose, newly retired as Whitman College president, wrote the script, adapting one he had written for a 1923 pageant titled *How the West Was Won*. The vogue for historical pageantry—in which huge numbers of costumed amateurs reenacted events tied to some historic milestone—had developed in Great Britain in the late nineteenth century, reached a peak in the eastern United States around World War I, and then found new relevance in the West. The pageants were invariably pioneer-centric, celebratory in nature, and designed to build a sense of community in young towns and cities. Walla Walla's centennial version presented history as a triumphal march of progress, beginning with dinosaurs emerging from a swamp and culminating in a Whitman College graduation ceremony. In a brief scene depicting indigenous people, Indian men lazed around while the women worked. The unmistakable message was that the Indians' traditional way of life was primitive and unproductive until the Whitmans arrived, bringing Bibles and civilization to the wilderness. The show ended with hundreds of people forming a "living flag" and singing the national anthem.[33]

More than three thousand local residents participated in the pageant as actors, singers, dancers, or musicians. Hundreds of others helped with costumes, sets, and other chores. The organizers tried to recruit cast members from the Confederated Tribes of the Cayuse, Umatilla, and Walla Walla Reservation in Pendleton, but records do not show how many signed up. At least some "Indians" in *Wagons West!* were white men wearing feather headdresses. Three young couples represented the Whitmans at different stages of life. The role of Narcissa discovering the body of her drowned toddler went to nineteen-year-old Vi Forrest. She remembered, decades later, that people in the audience cried during that scene. The pageant brought "a lot of pride" to the community, she commented. "Marcus and Narcissa were valued highly."[34]

The Whitman Centennial Corporation raised enough money to buy the land at the former mission site, but it took several years to clear legal hurdles and establish the Whitman National Monument. Archaeological work that began in 1941 was almost immediately suspended and did not resume until after World War II ended. An adobe storage shed, built by the Works Progress Administration to house archaeological finds and intended to last only a month or so, was turned into a rudimentary museum. It was not replaced until 1963. By then, the monument had doubled in area, to ninety-eight acres, and the name changed to the Whitman Mission National Historic Site. Throughout the 1950s and 1960s the historic site's interpretation of the Whitmans was consistently adulatory and nationalistic. "The work of the Whitmans at this mission places them with the noblest of the pioneers colonizing the West," a 1958 Park Service brochure declared. "Their indomitable spirit, energy, and determination carried the American flag to remote regions and contributed to our national expansion." The brochure's cover featured a drawing of a slender, sunbonneted woman in a long dress, a Bible in the crook of one arm, standing next to a tall, broad-shouldered man in a wide-brimmed hat, both gazing westward. The Cayuse got barely a mention, except as perpetrators of the "massacre" (a word that was repeated five times in the eight-page brochure).[35]

Park Service planners wanted visitors to appreciate the Whitmans' "devotion to God and country" and gain "inspiration and spiritual regeneration" from their example.[36] It was the height of the Cold War. Americans were fighting multifaceted wars against "Godless communists." Congress passed and President Dwight D. Eisenhower signed laws adding the words "under God" to the Pledge of Allegiance and requiring that the phrase "In God We Trust" be imprinted on US currency. That the Bible-toting Whitmans had played a role in Christianizing and "colonizing the West" was a point of pride—not opprobrium.

⁓

The Whitmans were markedly unsuccessful as missionaries—in their eleven years in Oregon they failed to convert a single Indian—yet historian Clifford Drury confidently declared in 1973 that "no Protestant missionaries in the history of the United States have been honored by so many monuments and memorials as Marcus and Narcissa Whitman."[37] A large mural installed in the Oregon State Capitol Rotunda in 1938 depicted John McLoughlin welcoming the Whitmans and the Spaldings to Fort Vancouver. Fort Whitman stood guard over Puget Sound from Goat Island until it was decommissioned and turned over to the Washington State Game Department in 1947. Elementary schools in Richland and Spokane, a middle school in Seattle, and a high school in Rushville, New York (Marcus Whitman's birthplace) were among the institutions that bore the missionary's name. A Presbyterian nonprofit acquired Narcissa's childhood home in Prattsburg, New York, restored it, and opened it to the public as a museum. Local historical societies and community boosters placed plaques, monuments, and roadside markers honoring the Whitmans in no fewer than ten states and the District of Columbia.

The Whitmans also made inroads into popular culture, through books, magazine articles, radio programs, and, briefly, a movie. A story by Oregon City writer Eva Emery Dye, a pioneer in the genre of historical fiction, inspired the script for a film to be titled *Martyrs of Yesterday*. Thirty members of the Confederated Tribes of the Cayuse, Umatilla, and Walla Walla signed on as extras. However, production was halted after an actress and a photographer died and five others were injured in a bus accident en route to a shoot near

Oregon City. Instead of the intended feature film, the producers cut the movie to a ten-minute short, released in late 1919 under the title *In the Land of the Setting Sun.*[38]

In 1930, NBC-affiliated stations broadcast a half-hour radio drama called *The Marcus Whitman Story.* At least seven novels about the Whitmans saw print in the 1950s. A standard plot line drew on the old rumor that Henry Spalding had once proposed to Narcissa, been rejected, and was forever jealous of her and Marcus. Drury, who dismissed the "spurned suitor" story as nonsense in his 1936 biography of Spalding, changed his mind and gave it a patina of authority in later books. Despite remarkably flimsy evidence (as noted in Chapter 3), the idea of Narcissa at the center of an enduring love triangle took hold in historical fiction, passed to a new generation as fact, and became embedded in history textbooks. It remains commonplace in narratives about the Whitmans to this day.[39]

A few scholars began to debunk the Whitman legend in the early twentieth century, but it proved remarkably hard to dislodge. As Whitman College professor G. Thomas Edwards wrote in his history of the school, "Americans wanted to believe in heroism and patriotism, and they generally dismissed the scholarship that demolished popular myths."[40] Historical myths about George Washington and the cherry tree, Paul Revere and his midnight ride, and Custer's last stand persisted long after they first faced challenges from inconvenient facts. Stephen Penrose, a key promoter of the mythical Marcus Whitman, never changed his story, despite encountering increasing skepticism as time went on. He even added some dramatic and entirely false details (for example, that the Whitmans had been scalped).[41] Penrose repeated the story so many times he became "captured" by it, Edwards wrote, and he clung to it until his death in 1954.[42]

The mythical Marcus Whitman had such broad appeal in the post–World War II era that the Washington State chapter of the

Federation of Business and Professional Women's Clubs initiated a campaign in 1947 to have him join the pantheon of heroes in the National Statuary Hall in Washington, DC. A federal law dating from the end of the Civil War allowed each state to honor two "deceased persons who have been citizens thereof" with statues, either marble or bronze, to be placed in a large, semicircular room near the Capitol Rotunda.[43] When the original hall became overcrowded, the display area was expanded into adjacent corridors. By the late 1940s nearly all the states had at least one statue somewhere in the Capitol and most had two. Washington had none. The businesswomen initially proposed to pay tribute to both Whitmans with a joint statue. After learning that Congress permitted only statues of individuals, they settled on Marcus and began lobbying the state legislature for the necessary authorization and funding. Senate Bill 32, introduced in the 1948–49 legislative session, endorsed the selection of Whitman and would have appropriated $15,000 to finance the project. "No other hero in the history of the state is more deserving of the honor of representation in Statuary Hall," a Tacoma legislator declared.[44]

A few voices were raised in dissent. A group calling itself the "Good Government League" mailed postcards to each of the state's 145 legislators claiming that "the Marcus Whitman legend is 90 percent fictitious"; that "hundreds" of other Washington citizens were more entitled to the honor; and the state would become "the laughing stock of the nation" if it put Whitman's statue in the US Capitol.[45] The bill's sponsors reacted by withdrawing the provision for funding. The amended bill passed by an almost unanimous vote and became law in March 1949. It proclaimed Whitman "a deceased resident of national renown," worthy of a statue commemorating his "fame and historic services as a great Washingtonian and a great American." (Never mind that Whitman was not, strictly speaking, a "Washingtonian"—the state was not created until 1889, forty-two years after his death.) The task of selecting a sculptor, approving a design, and raising the estimated $30,000 to pay for it was left in the hands of a twelve-person committee. Sculptor Avard Fairbanks, dean of the College of Fine Arts at the University of Utah, won the commission.[46]

Whitman already had been honored by one statue, a terra-cotta figure created in 1896 by Pennsylvania sculptor Alexander S. Calder for the façade of the United Presbyterian Church's headquarters in Philadelphia. Calder, father of famed mobilist Alexander Calder, presented Whitman as a stocky, middle-aged man, bundled in a fur-trimmed coat and hat, a muffler around his neck. The figure stands stoically by a wagon wheel, feet flat on the ground, empty handed, arms hanging at his sides. In contrast, Avard Fairbanks sculpted a man of action. His Whitman appears to be in motion, climbing an unbroken trail, buckskins taut against a muscled torso and thighs. The stoic missionary of the 1890s had been reimagined as a dashing frontiersman in the 1950s.

Washington added its second statue in Statuary Hall in 1980: Mother Joseph, a Canadian-born nun who designed and built schools and hospitals in Washington Territory in the mid-nineteenth century. Whitman, whose suspicion and distrust of "Papists" ran deep, would have been confounded to find himself sharing company in a hall of honor with a Catholic. Later, some people would wonder why notably secular Washington State should be represented in the nation's capitol by two nineteenth-century religious figures.

Whitman's statue was unveiled May 22, 1953, during ceremonies conducted in the Capitol Rotunda. Most of the state's congressional delegation attended, along with dozens of dignitaries, from then Vice President Richard M. Nixon to keynote speaker Supreme Court Justice William O. Douglas, a Whitman College graduate. In remarks more eloquent and nuanced than the usual Whitman tributes, Douglas said the claim that Whitman had kept Oregon out of the hands of the British was "probably too extravagant."

He mentioned the impact of the measles epidemic on the Cayuse, saying, "By their reckoning the tribe would soon be decimated. And so they decided Whitman should die." Douglas also outlined, at length, what he thought were Whitman's main contributions: proving that the Pacific Northwest was within the reach of anyone who could ride a horse or sit on a wagon; promoting "the manifest destiny of the Nation"; setting into motion "forces that increased the spiritual as well as the material inheritance of America"; and serving as a model of selfless public service. He ended his remarks by predicting that for years to come "Americans young and old who pass through this Hall will remember the example of the Whitmans, and, remembering, will find the confidence to face their own frontier."[47]

Two bronze copies of the statue were cast later. One was placed in the foyer of the Washington State Capitol in Olympia. The other found a home on the outskirts of the Whitman College campus in Walla Walla. Either late at night or early on a morning in October 2017, someone vandalized Walla Walla's statue by splashing it with red paint. It was a reminder that the past is a moving target, filtered through perspectives and values that change over time. Heroes and martyrs stand on shaky pedestals, even when, as in the case of Marcus Whitman, the pedestal is a seven-ton block of granite.

CHAPTER TEN:

REINTERPRETING
THE WHITMAN
"TRAGEDY"

The attack was the result of religious zeal and the greed for land. Columbia River people had always welcomed new technologies from any culture they contacted—French, British, Spanish and Hawaiian. None of those groups ever took the land.

—Stephanie Martin, park ranger, Whitman Mission National Historic Site

Our ancestors called this land home. We are still here. We will continue to be here.

—Confederated Tribes of the Cayuse, Umatilla, and Walla Walla

For ninety years a life-size painting of an idealized Narcissa Prentiss Whitman hung in the Great Room of Prentiss Hall, a women's residence and dining hall at Whitman College. The painting depicted Narcissa as a lovely young woman with large blue eyes, rosy cheeks,

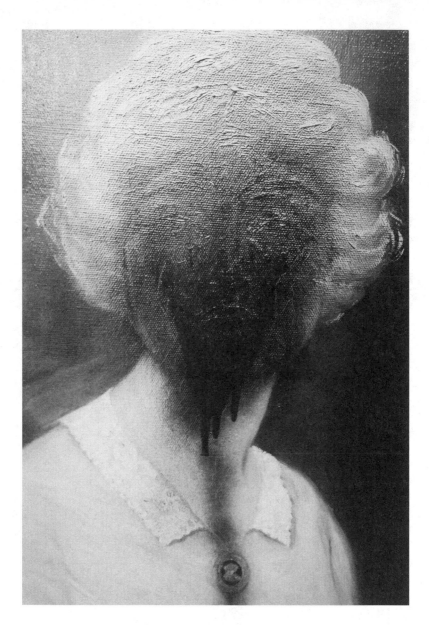

This romanticized portrait of Narcissa Prentiss Whitman was defaced with spray paint in October 2017. The painting (reproduced here in black and white) had been displayed in Prentiss Hall at Whitman College for ninety years. It was restored but then tucked away in storage, a symbol of changing attitudes toward the Whitmans and their legacy in the Northwest. *Photo courtesy The Cultured Pearl, Portland, and Whitman College, Walla Walla.*

a cupid's-bow mouth, and blond hair piled in thick, loose coils around the top of her head. The Narcissa Prentiss chapter of the Daughters of the American Revolution commissioned the work and donated it to the college in 1927.[1] Very late one night in October 2017, someone took a can of black spray paint into Prentiss Hall, aimed the nozzle directly at the painting, and squeezed, obliterating the heart-shaped face and sending rivulets of black down the V-necked pastel bodice and full hoop skirt. That same night, or possibly predawn morning, someone (perhaps the same "person or persons unknown") sprayed red paint on the hands, torso, and pedestal of the Marcus Whitman statue at the edge of campus.

The vandalism was meant to be discovered on Monday, October 9, a day recognized by some as Columbus Day and by others as Indigenous Peoples Day. The color choices seemed deliberate: black in reference to white people using blackface as a tool of racial derision; red to suggest that Whitman had blood on his hands. An anonymous note, posted with the painting, denounced the Whitmans as "colonizers, racists, murderers" who "brought disease, stole native peoples' land, claimed it for themselves, and actively recruited others to do the same."[2] A sympathetic faculty member described the clandestine deeds as "acts of resistance against landscapes of white supremacy."[3] The paint was scrubbed off the statue. The painting was cleaned and restored and then hung upside down in a special exhibit at the college's Maxey Museum. The exhibit explored the ways in which the college—founded as a "living monument" to Whitman in 1859—had promoted and benefited from the image of the Whitmans as heroic Christian martyrs. When the exhibit closed, in December 2018, the painting was packed away and put in storage, a reflection of changing attitudes toward the sanctity of the pioneer past and the Whitmans' place in it.

The challenges to Whitman iconography in Walla Walla came during a contentious national debate about who and what should be remembered in America. In 2015 a white supremacist's massacre of nine black congregants at a church in Charleston, South Carolina, sparked a campaign to banish from the public square monuments, plaques, and place-names that paid homage to the Confederacy. The campaign quickly expanded to include memorials related, in one way or another, to the conquest of indigenous peoples. Just two weeks after the spray cans were aimed at the Whitmans, a group calling itself the Monument Removal Brigade poured red paint on the marble pedestal of a bronze statue of President Theodore Roosevelt at the entrance to the American Museum of Natural History in New York. The statue, installed in 1940, features a powerful Roosevelt on horseback, flanked at stirrup level by two half-nude figures—one African, the other American Indian—both on foot and carrying his rifles, like porters. A *New York Times* art critic described it as "quite literally an emblem of white-man-on-top."[4]

The Roosevelt statue had been the target of periodic protests for decades, as had an equally blunt tribute to racial hierarchy in downtown San Francisco called *Early Days*. Dedicated in 1894 as part of a massive monument to colonialism, *Early Days* featured a nearly naked Indian cowering at the feet of a Catholic missionary and a Spanish cowboy. The American Indian Movement Confederation condemned it in 1995 as a symbol of the "humiliation, degradation, genocide, and sorrow inflicted upon this country's indigenous people by a foreign invader through religious persecution and ethnic prejudice." The city added a small plaque about "mistreatment" of Indians but otherwise shrugged off the opposition as a niche issue, important only to an insignificant minority. The violence in Charleston two decades later, followed by the 2017 death of a counterprotester during a white supremacist rally in Charlottesville, Virginia, led to new demands that the sculpture be removed. This time San Francisco responded by quietly carting it off to storage.[5]

To Kevin Gover, director of the Smithsonian's National Museum of the American Indian, the end of *Early Days* marked "a tipping point for the politics of Native American memory." As a nation, he said, "we still live with symbols of white supremacy in our public spaces and popular culture. But we are also at a stage where we can have an honest discussion about their origins and meaning and address the harm they do."[6]

Scholars use the phrase "politics of memory" to describe how narratives about the past and the objects chosen to represent those narratives reflect and reinforce the politics of the present. Most of the Confederate statues in the South were erected during the Jim Crow era, especially from the 1890s through the 1920s. More appeared in the late 1940s and 1950s, in response to efforts to desegregate American military forces, public schools, and public accommodations. These statues and monuments romanticized the Confederacy as a noble and heroic "Lost Cause" and downplayed the role of slavery in the Civil War. They also served as subtle tools of intimidation, aimed at black people trying to assert their civil rights. The same period saw the proliferation of monuments idealizing the virtues and sacrifices of white colonizers in the American West while ignoring the impact of conquest, both physical and cultural, on indigenous peoples. Glorifying the pioneers was a way to justify what had been done in the past and perhaps ease anxieties about the future—the solidity of stone and metal suggesting that the sons and daughters of the pioneers would continue to prevail.

A competing narrative began to resonate with many Americans in the late 1960s. Books such as Dee Brown's best-selling *Bury My Heart at Wounded Knee* and popular films such as *Soldier Blue* and *Little Big Man* (all released in 1970) helped reframe the story by presenting Indians in a sympathetic if sometimes one-dimensional light. Many of these works tended to portray Indians as passive victims of white mendacity. "It's as if it didn't matter what Indians did, only what whites did to them," influential historian Richard White once said. But they helped generate interest, from a new generation of historians as well as from the general public, in western history that included nonwhite, nondominant points of view. White acknowledged that as a young scholar, he had found inspiration in *Bury My Heart*, despite its flaws.[7]

Perhaps more than any other period in American history, the late 1960s and 1970s were marked by broad challenges to the conventions of the past. Opposition to the Vietnam War gave rise to new critiques of nineteenth-century US military campaigns against Indians. The gains and tactics of the civil rights movement stimulated demands for justice from other previously marginalized groups, including Hispanics, farmworkers, women, and—most relevant to this book—American Indians. The American Indian Movement, founded in Minneapolis in 1968, launched a "Red Power" campaign with several attention-getting protests, including sit-ins at the federal Bureau of Indian Affairs in 1972 and the 1973 occupation of the site of the Wounded Knee massacre on the Pine Ridge Reservation in South Dakota. Whether these political developments spurred or mirrored social change is hard to say, but guides at the Whitman Mission National Historic Site began noticing "a certain cynicism among some of our visitors—a feeling that the Whitmans were meddling where they didn't belong and deserved their fate."[8]

The US Congress responded to pressure from Indian activists by passing the American Indian Religious Freedom Act in 1978. The legislation made it the official policy of the United States to "protect and preserve" traditional spiritual and cultural practices. It was a repudiation of the very objectives that had drawn the Whitmans and their fellow missionaries to the West in the first place. The new law prompted a shift in the interpretive tone at the Whitman Mission National Historic Site. Marjorie Waheneka, a descendant of Cayuse, Palouse, Nez Perce, and Warm Springs Indians, joined the staff as a ranger and interpreter in 1980, the first member of the Confederated Tribes of the Umatilla to work full-time at the mission. Some of her relatives warned her about taking the job. "At first people said, 'How can you work there? Don't you remember what happened to your people?'" Waheneka recalled in a 1993 interview. "But people don't get mad anymore. Now they say, 'It's about time.'"[9]

The National Park Service, which operates the Whitman Mission site, redesigned the exhibits and expanded the programming in the mid-1980s to put more emphasis on Cayuse history. "Clash of cultures" replaced "heroic pioneers" as the governing motif. "We're trying to get across the idea that the Cayuse culture was here and the Anglos just slammed into them," one ranger said. The staff stopped conducting annual memorial services at the "Great Grave" on the Saturday closest to the date of the attack, a practice that had been carried on for more than half a century. Interest had dwindled, the ranger said, and besides, the ceremony seemed "inappropriate."[10] New displays reflected Indian and non-Indian perspectives in almost equal measure. One exhibit focused on the "seasonal round" and life for the Cayuse and their relatives before contact with whites. A sample caption read: "There were no fences then and no one owned the land." Another exhibit attempted to put the Whitmans into historical context, noting the twin influences of Manifest Destiny and religious revivalism. "You can't have thirteen people killed and not have an emotional issue," Park Superintendent Terry Darby remarked, "and you can't live this close to an Indian community and not be sensitive to their view. We want to show both points of view and not alienate one. So if it sounds like I'm waltzing through a minefield, I am."[11]

In 1991, when Washington State Senate Majority Leader Jeanette Hayner, a Republican from Walla Walla, announced plans to install a Whitman statue (a replica of the one in the US Capitol) in her hometown, the reaction was at best lukewarm. The Salt Lake City artist who created the original sculpture had died. The mold was still in his studio and his heirs wanted to be rid of it. They offered Washington State officials the chance to use it one more time before they destroyed it. Hayner, one of the legislature's most powerful members, declared the lawmakers "would be derelict in our duty" if they did not authorize a copy of the statue for "the place where it has the most significance."[12] Critics said it would be more fitting to put up a monument to Walla Walla chief PeoPeoMoxMox, who was murdered and mutilated by Oregon militiamen while trying to negotiate an end to the Walla Walla War in 1855. But Hayner pushed an appropriation of $53,000 through the legislature and the mold yielded a third and final casting. The resulting statue found a home at a five-way stop facing Walla Walla's Main Street after suggestions for a more central location were rejected.[13] PeoPeoMoxMox eventually got his own statue, commissioned by a local community group and installed in a plaza across from City Hall in June 2005. In the end, the prime real estate went to the Indian, not the missionary.

Six decades after Marcus Whitman was ensconced in the National Statuary Hall, there were calls for his eviction. A *Seattle Times* columnist wondered in 2014 whether a man who died more than forty years before Washington was even a state is "the best we've got."[14] In January 2019 a Seattle legislator introduced a bill to replace the statue (and its copy in Olympia) with a more contemporary hero, to be chosen by a ten-member task force. In the stilted language of the bill: "The legislature finds that under rigorous, objective review Marcus Whitman does not meet the standards of being one of our state's top honorees with a statue display in Olympia and the statuary hall in the United States capitol."[15] Compare that to the accolades heaped upon Whitman when the original statue was dedicated in 1953, including this one from Governor Arthur Langlie: "America honors itself by honoring him."[16]

University of Washington history professor John Findlay was among those who suggested that a suitable replacement would be a statue of Billy Frank Jr., a Nisqually Indian fishing activist who died in 2014 at age eighty-three, after a lifetime of defending the treaty fishing rights of Northwest tribes and working with non-Indians to restore salmon runs. Elmer Ward, an attorney and member of the Yakama Nation, seconded the motion, saying of Billy Frank, "He didn't try to change anyone's religion or status or rights."[17] There was pushback. Whitman's defenders pointed out that he was not a slave owner or a Confederate hero, unlike many others who are enshrined in the US Capitol. He did not order the forcible removal of Indians from their homeland, unlike Andrew Jackson, one of Tennessee's honorees. He did not imprison and mistreat indigenous people who refused to convert to Christianity, unlike Junipero Serra, an eighteenth-century friar who represents California in the Statuary Hall. In other words, Whitman wasn't that bad.

Rowland Thompson, a longtime lobbyist in Olympia (and Whitman College graduate) noted that President Thomas Jefferson, explorer Meriwether Lewis, and Manifest Destiny champion Thomas Hart Benton—all of whom have counties in Washington State named for them—owned slaves; and Franklin Roosevelt, whose name is attached to the reservoir behind Grand Coulee Dam, sent Japanese citizens to internment camps during World War II. Roger Harnack, editor and publisher of two weekly newspapers in northeastern Washington, accused the bill's sponsors of attempting "a second Whitman Massacre" by assassinating the character of a man who had earned his place in history. "If we sit idly by and let his statues be removed, emboldened revisionists will take aim at schools and other places named in honor of Marcus Whitman," Harnack warned.[18] The bill died in committee. The statues stayed put.

The sesquicentennial of the Cayuse attack on the Whitman Mission passed with little notice in 1997. In contrast to the fanfare surrounding the fiftieth anniversary a century earlier, there were no parades, grand speeches, or somber ceremonies at the mission site. Instead, Whitman College and the Whitman Mission National Historic Site cosponsored a two-day symposium at the college with the decidedly noncelebratory title "Examining the Collision of Cultures in the Age of Multiculturalism: The Whitman Tragedy, 1847–1997." Representatives of the Confederated Tribes participated. The goal was to show that the "tragedy" was not one-sided, affecting only whites; it also led to death, loss, dispossession, and pain for Indians.[19]

The keynote speaker was Patricia Limerick, University of Colorado professor and a leading scholar of the so-called "new western history"—a more inclusive, less sentimental approach to the history of the American West. Limerick included a section on the Whitmans in her groundbreaking book *Legacy of Conquest*, published in 1986. She depicted them as neither villains nor "martyred innocents" but simply as human. "Given the inability of Cayuses to understand Presbyterians, and the inability of Presbyterians to understand Cayuses, the trouble could only escalate," she wrote. She asked her readers to see that "real Westerners, contrary to the old divisions between good guys and bad guys, combined the roles of victim and villain." Acknowledging this moral complexity, Limerick wrote, does not debunk history but enriches it.[20]

Limerick was in the vanguard of a generation of historians and other scholars who asked new questions, uncovered new evidence, and brought new analysis to the interactions between Euro-Americans and indigenous peoples in the West. Christopher L. Miller, in his 1985 book *Prophetic Worlds*, examined the surprisingly similar millennial visions of Plateau Indian prophets and evangelical Christians, including the Whitmans. Julie Roy Jeffrey published a revisionist biography of Narcissa Whitman in 1991. Albert Furtwangler, in his 2005 work *Bringing Indians to the Book*, found it inevitable that misunderstandings would develop between missionaries, steeped in the traditions of literate Europe and Britain, and indigenous people, who passed on their values, learning, and history through words that were spoken or sung, not written. These and other writers emphasized the complicated dynamics that developed between various groups in the historic West. But much of what filtered into public consciousness still reflected what Limerick called "old divisions between good guys and bad guys." The difference was that missionaries were now cast as bad guys.

This emphasis on good versus bad seemed particularly true at Whitman College. G. Thomas Edwards, a longtime history faculty member who helped organize the bicentennial symposium in 1997, remarked that Marcus Whitman had become almost persona non grata at his namesake institution, like a disgraced relative no one wanted to talk about. "It would be easier if the school were named Lewis and Clark," he commented, a little ruefully. "Everyone likes them." When Edwards began teaching at Whitman in 1964, tours of the Whitman Mission site were mandatory for first-year students. He was still leading tours in the late 1990s, but few attended. "The college does virtually nothing to recognize Marcus Whitman," one student said. "What Whitman was attempting to do 150 years ago is un-PC in our world, and I think it scares some people."[21]

Marcus and Narcissa Whitman may be convenient symbols of white arrogance and oppression when viewed through a twenty-first-century lens, but they should be understood first as products of their own time and culture. They arrived in Oregon Country as idealistic young people who deeply believed that those who did not understand God in the way they did were doomed to burn in hell for all eternity. They knew they would face hardships and dangers, certainly from nature, possibly from the humans they expected to meet in the West, whether "wild" Indians or wilder mountain men. They accepted the risks because they were convinced that God wanted them to tell Indians about Jesus and the path to salvation. Their zeal may be difficult to understand in our more secular age, but they tried to do what they thought was the right thing. And at least initially, many of the Indians the Whitmans encountered were receptive to their message and folded elements of it into their own spiritual practices.

The same proselytizing impulse took John Allen Chau, a twenty-six-year-old missionary from Vancouver, Washington, to a remote island in the Indian Ocean in November 2018. He was killed by arrows shot at him by the island's inhabitants while he was trying to tell them that Jesus loved them.[22] The Whitmans were venerated as martyrs after they died; Chau was excoriated as an ignorant, arrogant, self-serving cultural imperialist. "He has reinforced the stereotype of all missionaries as brash young colonizers trying to tame 'primitive' tribes," a former Methodist missionary wrote in a letter to the *New York Times*.[23] No one organized a militia to punish the villagers; no one erected monuments in Chau's honor. He was a man, it would seem, out of his time.

The Whitmans were undeniably brave, tough, determined, and hardworking. Narcissa was in the late stages of pregnancy during the most strenuous part of the journey to Oregon. She often cooked three meals a day for a dozen or more people at the mission, and for the first five years, until she got a stove, she did it all over an open fire. Marcus ended many days bent with fatigue from the sheer physical labor involved in establishing and expanding his mission and farm. But they were woefully unprepared for missionary work.

Their understanding of what Indians wanted or needed was based on hearsay and imagination. The primary qualifications for appointment by the American Board of Commissioners for Foreign Missions were piety and good health. The board did not provide cross-cultural training. It did not expect candidates to show respect for or solidarity with the people they were to live with. In their surviving letters, neither of the Whitmans ever expressed any admiration or appreciation for native traditions, technology, or values. They had been drawn to Oregon by the idea of saving Indian souls, but they felt no affinity for the Indians they actually encountered.

The missionaries set out to transform every aspect of Cayuse culture—from diet and dress to shelter, work, and worship. They favored Indians who dressed like white people over those who wore traditional clothing. To replace a diet of wild game and native plants, they promoted one based on domesticated animals and cultivated plants. They wanted Indians to give up their seasonal rounds of hunting, fishing, and gathering and become farmers and, above all, abandon their traditional spiritual practices and fully embrace Christianity, specifically Presbyterianism. Nuclear families of Christianized Indians would then live in frame houses, not multi-family tule lodges; they would stay put; tend their fields, gardens, hogs, and cows; and accept white Christians' notions about everything from property to gender roles.

Despite their ambitious agenda, the Whitmans gave relatively little time and attention to Indians after they reached Oregon. They were preoccupied first by the struggle to make a home in what was, for them, a wilderness. Before long, they also had to house, feed, and support the missionaries who came to "reinforce" them. The ever-increasing flow of emigrants was an added burden and distraction. Narcissa was hobbled by grief after the drowning of her daughter. Both she and Marcus suffered from repeated bouts of illness. Unrealistic expectations, lack of preparation for understanding another culture, loneliness, privation, and poor health took a toll, and not only on the Whitmans. As one writer put it, the Protestant mission field in Oregon was "littered with disillusioned missionaries."[24] Mourning "the fate of the heathen" from the comforts of the East proved to be easier than engaging with Indians as people. The Methodist Mission Board (the first to establish a presence in Oregon) ultimately sold out to the American Board; half of the missionaries dispatched by that group left the field, and the Whitmans were on the verge of leaving when their mission was attacked.

Self-imposed isolation and loneliness marked the final years of Narcissa's life. She yearned for the company of other white women, but she disliked the four who arrived with their husbands on assignment from the American Board in 1838. They were not like the "warm-hearted revival Christians" she had grown up with.[25] She felt more comfortable with the Methodists at The Dalles and in the Willamette Valley, but she was rarely able to see them. She had occasional contact with the métis wives of Hudson's Bay Company officials, but she drew no emotional support from those relationships. She never attempted to establish friendships with Indian women. Marcus was absorbed by the demands of running what had become less a mission than a trading post and rest stop for colonists. Both of them were "out of their proper sphere," Henry K. W. Perkins, a former Methodist missionary at The Dalles, wrote in a frank appraisal to Narcissa's sister Jane a year after the Whitmans' deaths. "They were not adapted to their work. They could not possibly interest & gain the affections of the natives."

Perkins knew both Whitmans well. Narcissa spent months at The Dalles with him and his wife, Elvira, while Marcus was gone on his trip East. The Indians "*feared* the Doctor [but] did not *love* him," Perkins wrote. "They did not love your sister." He thought Marcus was simply too impatient and arrogant to succeed as a missionary. "Dr. Whitman in pursuing his missionary labors never so identified himself with the natives as to make their interests *paramount*," Perkins added. "He looked upon them as an inferior race & doomed at no distant day to give place to a settlement of enterprising Americans. Indeed it might almost be doubted whether he felt half the interest in the natives that he did in the *prospective* white population." As for Narcissa, "she loved company, society, excitement & ought always to have enjoyed it. The self-denial that took her away from it was suicidal."[26]

Marcus Whitman picked a level site for his mission, snugged up against the base of a tall hill, topped by what the National Park Service now prefers to call the Whitman Memorial Obelisk (in view of snarky comments about the original name, the "Whitman Shaft"). Visitors standing next to the obelisk have a panoramic view of the Walla Walla Valley. The Blue Mountains curve east and south in the distance. Rolling hills, as rumpled as an unmade bed, stretch for miles to the west, many topped with long-bladed wind turbines. The region has become a major producer of wind- and solar-powered energy, aided in part by investments from the Confederated Tribes of the Umatilla Indian Reservation.

Closer in, the landscape is slotted with vineyards and wineries—an ironic touch, given the Whitmans' unfailing opposition to all things alcohol.[27] In spring and fall the air here is often gritty with windblown dust, churned up by the plowing, planting, and harvesting of crops on nearby farm fields. There would have been less dust during the missionary era, when fewer than sixty acres of land were under cultivation and thigh-high grasses held the rest in place. Native grasses now flourish on parts of the mission grounds, the result of a revegetation process that began in the 1950s. Ring-necked pheasants are among the habitués. The birds, now so common throughout the United States that they seem to be a native species, have a little-known connection to the Whitmans. They were introduced to the Willamette Valley from China in 1881 by Gertrude Hall Denny and her husband, Owen Denny, then the US consul general in Shanghai. Gertrude was a daughter of Peter D. Hall, the emigrant who escaped from Waiilatpu at the beginning of the attack on the mission, reached Fort Walla Walla, and then disappeared, presumably drowned. His wife and five daughters, including ten-year-old Gertrude, were among the hostages. When Gertrude died, in 1933, she was the last survivor of the "Whitman Massacre."[28]

A roadside marker just outside the entrance to the Whitman Mission National Historic Site summarizes the history of the mission in five neutral, measured sentences, including these: "Cultural differences, climaxed by a measles epidemic that killed many Cayuse, ended the missionary effort. A few suspicious Cayuse took the lives of Marcus and Narcissa and 11 others on November 29, 1847." The sign is notable for words that do not appear: martyrs, massacre, murder, or anything to do with the "saving" of Oregon or Indian souls.

The same measured tone prevails at the mission itself, summed up in a headline on the official website: "Retribution or Revenge?" Visitors are asked to ponder whether the attack was "justified legal retribution, an act of revenge, or some combination of both."[29] Tiloukaikt and other Cayuse leaders provided their own answer to that question during the council hosted by Bishop Blanchet at the Catholic mission on the Umatilla just a few weeks after the killings. The Cayuse described the devastating effects of the measles epidemic and explained how and why they had come to believe that Marcus Whitman, assisted by his wife, was the cause. None of them took direct responsibility for the attack, but they strongly asserted that it was carried out within the boundaries of tribal law.[30] In 1850, when Tiloukaikt and four others were tried for murder, their lawyers made similar arguments. The lawyers also contended, to no avail, that

Americans had no legal jurisdiction in the case because the Cayuse had not yet ceded any of their homelands to the United States, and Cayuse law should prevail.[31]

Cayuse traditions regarding healers who did not heal were fairly well documented. Samuel Black, chief trader at Fort Walla Walla from 1825 to 1830, reported that "they Kill 2 or 3 of their Doctors every year," acts usually carried out by enraged relatives seeking revenge for deaths attributed to the malevolence of shamans (or *te-wats*) who had been corrupted in one way or another.[32] Black's immediate successor, Simon McGillivray Jr., also made note of the practice, as did Archibald McKinlay, chief trader from 1841 to 1846, who claimed that between them the Cayuse and Walla Walla "shot seven of their own medicine men right by the fort during my five years' stay there, and probably over three times that number altogether."[33] The Whitmans were fully aware of the tenuous position of *te-wats* in Cayuse culture. As Narcissa wrote to her parents just a few months after settling in at Waiilatpu, physicians who lost patients were "in great danger of being killed" themselves.[34]

The Cayuse killed eleven other people at the Whitman Mission in 1847: nine men and two teenage boys (old enough to have been considered adults in Cayuse culture), all Americans. Two American men and their adult sons who were working for Whitman at the lumber mill were spared because they claimed to be British. In contrast to the often indiscriminate attacks against Indians carried out by white militiamen and federal troops, the targeted violence at the mission was in keeping with traditional notions about warfare: kill the enemy's men and capture the women and children. The bloodshed can also be seen as an act of self-defense, part of a struggle by Indians to regain control of their land, resources, and way of life. "I don't know of any people on this earth who would not have done something similar given the same stress we were facing," commented

Roberta Conner, director of the Tamástslikt Cultural Institute, adding, "I always look at it and think, was it justifiable homicide?"[35]

Justified or not, the Cayuse as a tribe paid a heavy price for the attack. Many were driven into hiding in the Blue Mountains; all faced harassment by volunteer militias. At the Walla Walla Treaty Council in 1855, weakened by persecution and warned that more settlers would soon overwhelm them entirely, the tribe ceded millions of acres of homelands and agreed to live on a reservation alongside people with whom they had sometimes clashed. When government surveyors finally marked the boundaries of the reservation in 1859, they included only 245,699 acres—half what had been promised—and the future town of Pendleton sat on some of the land. Federal legislation in and after 1887 led to further erosion of the tribal land base, by enabling non-Indians to acquire parcels of land allotted to individual Indians. By the early 1930s the reservation set aside for the Cayuse, Umatilla, and Walla Walla had shrunk to 158,000 acres, and nearly half of it was in the hands of non-Indians. Dams, mining, railroad construction, and agricultural activities severely reduced the tribes' ability to fish, gather, and hunt in their "usual and customary places," as promised by treaty.

The three tribes took a series of steps, beginning in the 1940s, to reclaim sovereignty over their affairs. In 1949 they voted, by a narrow margin, to establish a single tribal government, a controversial move at the time because it diminished the role of traditional headmen. As the newly named Confederated Tribes of the Umatilla, they filed two major lawsuits against the federal government. The first sought damages for the loss of fisheries due to the construction of The Dalles dam on the Columbia River at Celilo Falls. The government paid the Confederated Tribes $4.6 million to settle that claim in 1953. The second suit, seeking compensation for the hundreds of thousands of acres of land illegally excluded from the reservation, dragged on for years before it was settled in 1965 for $2.4 million.[36] Meanwhile, the tribes successfully lobbied for the return of some 14,000 acres in the Johnson Creek area southeast of Pilot Rock, Oregon, bringing the reservation to its current size of about 172,000 acres—a third of the 512,000 acres promised by treaty.

The tribes marked the 150th anniversary of the Treaty Council in 2005 with "a victory celebration of survival" in Walla Walla. It began with a ceremonial procession of fifty mounted riders in full regalia, an echo of the thousands of Nez Perce and Cayuse horsemen who made a spectacular grand entry into the treaty grounds in 1855. "It was a proud moment and wonderful to see Indians with the warbonnet headdresses, on horseback, singing and *hayaytám* 'war whooping,'" wrote Antone Minthorn, former chair of the Confederated Tribes of the Umatilla Indian Reservation. "Our history is our strength. Our traditional cultures define us."[37]

The Tamástslikt Cultural Institute helps preserve and convey that history. The institute, located on the reservation near Pendleton, 38 miles south of Walla Walla, is the only Indian-owned museum and research center on the 2,170-mile-long Oregon Trail. "If you want to hear about western expansionism from a tribal point of view, this is the best place to come," says Roberta Conner, its founding director. "I'm proud to say we tell it better than anybody else."[38] Tamástslikt takes its name from a Sahaptin word meaning to "turn over" or "interpret." Its forty-five-thousand-square-foot building is a striking piece of architecture. The main exhibit space is divided into three sections: "We Were," "We Are," and "We Will Be." A recurring theme is the tribes' relationship to horses. One of the more poignant displays is a stack of cans of dog food, representing a period in the 1930s when thousands of Cayuse horses were rounded up by the federal government, loaded into railroad boxcars, and sent to Portland for slaughter and packaging as dog food. To area farmers, herds of free-roaming horses were a nuisance.

When anthropologist Theodore Stern began his acclaimed study of the Confederated Tribes in the early 1950s, he expected to find that they had "lost their Indian qualities" and succumbed to pressures to assimilate, living as they were on a small reservation close to a major town. Instead, he found "a tenacious adherence to their cultural heritage," as demonstrated, for example, by the persistence of the traditional *Washat* or Seven Drums religion (sometimes practiced in secret in those days). "On the reservation when I began my research," Stern wrote, "there were echoes of days lived in freedom and in the subsequent bitterness of its loss."[39]

One avenue for the expression of that cultural identity has been the Pendleton Round-Up, consistently rated one of the nation's top-ten rodeos. The Cayuse, Umatilla, and Walla Walla tribes have been an integral part of Round-Up since its beginning, in 1910. They host a week-long encampment that typically includes more than three hundred teepees—a grand village reminiscent of gatherings their ancestors held at favorite fishing or gathering sites. Many tribal members participate in an outdoor historical pageant called *Happy Canyon*. Roles in the pageant are often passed down within families, from one generation to the next. It may be puzzling that Indians support an event that in some ways celebrates the people responsible for the tribes' displacement, but for many Round-Up was, and is, a "a kind of blessing," according to Conner—a way to remember life as it once was, before the wounds created by the loss of land and freedom.[40]

The attack on the Whitman Mission in November 1847 by a group of Cayuse warriors led to the first Indian war in the Northwest, the creation of Oregon Territory as a federal entity, and eventually a treaty that stripped the tribe of most of its land. But that was not the end of the story for the Indians. As historian Clifford Trafzer has written, "their lives did not end in the last century, and their cultures did not fade away."[41] The Cayuse survive as part of the Confederated Tribes of the Umatilla Indian Reservation (CTUIR), with more than thirty-one hundred enrolled members and an annual operating budget of some $250 million. Roughly half the tribal members live on the reservation, along with about three hundred Indians enrolled in other tribes and fifteen hundred non-Indians. The tribes own the Wildhorse Resort (which includes a casino, hotel, recreational vehicle park, and eighteen-hole golf course) and Cayuse Technologies (a software development and training enterprise). They also have investments in wind, solar, and geothermal energy, among other business interests, and have made substantial commitments to environmental sustainability—from working to restore fish and eel runs in the Umatilla River to improving energy efficiency in tribal facilities.[42] With some eighteen hundred employees and an annual payroll of about $60 million, the CTUIR is one of the largest employers in northeastern Oregon.[43]

"Many people romanticize about American Indian culture," Roberta Conner told an interviewer who was studying native perspectives on sustainability in 2007, "but fundamentally they don't understand that this has always been about land. Not about ownership, but about responsibility, accountability, and stewardship." For Conner, that deeply rooted connection to the land means: "We're not leaving. We're not giving up. We're not giving in. We're here for the long term.

"We're here forever."[44]

ACKNOWLEDGMENTS

This book began as a series of articles for HistoryLink.org, the online encyclopedia of Washington State history. I am grateful to Marie McCaffrey, cofounder (with her late husband, Walt Crowley) of HistoryLink; to Priscilla Long, word maven, who edited most of the resulting work; to Jennifer Ott, assistant director, who provided valuable feedback on drafts of several chapters in manuscript form; and to all my other colleagues at HistoryLink for their support and encouragement over the many years that it took me to finish up. As Marie once commented, "Cassandra has been working on this for so long that if her book was a person, it could already have had children."

That it exists as a book at all is due in no small measure to Sandra Chait, my writing partner; and Alexandra "Sasha" Harmon, professor emerita of American Indian studies at the University of Washington. I'd probably still be staring at my computer screen if Sandra had not laid down deadlines. The book is much better than it would have been without Sasha's insights, expertise, and impatience with the passive tense. Both of them did me the great favor of reading the entire manuscript in draft form, parts of it several times. The flaws in the final product belong entirely to me.

Roberta Conner, director of the Tamástslikt Cultural Institute, was an invaluable resource. She generously and patiently answered my many questions during several interviews, both in person and on the phone. Tamástslikt, on the Confederated Tribes of the Umatilla Indian Reservation near Pendleton, Oregon, is the only museum and interpretive center on the Oregon Trail that tells the story of western expansionism from a tribal point of view. I relied heavily on two books published by the institute: *Wiyaxayxt / Wiyaakaa'awn / As Days Go By: Our History, Our Land, and Our People*, edited by Jennifer Karson; and *Čáw Pawá Láakni / They Are Not Forgotten: Sahaptian Place Names Atlas of the Cayuse, Umatilla, and Walla Walla*, edited by Eugene S. Hunn.

Archivists and librarians are indispensable to anyone who writes history. Among those who were particularly obliging and helpful to me were Dana Bronson at the Penrose Library and Northwest Archives, Whitman College, Walla Walla; Elizabeth Miller at Whitman College's Maxey Museum; Cheryl Gunselman and Trevor Bond at the Manuscripts, Archives, and Special Collections Department, Washington State University, Pullman; and Arlene Gehmacher at the Royal Ontario Museum, Toronto. I'm also grateful to the rangers and interpreters at the Whitman Mission National Historic Site, near Walla Walla; the Nez Perce National Historic Park, at Lapwai; and the Fort Vancouver National Historic Site, at Vancouver, Washington. Staff at libraries and historical societies in Rushville, Bath, Angelica, Prattsburg, and Holland Patent in upstate New York were immensely helpful in expanding my understanding of the background and personalities of the Whitmans, the Spaldings, and their fellow missionaries.

I benefited from a wide circle of readers who plowed through drafts of this book in various forms, including UW historians Richard Johnson, Carol Thomas, and John Findlay, all of whom pushed me beyond my comfort zone by asking that I not just tell the story but try to explain what it means. Stephanie Martin, park ranger at the Whitman Mission National Historic Site, read the manuscript chapter by chapter and then as a whole and saved me from many embarrassing errors. My sister-in-law, Kathleen Cain, helped steer me away from too much jargon and too many fuzzy sentences.

My thanks also to my friend Sheila Farr, who introduced me to Anne Depue, agent extraordinaire, who sold the book to Sasquatch and helped guide it from proposal to finished product. Editor Gary Luke commissioned the project; his successor, Jennifer Worick, took it through the production process. I deeply appreciate the skill and professionalism of Jennifer and her team.

I'm surprised that I have any friends left at the end of this long and isolating process, but I know you're out there and I want to thank you all for sticking with me, for letting me drone on about my research, and for not asking, too many times, "Are you done yet?" I'm grateful beyond measure for the love and support of my family, including my daughter, Linnea; grandchildren, Emma and Sam; siblings John, Michael, and Pam (and honorary siblings Richard and Sharon); nieces Shelly and Liz; and, above all, my husband, Glenn Drosendahl, who makes everything possible.

NOTES

In citing works in the notes, short titles have been used whenever a full citation appears in the selected bibliography, and primary documents are reproduced with original spelling, capitalization, and grammar.

INTRODUCTION

1. Associated Press, "Statue of Marcus Whitman Unveiled in Capitol Rotunda," *Spokesman-Review* (Spokane), May 23, 1953.

2. *Acceptance of the Statue of Marcus Whitman Presented by the State of Washington*, 57, 63.

3. Neuberger, *Our Promised Land,* 14.

4. Gwartney, *I Am a Stranger Here Myself,* 14.

CHAPTER ONE

Epigraph: William McBean, report to Board of Management, Fort Vancouver, November 30, 1847, *Oregon Spectator*, December 9, 1847.

1. Marcus Whitman to Alanson Hinman, October 23, 1847, in Narcissa Whitman, *Letters of Narcissa Whitman*.

2. "About thirty souls of the Cayuse tribe died, one after another, who evidently believed the Doctor poisoned them" (William McBean, report to Board of Management, November 30, 1847, *Oregon Spectator*, December 9, 1847).

3. Henry Spalding, *Oregon American and Evangelical Unionist*, July 19, 1848, in Drury, *Henry Harmon Spalding*, 332.

4. "Excerpts from Lectures by Henry H. Spalding," *Albany* (Oregon) *States Rights Democrat*, reprinted in Warren, *Memoirs of the West*, 116.

5. Catherine Sager Pringle to Frederic Sager, Salem, December 21, 1854, *Oregon Historical Quarterly* 37, no. 7 (December 1936): 357.

6. Brouillet, *Authentic Account of the Murder*, 50–51; Henry Spalding to David Greene, January 8, 1848, American Board of Commissioners for Foreign Missions (hereafter ABCFM Archives), Houghton Library, Harvard University.

7. Eliza Spalding's 1916 memoir as cited in Warren, *Memoirs of the West*, 23.

8. Kelman, *Misplaced Massacre*, 8.

9. Roberta Conner, phone interview with the author, May 30, 2018.

10. John D. Manson, July 29, 1884, in Drury, *Marcus and Narcissa Whitman*, 2: 352–53.

11. Matilda Sager as cited in Delaney, *Survivor's Recollections*, 15.

12. Elizabeth Sager as cited in Drury, *Marcus and Narcissa Whitman*, 2: 255.

13. Delaney, *Survivor's Recollections*, 16; and Elizabeth M. Sager to Frederick Sager, December 21, 1854, *Oregon Historical Quarterly* 37, no. 7 (December 1936): 358.

14. "Within ten minutes after they commenced all were killed who were killed, with the exception of one or two," wrote survivor Nathan Kimball, who was thirteen at the time of the attack; in Oregon Pioneer Association, *Transactions of the Oregon Pioneer Association* 31 (1903): 189.

15. Matilda Sager as cited in Delaney, *Survivor's Recollections*, 17.

16. Nancy Osborn Jacobs, paper read at Walla Walla, May 29, 1912, reprinted in *Waitsburg* (Washington) *Times*, February 2, 1934, clipping in Marcus and Narcissa Whitman Collection, Whitman College and Northwest Archives, Walla Walla (hereafter Whitman College Archives).

17. Matilda Sager as cited in Delaney, *Survivor's Recollections*, 18.

18. Catherine Sager Pringle to Frederic Sager, December 21, 1854, in *Oregon Historical Quarterly* 37, no. 4 (December 1836): 354–60.

19. Eliza Spalding as cited in Warren, *Memoirs of the West*, 24.

20. Eliza Spalding as cited in Warren, *Memoirs of the West*, 24–25.

21. Deposition of Lorinda Bewley, December 12, 1848, G. Walling, Justice of the Peace, Clackamas County, Oregon Territory, in Gray, *History of Oregon*, 487.

22. Interview with Elizabeth Sager Helm, "The Last Day at Waiilatpu," in *Transactions of the Oregon Pioneer Association* 24 (1896): 120–28, esp. 124.

23. Eliza Spalding as cited in Warren, *Memoirs of the West*, 24–25; and Matilda Sager as cited in Delaney, *Survivor's Recollections*, 19. In his account of the day's events, written from Fort Vancouver in early January 1848, Henry Spalding reported that "Mrs. Whitman died immediately"; Henry Spalding to David Greene, January 8, 1848, ABCFM Archives.

24. Marcus Whitman to Alanson Hinman, November 8, 1847, in Drury, *More about the Whitmans*, 15–16.

25. Nancy Osborn Jacobs, paper read at Walla Walla, May 29, 1912, reprinted in *Waitsburg Times*, February 2, 1934.

26. Eliza Spalding as cited in Warren, *Memoirs of the West*, 25.

27. Nancy Osborn Jacobs, paper read at Walla Walla, May 29, 1912, reprinted in *Waitsburg Times*, February 2, 1934.

28. Saunders, *Whitman Massacre*, 23.

29. Statement of John Mix Stanley, March 10, 1848, in Brouillet, *Authentic Account of the Murder*, 77. In his letter to the HBC Board of Management at Fort Vancouver, November 30, 1847, McBean said he had only five men to help him defend what he called Fort Nez Percés (*Oregon Spectator*, December 9, 1847).

30. Saunders, *Whitman Massacre*, 34.

31. Brouillet, *Authentic Account of the Murder*, 49.

32. Brouillet to Col. Gilliam, March 2, 1848, in Brouillet, *Authentic Account of the Murder*, 51.

33. Delaney, *Survivor's Recollections*, 22.

34. "Recollections of Nathan Kimball," *Transactions of the Oregon Pioneer Association* 31 (1903): 189–95, esp. 190.

35. Eliza Spalding as cited in Warren, *Memoirs of the West*, 27.

36. Drury, *Marcus and Narcissa Whitman*, 2: 272. See also the affidavit by Lorinda Bewley, December 12, 1848, recorded by G. Walling, Justice of the Peace, Clackamas County, Oregon Territory, in Gray, *History of Oregon*, 488.

37. Deposition of Daniel Young, January 20, 1849, Tualatin Plains, Oregon Territory, G.W. Coffinbury, Justice of the Peace, in Gray, *History of Oregon*, 474–77.

38. Drury, *Henry Harmon Spalding*, 345. Drury counted forty-seven hostages but apparently included the two children who died of measles a few days after the initial attack. The *Oregon Spectator* published the names of the forty-five captives in the January 20, 1848, edition (see p. 2).

CHAPTER TWO

Epigraph: Narcissa Whitman, diary entry of October 18, 1836, in Drury, *Where Wagons Could Go*, 108.

1. Roberta Conner, interview with the author, June 14, 2018, Seattle.

2. Roberta Conner, phone interview with the author, May 30, 2018. Conner later pointed out that "back then no one was routinely talking about tribal identity; we were busy dealing with poverty, racism, getting by"; Roberta Conner email to author, November 15, 2019.

3. Roberta Conner, interview with the author, July 21, 2009, Pendleton.

4. Haruo Aoki, "A Cayuse Dictionary Based on the 1829 Records of Samuel Black, the 1888 Records of Henry W. Henshaw and Others," unpublished manuscript, 1998, Confederated Tribes of the Umatilla Indian Reservation archives.

5. Hunn, *Čáw Pawá Láakni / They Are Not Forgotten*, 125.

6. Kane, entry dated July 11, 1847, *Wanderings of an Artist*.

7. Ross, *Fur Hunters of the Far West*, 176.

8. Douglas, *Journal Kept by David Douglas*, 159.

9. Farnham, *Travels in the Great Western Prairies*, 2: 141.

10. Verne F. Ray, "Tribal Distribution in Northeastern Oregon," *American Anthropologist* 40, no. 3 (1938): 384–95; and Ruby and Brown, *Cayuse Indians*, 3–4.

11. Nancy J. Turner and Harriet V. Kuhnlein, "Camas and Riceroot: Two Liliaceous 'Root' Foods of the Northwest Coast Indians," *Ecology of Food and Nutrition* 13, no. 4 (November 1983): 189–219, esp. 216.

12. Eugene Hunn, "Mobility as a Factor Limiting Resource Use," in *Resource Managers: North American and Australian Hunter-Gatherers*, edited by Nancy Williams and Eugene Hunn, 156–72 (Boulder, CO: American Association for the Advancement of Science, 1982). See also Vibert, *Traders' Tales*, 130.

13. Stern, *Chiefs and Chief Traders*, 42.

14. Slavery was commonplace among some American Indian tribes in the precolonial era, including those in the Northwest, usually involving captives from other tribes. See Elsie Frances Dennis, "Indian Slavery in the Pacific Northwest," *Oregon Historical Quarterly* 31, no. 1 (March 1930): 69–81. Sacagawea, who traveled west with the Lewis and Clark Expedition, was a Shoshone woman who had been taken captive at about age twelve by a group of Hidatsas from what is now North Dakota. She was later sold to a French Canadian trapper named Toussaint Charbonneau. Both she and Charbonneau joined the expedition as interpreters. She was reunited with her relatives, including her brother, when the explorers crossed into her homeland in present-day Idaho. Clark recorded her reaction, using his distinctive spelling: "The Intertrepeter & Squar who were before me at Some distance danced for the joyful Sight, and She made signs to me that they were her nation" (William Clark, entry dated August 17, 1805, in Moulton, *Journals of the Lewis and Clark Expedition*).

15. Ruby and Brown, *Cayuse Indians*, 17–18.

16. Henry K. W. Perkins to "Bro. Pitman," December 4, 1843, in Boyd, *People of The Dalles*, appendix 1, 292; and Perkins journal entry, early winter 1842, quoted in Boyd, *People of The Dalles*, 269.

17. Hunn, *Čáw Pawá Láakni / They Are Not Forgotten*, 13.

18. Vibert, *Traders' Tales*, 27.

19. Phillip E. Cash Cash, "Oral Traditions of the Natítaytma," in Karson, *Wiyaxayxt / Wiyaakaa'awn / As Days Go By*, 5–19, esp. 6.

20. Mithun, *Languages of Native North America*, 375.

21. Vibert, *Traders' Tales*, 124; and James P. Ronda, "Down the Columbia," chapter 7 of *Lewis and Clark Among the Indians*, https://lewisandclarkjournals.unl.edu/item/lc.sup.ronda.01.07, accessed October 2019.

22. West, *Last Indian War*, 18.

23. Robert T. Boyd, "Smallpox in the Pacific Northwest: The First Epidemics," *BC Studies*, no. 101 (Spring 1994): 5–40, quote on 29.

24. Robert T. Boyd, "Introduction of Infectious Diseases among the Indians of the Pacific Northwest, 1774–1874," PhD diss., University of Washington, 1985.

25. Hunn, *Nch'i-Wana*, 241.

26. Thompson, *David Thompson's Narrative*, 337.

27. Miller, *Prophetic Worlds*, 41–42, 44.

28. Ruby and Brown, *Spokane Indians*, 31–33.

29. Yureerachen as cited in Wilkes, *Narrative of the United States Exploring Expedition*, 4: 439.

30. Miller, *Prophetic Worlds*, 42–44.

31. William Clark, entry dated October 19, 1805, in Moulton, *Journals of the Lewis and Clark Expedition*. See also note 1 in that entry.

32. Ronda, "Down the Columbia."

33. William Clark, entry dated April 25, 1806, in Moulton, *Journals of the Lewis and Clark Expedition*.

34. Meriwether Lewis, entry dated April 28, 1806, in Moulton, *Journals of the Lewis and Clark Expedition*. See also Clark's entry, same date.

35. William Clark, entry dated April 28, 1806, in Moulton, *Journals of the Lewis and Clark Expedition*.

36. The Cayuse population at time of contact is a slippery number. The Hulberts, authors of the three-volume *Marcus Whitman, Crusader*, estimated that there were probably twelve hundred Cayuses at their peak (part of their eight-volume *Overland to the Pacific*, 6: 75). At the top range was this estimate, from the editor of a 1970 book about the Nez Perce: "There were probably at least 3,000 Cayuse" at time of contact with Lewis and Clark (in Feathers, *These Are the Nez Perce Nation*, 20). Lewis and Clark estimated only 250; see William Clark, "Estimate of Western Indians," supplement, in Moulton, *Journals of the Lewis and Clark Expedition*, https://lewisandclarkjournals.unl .edu/item/lc.jrn.1805-1806.winter.part2#n3029. Ruby and Brown, in *Cayuse Indians*, accept five hundred as the population in 1780, citing James Mooney, *The Aboriginal Population of America North of Mexico* (Washington, DC: The Smithsonian Institution, 1938), 18.

37. Alexandra Harmon, email to author, June 27, 2019.

38. Thompson, *David Thompson's Narrative*, 489–91.

39. Ross, *Adventures of the First Settlers*, 126–27.

40. Ross, *Adventures of the First Settlers*, 129, 131.

41. Josephy, *Nez Perce Indians*, 69–70; Stark, *Astoria*, 266–68; and Ross, *Adventures of the First Settlers*, 212–14.

42. Ross, *Fur Hunters of the Far West*, 5–8.

43. Ross, *Fur Hunters of the Far West*, 167, 171.

44. Harmon, *Indians in the Making*, 15.

45. Ross, *Fur Hunters of the Far West*, 165–66; and Hunn, *Čáw Pawá Láakni / They Are Not Forgotten*, 96.

46. Karson, *Wiyaxayxt / Wiyaakaa'awn / As Days Go By*, 46.

47. Samuel Black (chief trader at Fort Walla Walla, 1825–1830) said the Cayuse produced about two-thirds of the furs traded at the post; see Vibert, *Traders' Tales*, 207.

48. "Establishment of Fort Nez Perces," http://trailtribes.org/umatilla/establishment-of-fort-nez-perces.htm, accessed October 2019.

49. Addis, "Whitman Massacre."

50. Ruby and Brown, *Cayuse Indians*, 65.

51. Stern, *Chiefs and Change in the Oregon Country*, 18.

52. Townsend, *Narrative of a Journey across the Rocky Mountains*, 246.

53. Narcissa Whitman, January 2, 1837, in Drury, *Where Wagons Could Go*, 123–24.

54. Miller, *Prophetic Worlds*, 59.

55. Josephy, *Nez Perce Indians*, 94, 96. See also Robert Lee Sappington et al., "Alice Cunningham Fletcher's 'The New Perce Country,'" *Northwest Anthropological Research Notes* 29, no. 2 (Fall 1995): 177–220.

56. Clark's report to Cass is cited in Clifford Drury, "1830 Report on the Fur Trade by General William Clark," *Oregon Historical Quarterly* 48, no. 1 (March 1947): 31–33.

57. Clark's private letter to Cass is cited in Baird, Mallickan, and Swagerty, *Encounters with the People*, 178, citing National Archives and Records Administration, RG 75, Letters Received by the Commissioner of Indian Affairs, Letters Received from the Saint Louis Superintendency, 1824–51, Roll 749.

58. Baird, Mallickan, and Swagerty, *Encounters with the People*, 177, citing *The Book of Sepultures, 1781–1832, of the St. Louis Cathedral*.

59. Catlin, *Letters and Notes*, 2: 108–10.

60. *Christian Advocate and Journal and Zion's Herald*, March 1, 1833, and March 22, 1833.

61. Furtwangler, *Bringing Indians to the Book*, 41.

62. Lee and Frost, *Ten Years in Oregon*, 122.

CHAPTER THREE

Epigraph: Roberta Conner, interview with the author, June 14, 2018, Seattle.

1. Lewis Cass, "Removal of the Indians," *North American Review* 30, no. 1 (January 1830): 62–64. See also Thornton, *American Indian Holocaust and Survival*, 26–32.

2. Catlin, *Letters and Notes,* 1: 261–62.

3. Catlin, *My Life amongst the Indians*, 4.

4. Henry Spalding to David Greene, April 21, 1838, ABCFM Archives. Narcissa often wrote about the "dear heathen," as in this November 5, 1838, letter to Elvira Perkins, a Methodist missionary (in *Letters of Narcissa Whitman*): "I, too, desire to be freed from so many worldly cares and perplexities, and that my time may be spent in seeking the immediate conversion of these dear heathen to God. O, what a thought to think of meeting them among the blood-washed throng around the throne of God!"

5. Eliza Hart Spalding, "Diary of Eliza Hart Spalding," entry dated May 27, 1836, in Henry Harmon Spalding Papers, Cage 143, Box 2, Folder 31, Manuscripts, Archives, and Special Collections, Washington State University Libraries, Pullman; published in Drury, *Where Wagons Could Go* (hereafter Eliza Hart Spalding, "Diary").

6. Henry Spalding to Henry Green, July 8, 1836, cited in Drury, *Henry Harmon Spalding*, 168.

7. West, *Last Indian War*, 43–44.

8. Marcus Whitman to Stephen Prentiss, 1844, in *Letters of Narcissa Whitman*.

9. B. F. Nichols, "Recollections of the Whitman Mission," *Whitman College Quarterly* 1, no. 3 (October 1897): 17–20, quote on 19.

10. Drury, *Marcus and Narcissa Whitman*, 2: 382.

11. Marcus Whitman to David Greene, April 13, 1846, ABCFM Archives.

12. "Statement of Mrs. Calkins of Naples, daughter of Mrs. Wisewell, who was sister of Marcus Whitman," undated, Marcus and Narcissa Whitman Papers, Cage 142 (Box 1, Folder 16), Manuscripts, Archives, and Special Collections, Washington State University Libraries, Pullman (hereafter WSU).

13. Marcus Whitman to David Greene, June 3, 1834, ABCFM Archives.

14. "Statement of Mrs. Calkins of Naples, daughter of Mrs. Wisewell, who was sister of Marcus Whitman," undated, Marcus and Narcissa Whitman Papers, WSU.

15. Marcus Whitman to David Greene, June 3, 1834, ABCFM Archives.

16. In a May 27, 1843, letter to his mother from the Missouri frontier, on his way back to Oregon after having visited her, Whitman wrote: "I feel most desirous to know that my Dear Mother has determined to live the rest of her days witnessing a good profession of godliness. What keeps you from this? Is it that you are not a sinner, or if not that, is it that there is no Saviour of sinners, or is it that you have not too long refused & neglected to love & obey him. Has not his forbearance & his mercy been very long expended towards you?" (letter cited in Drury, *Marcus and Narcissa Whitman*, 1: 71).

17. Marcus Whitman to David Greene, June 27, 1834, ABCFM Archives.

18. Joel Wakeman, "A Venerable Name from Old Franklin," *Prattsburg News*, August 17, 1893, in Joel Wakeman Papers, WSU, typescript, p. 10.

19. Marcus Whitman to David Greene, June 27, 1834, ABCFM Archives.

20. Gray, *History of Oregon*, 107.

21. Marcus Whitman to David Greene, December 2, 1834, ABCFM Archives.

22. Samuel Parker to David Greene, December 17, 1834, ABCFM Archives; and David Greene to Samuel Parker, December 24, 1834, ABCFM Archives.

23. Narcissa Whitman to her parents, November 19, 1841, in *Letters of Narcissa Whitman*.

24. Narcissa Prentiss to ABCFM, February 23, 1835, ABCFM Archives.

25. Joel Wakeman, "Pleasant Memories," *Prattsburg News*, January 20, 1898, in Joel Wakeman Papers, WSU, typescript, p. 17.

26. Drury cites a reminiscence published in 1897 by Rev. Levi Fay Waldo, a descendant of an old Prattsburg family and a relative of the Prentiss family: "From my earliest recollection he [Stephen Prentiss] was always known as Judge Prentiss, having served one term as County or Probate Judge. He carried on his business about one-half mile southeast of the public square, where he had a saw-mill, a gristmill, and a distillery. . . . My uncle, Prentiss Fay, a most excellent Christian man, worked for his uncle in the distillery, where I am told they kept the Bible depository and held mid-week prayer meetings." Drury (in *Marcus and Narcissa Whitman,* 1: 100) points out that churches on the frontier were slow to promote temperance, and it was not unusual for the devout, including ministers, to imbibe strong liquor without invoking disapproval.

27. Narcissa Prentiss to ABCFM, February 23, 1835, ABCFM Archives.

28. Joel Wakeman, "Pleasant Memories," *Prattsburg News*, February 3, 1898, in Joel Wakeman Papers, WSU, typescript, p. 22.

29. Marcus Whitman to David Greene, June 3, 1834, ABCFM Archives.

30. Marcus Whitman to Jane Prentiss, May 17, 1842, in *Letters of Narcissa Whitman*.

31. Marcus Whitman to Narcissa Prentiss, April 30, 1835, in Mowry, *Marcus Whitman and the Early Days of Oregon*, 56. The original cannot be located.

32. Marcus Whitman to David Greene, May 10, 1839, ABCFM Archives.

33. W. G. Rae to James Hargrave, March 20, 1836, in G. P. Glazebrook, ed., *The Hargrave Correspondence, 1821–1843* (Toronto: The Champlain Society, 1938), 234–35. Rae, a company employee on temporary duty at Fort Nez Percés, encountered Parker at Fort Vancouver sometime around February 14, 1836.

34. Marcus Whitman Journal of 1835, typescript prepared by Clifford M. Drury, in Marcus and Narcissa Whitman Papers, Cage 142, Box 1, Folder 25, WSU.

35. Marcus Whitman to Narcissa Prentiss, June 21, 1835, cited in Mowry, *Marcus Whitman and the Early Days of Oregon,* 60.

36. Whitman, journal entry dated August 12, 1835, as cited in Young, "Journal and Report by Dr. Marcus Whitman."

37. Parker, *Journal of an Exploring Tour*, 80.

38. Young, "Journal and Report by Dr. Marcus Whitman," entry dated August 17, 1835.

39. Young, "Journal and Report by Dr. Marcus Whitman," entries dated August 16 and August 18, 1835.

40. David Greene to Marcus Whitman, December 8, 1835, in Drury, *Marcus and Narcissa Whitman*, 1: 144.

41. Henry Spalding to Rachel Smith Spalding, May 3, 1871, in Drury, *Henry Harmon Spalding*, 24. Note that in his initial letter of application to the ABCFM, Spalding said he had been sent to a foster home when he was sixteen months old: "I was from infancy separated from all friends, bound out to strangers at the age of 16 months"; see Spalding, "Applic. To Board," August 7, 1835, in Hulbert and Hulbert, *Overland to the Pacific,* 5: 30.

42. Drury, *Henry Harmon Spalding*, 42. The phrase "serious turn of mind" is from Gray, *History of Oregon*, 110.

43. Henry Spalding to Levi Hart, September 1833, RG 283, Box 1, Folder 2, Presbyterian Historical Society, Philadelphia.

44. Drury, *Henry Harmon Spalding*, 49.

45. Henry Spalding to Levi Hart, September 1833, Presbyterian Historical Society.

46. Rev. George Rudd and Rev. James H. Hotchkin to ABCFM, August 6, 1835; and Artemas Bullard to ABCFM, August 14, 1835, ABCFM Archives.

47. Levi Hart, Eliza's father, died in 1846. In his will, he stipulated that Eliza could receive her share of his estate only if she collected it in person: "that is to Say it must be paid into her hand"; "The Last Will and Testament of Levi Hart, (of the Fox Road), Town of Trenton, County of Oneida and State of New York," January 20, 1845, Oneida County Clerk's Office, Book of Deeds 186, copy in Holland Patent history binder, Holland Patent Free Library.

48. Lavender, *Land of Giants*, 174.

49. Drury, *Marcus Whitman, M.D.*, 84.

50. According to Drury, the letter, dated January 11, 1893, was written by Narcissa's youngest sister, Harriet (Mrs. John W. Jackson), then living in Oberlin, Ohio, to Eva Emery Dye, and the original was in the collections of the Oregon Historical Society (OHS) in Portland. The OHS holds four letters from Harriet Prentiss Jackson to Eva Emery Dye, dated December 8, 1892; January 11, 1893 (the date of the letter cited by Drury); February 28, 1893; and March 3, 1893. None of them say anything about Henry Spalding. Eva Emery Dye Papers, Mss 1089, Box 2, Folder 1, OHS Research Library, Portland.

51. Henry Spalding to David Greene, December 28, 1835, ABCFM Archives.

52. David Greene to Marcus Whitman, January 22, 1836, ABCFM Archives.

53. Eliza Hart Spalding, entry dated February 20, 1836, "Diary."

54. Narcissa Whitman as cited in Eells, *Marcus Whitman,* 28.

55. Letter to the editor from Mrs. George Hunter, who said she had witnessed the scene, published in *Prattsburg* (New York) *News,* March 2, 1882, photocopy in Marcus and Narcissa Papers, WSU, Box 1, Folder 22. See also Drury, *Marcus and Narcissa Whitman,* 1: 163.

CHAPTER FOUR

Epigraphs: Henry Spalding to David Greene, July 8, 1836; and Marcus Whitman to Greene, July 16, 1836, ABCFM Archives.

1. Eliza Hart Spalding, entry dated February 1, 1836, "Diary."

2. Narcissa Whitman, March 15, 1836, in *Letters of Narcissa Whitman.*

3. Narcissa Whitman, March 28, 1836, in *Letters of Narcissa Whitman.*

4. Eliza Hart Spalding, entry dated March 22, 1836, "Diary"; Narcissa Whitman, April 7, 1836, in *Letters of Narcissa Whitman.*

5. Narcissa Whitman, March 30, 1836, in *Letters of Narcissa Whitman.* In a lengthy letter to her family from the rendezvous in Wyoming, Narcissa again insisted, "I do not regret coming"; July 15–19, 1836, in Marcus and Narcissa Whitman Collection, Box 1, Whitman College Archives.

6. Eliza Hart Spalding, entry dated March 25, 1836, "Diary."

7. Narcissa Whitman, March 28 and March 29, 1836, in *Letters of Narcissa Whitman.*

8. Narcissa Whitman, March 29, 1836, in *Letters of Narcissa Whitman.*

9. "Diary of Myra Eells," entry dated April 9, 1838, in Drury, *On to Oregon,* 56.

10. Elkanah Walker to David Greene, October 15, 1838, ABCFM Archives.

11. Eliza Hart Spalding, entry dated March 31, 1836, "Diary."

12. Eliza Hart Spalding, entry dated April 1, 1836, "Diary"; Henry Spalding to David Greene, May 20, 1836, ABCFM Archives.

13. Narcissa Whitman, April 4 and March 15, 1836, in *Letters of Narcissa Whitman.*

14. Drury, *Henry Harmon Spalding*, 127.

15. Four other missionary women, sent to Oregon with their husbands in 1838, also rode sidesaddles over the mountains. The saddle used by one of them—Mary Richardson Walker—is in the Oregon Historical Society's museum in Portland.

16. "Dr. Whitman and Messrs. Spalding and Gray were at the Otoe Agency near the mouth of the Great Platte river, May 20, in good health. Having been disappointed in securing a passage, as they expected, on a steamboat which proceeds high up the Missouri River, they were obliged to prepare themselves for making the whole journey by land" ("Brief Notices: Rocky-Mountain Indians," *Missionary Journal* 32, no. 8 [August 1836]: 317).

17. Henry Spalding to David Greene, May 20, 1836, ABCFM Archives.

18. Eliza Hart Spalding, entry dated May 27, 1836, "Diary."

19. Narcissa Whitman, June 3, 1836, in *Letters of Narcissa Whitman*.

20. Asa B. Smith, "Journal across the Rocky Mountains," June 11, 1838, ABCFM Archives microfilm edition, reel 784.

21. Narcissa Whitman, June 4, 1836, in *Letters of Narcissa Whitman*.

22. Eliza Hart Spalding, entry dated June 21, 1836, "Diary."

23. Eliza Hart Spalding, entry dated June 15, 1836, "Diary."

24. Narcissa Whitman, June 27, 1836, in *Letters of Narcissa Whitman*.

25. Marcus Whitman to David Greene, July 16, 1836, ABCFM Archives.

26. Eliza Hart Spalding, entry dated July 4, 1836, "Diary."

27. "An Evening with an Old Missionary," *The Advance* (Chicago), December 1, 1870, in "Letter from the Secretary of the Interior," February 8, 1871, Senate Executive Document No. 37, 41st Congress, 3rd Session, 8–12.

28. George Ludington Weed, "When Dr. Whitman Added Three Stars to Our Flag / How Oregon Was Saved for the Union," *Ladies Home Journal*, November 1897, p. 9 (https://babel.hathitrust.org/cgi/pt?id=mdp .39015012341627;view=1up;seq=429;size=200). The drawing by Alice Barber Stephens was captioned "Dr. Whitman and party celebrating the Fourth of July at South Pass. 1836." It was reprinted in *Whitman College Quarterly* 1, no. 1 (January 1897) and *Whitman College Quarterly* 12, no. 4 (October 1909); Eells, *Marcus Whitman*; and elsewhere.

29. Oliver W. Nixon, *Whitman's Ride through Savage Lands*, drawing captioned "Pacific Springs, July 4, 1836," opposite p. 57.

30. Eliza Hart Spalding, entry dated July 6, 1836, "Diary."

31. Marcus Whitman to David Greene, July 16, 1836, ABCFM Archives.

32. Narcissa Whitman, July 16, 1836, in *Letters of Narcissa Whitman*.

33. Victor, *River of the West*, 207.

34. Gray, *History of Oregon*, 123.

35. Narcissa Whitman to Stephen and Clarissa Prentiss, October 20, 1836, Narcissa Prentiss Whitman Journal, Marcus and Narcissa Whitman Collection, Box 3, Whitman College Archives.

36. Marcus Whitman to David Greene, May 10, 1839, ABCFM Archives.

37. Henry Spalding to the ABCFM, postscript to letter dated July 8, 1836, in Drury, *Where Wagons Could Go*, 70.

38. Narcissa Whitman, July 26 and 29, 1836, in *Letters of Narcissa Whitman*.

39. Narcissa Whitman, July 23 and 27, 1836, in Drury, *Where Wagons Could Go*, 73–75.

40. Narcissa Whitman, July 28, 1836, in *Letters of Narcissa Whitman*.

41. Narcissa Whitman, July 28, 1836, in *Letters of Narcissa Whitman*.

42. Miles Goodyear as cited in Gray, *History of Oregon*, 133.

43. Narcissa Whitman, August 5, 1936, in Drury, *Where Wagons Could Go*, 80–81.

44. Narcissa Whitman, August 29, 1936, in Drury, *Where Wagons Could Go*, 90–91.

45. [William] Henry Gray to David Ambler, September 9, 1836, in Hulbert and Hulbert, *Overland to the Pacific,* 6: 226–27.

46. Narcissa Whitman, March 14, 1838, in *Letters of Narcissa Whitman*.

47. Townsend, *Narrative of a Journey across the Rocky Mountains*, 249.

48. William H[enry] Gray to David Ambler and Family, September 9, 1836 (written from "Columbia River, Breakfast Harbour," en route to Fort Vancouver), in Hulbert and Hulbert, *Overland to the Pacific,* 6: 227.

49. Marcus Whitman to David Greene, May 5, 1837, ABCFM Archives.

50. Narcissa Whitman, September 8, 1836, in Drury, *Where Wagons Could Go,* 97.

51. Townsend, *Narrative of a Journey across the Rocky Mountains*, 250.

52. Narcissa Whitman to her mother, December 5, 1836, in *Letters of Narcissa Whitman*.

53. Narcissa Whitman, September 12, 1836, in *Letters of Narcissa Whitman*. For more about Fort Vancouver, see also Morrison, *John McLoughlin and the Far Northwest*.

54. Narcissa Whitman, September 12, 1836, in *Letters of Narcissa Whitman*.

55. Eliza Hart Spalding, entry dated September 14, 1836, "Diary."

56. Narcissa Whitman, September 12, 1836, in *Letters of Narcissa Whitman*.

57. Dietrich, *Northwest Passage*, 163.

58. Narcissa Whitman, September 30, 1836, in *Letters of Narcissa Whitman*.

59. Narcissa Whitman, September 12, 1836, in *Letters of Narcissa Whitman*.

60. Hunn, *Čáw Pawá Láakni / They Are Not Forgotten*, 125.

61. Marcus Whitman to Samuel Parker, October 8, 1836, in Drury, *Marcus and Narcissa Whitman*, 1: 244.

CHAPTER FIVE

Epigraph: Marcus Whitman to David Greene, March 24, 1838, ABCFM Archives.

1. Henry Spalding to William and Edward Porter, Prattsburg, New York, from Fort Walla Walla, October 2, 1836, in Henry Harmon Spalding Papers, Box 1, Folder 1, WSU.

2. Narcissa Whitman, December 8, 1836, in *Letters of Narcissa Whitman*.

3. Narcissa Whitman to her mother, December 5, 1836, in Drury, *Where Wagons Could Go*, 119–20.

4. Henry Spalding to ABCFM, February 16, 1837, reprinted in "Indians West of the Rocky Mountains: Letter from Mr. Spalding, Dated Feb. 16, 1837," *Missionary Herald* 33, no. 12 (December 1837): 497.

5. Drury, *Henry Harmon Spalding*, 161.

6. Narcissa Whitman to her mother, December 5, 1836, in Drury, *Where Wagons Could Go*, 119–20.

7. Jeffrey, *Converting the West*, 101.

8. Narcissa Whitman to her mother, December 5, 1836, in Drury, *Where Wagons Could Go*, 119–20.

9. Narcissa Whitman to her parents, December 26, 1836, in Drury, *Where Wagons Could Go*, 119–20.

10. Narcissa Whitman to her parents, December 26, 1836, and February 18, 1837, in Drury, *Where Wagons Could Go*, 121–22 and 124–25.

11. Garth, "Report on the Second Season's Excavations at Waiilatpu."

12. Narcissa Whitman, January 2, 1837, in Drury, *Where Wagons Could Go*, 123.

13. Terry O'Driscoll et al., "Traditional First Nations Birthing Practices: Interviews with Elders in Northwestern Ontario," *Journal of Obstetrics and Gynecology* 33, no. 1 (January 2011): 24–29.

14. Narcissa Whitman to her family, March 30, 1837, in Drury, *Where Wagons Could Go*, 126–27.

15. Narcissa Whitman to her family, March 30, 1837, in Drury, *Where Wagons Could Go*, 126–27.

16. Narcissa Whitman to her family, May 3, 1837, in *Letters of Narcissa Whitman*.

17. Narcissa Whitman to her family, March 30, 1837, in Drury, *Where Wagons Could Go*, 126–27.

18. Narcissa Whitman to her family, May 3, 1837, in *Letters of Narcissa Whitman*.

19. Marcus Whitman to David Greene, May 5, 1837, ABCFM Archives.

20. Marcus Whitman to David Greene, May 8, 1838, ABCFM Archives.

21. Marcus Whitman to David Greene, May 8, 1838, ABCFM Archives.

22. Henry Spalding to [David Greene?], April 1, 1840, in Drury, *Henry Harmon Spalding*, 204–05.

23. Marcus Whitman to David Greene, May 5, 1837, ABCFM Archives.

24. Marcus Whitman to David Greene, March 27, 1840, ABCFM Archives.

25. Townsend, *Narrative of a Journey across the Rocky Mountains*, 245.

26. Narcissa Whitman to her mother, December 5, 1835, in Drury, *Where Wagons Could Go*, 119–20.

27. Narcissa Whitman to her family, May 2, 1837, in *Letters of Narcissa Whitman.*

28. Narcissa Whitman to her sister Mary Ann, September 25, 1838, in *Letters of Narcissa Whitman.*

29. Marcus Whitman to David Greene, May 5, 1837, ABCFM Archives; and Spalding to Samuel Parker, February 21, 1837, in Drury, *Marcus Whitman, M.D.,* 172.

30. Joel Palmer, a member of the 1845 emigration, Superintendent of Indian Affairs in 1847, included a glossary of helpful words and phrases in Chinook Jargon and Nez Perce in his *Journal of Travels over the Rocky Mountains, 1845–46,* originally published in 1847 (reprinted in 1851 and 1853) and intended as a guidebook for emigrants.

31. Margaret Smith, Fort Vancouver, to her father, April 10, 1838, in *Oregonian and Indian's Advocate* 1, no. 2 (November 1838): 60.

32. Marcus Whitman to David Greene, October 30 and March 24, 1838, ABCFM Archives.

33. Marcus Whitman to David Greene, March 12, 1838, ABCFM Archives.

34. Narcissa Whitman to her parents, April 11, 1838, in *Letters of Narcissa Whitman.*

35. Marcus Whitman to David Greene, March 24, 1838, ABCFM Archives.

36. Marcus Whitman to David Greene, May 8, 1838, ABCFM Archives.

37. Henry Spalding and Marcus Whitman to the American Board, April 21, 1838, in Drury, *Henry Harmon Spalding,* 183. See also Jones, *Great Command,* 172–74.

38. David Greene to Marcus Whitman, January 7, 1837, in Hulbert and Hulbert, *Overland to the Pacific,* 6: 261.

39. David Greene to Henry Spalding and Marcus Whitman, July 6, 1837, in Hulbert and Hulbert, *Overland to the Pacific,* 6: 285.

40. David Greene as cited in Jones, *Great Command,* 172, 175.

41. William Henry Gray to Mary Augusta Dix, February 15, 1838, in Drury, *Where Wagons Could Go,* 239–40.

42. Mary Richardson Walker, *Diary,* entry dated May 27, 1838, in Drury, *On to Oregon.*

43. Constitution of the Columbia Maternal Association, Columbia Maternal Association Collection, 1839–1940, WCMss.653, Whitman College and Northwest Archives, Walla Walla.

44. Mary Walker, *Diary*, entry dated June 10, 1838, in Drury, *On to Oregon*.

45. Mary Walker, *Diary*, entry dated June 10, 1838, in Drury, *On to Oregon*.

46. Narcissa Whitman to Jane Prentiss, May 17, 1839, in *Letters of Narcissa Whitman*.

47. Mary Walker, *Diary,* entry dated December 12, 1838, in Drury, *On to Oregon*.

48. Narcissa Whitman to her family, September 18, 1838, in *Letters of Narcissa Whitman*.

49. Narcissa Whitman to Elvira Perkins, March 8, 1839, in *Letters of Narcissa Whitman*.

50. Mary Walker, *Diary,* entry dated June 24, 1839, in Drury, *On to Oregon*.

51. Narcissa Whitman to her family, September 30, 1839, in *Letters of Narcissa Whitman*.

52. Narcissa Whitman to her mother, October 9, 1839, in *Letters of Narcissa Whitman*.

53. Marcus Whitman to David Greene, October 15, 1840, in Drury, *Henry Harmon Spalding*, 224.

54. Narcissa Whitman to Jane Prentiss, May 17, 1839, in *Letters of Narcissa Whitman*.

55. Narcissa Whitman to her father, April 30, 1840, in *Letters of Narcissa Whitman*.

56. Narcissa Whitman to Elvira Perkins, January 1, 1840, in *Letters of Narcissa Whitman*.

57. See Garth, "Report on the Second Season's Excavations at Waiilatpu."

58. Narcissa Whitman to her mother, May 2, 1840, in *Letters of Narcissa Whitman*.

CHAPTER SIX

Epigraph: Marcus Whitman to David Greene, November 11, 1841, ABCFM Archives.

1. "Mr. Parker's Exploring Tour Beyond the Rocky Mountains," *Methodist Magazine and Quarterly Review* 21, no. 1 (January 1839): 71.

2. Brouillet, *Authentic Account of the Murder*, 23–24.

3. Narcissa Whitman to Elvira Perkins, January 1, 1840, in *Letters of Narcissa Whitman.*

4. Narcissa Whitman to her parents, January 2, 1837, in Drury, *Where Wagons Could Go,* 123.

5. Samuel Parker said the most telling example of "opposition to the truths of the gospel" that he encountered in Cayuse country involved the issue of "a plurality of wives." One Cayuse chief insisted he would never part with any of his wives, and if that meant he was bound for hell, "he would go in all his sins, and would not alter his life" (Parker, *Journal of an Exploring Tour,* 181–82).

6. Marcus Whitman to David Greene, October 15, 1840, ABCFM Archives.

7. Narcissa Whitman to her father, October 19, 1840, in *Letters of Narcissa Whitman.*

8. Cebula, *Plateau Indians,* 100.

9. Archibald McKinlay to W. Fraser Tolmie, May 12, 1884, in *Transactions of the Oregon Pioneer Association* 12 (1884): 34.

10. John Young, an emigrant who worked for Whitman during the winter of 1846, said Whitman laughed when he told Young that three Indians had been seriously sickened by poisoned meat that had been set out as bait for wolves during a particularly brutal cold spell that winter. According to Young, Whitman said the Indians would have died if they had not induced vomiting by drinking large quantities of water. Young quoted Whitman as saying, "I had told them very often not to eat of that meat which we distributed for the wolves, that it would kill them; they will take care now, I suppose" (in Drury, *Marcus and Narcissa Whitman,* 2: 235).

11. Marcus Whitman to David Greene, April 8, 1845, ABCFM Archives.

12. Archibald McKinlay, chief trader at Fort Walla Walla from 1841 to 1846, claimed that between them the Cayuse and Walla Walla "shot seven of their own medicine men right by the fort during my five years' stay there, and probably over three times that number altogether." Archibald McKinlay to W. Fraser Tolmie, May 12, 1884, in *Transactions of the Oregon Pioneer Association* 12 (1884): 35.

13. Narcissa Whitman to her parents, May 3, 1837, in *Letters of Narcissa Whitman.*

14. Marcus Whitman detailed these events in a letter to David Greene, November 11, 1841, ABCFM Archives.

15. Narcissa Whitman to her parents, October 9, 1839, in *Letters of Narcissa Whitman.*

16. Carol L. Higham, "Christian Missions to American Indians," American History, Oxford University Encyclopedias, http://americanhistory .oxfordre.com/view/10.1093/acrefore/9780199329175.001.0001 /acrefore-9780199329175-e-323 (accessed May 2016).

17. Marcus Whitman to David Greene, October 29, 1840, ABCFM Archives.

18. Sally Thompson, "Missionaries and Early Settlers," PhD diss., https:// trailtribes.org/umatilla/missionaries-and-early-settlers.htm, accessed March 2019.

19. Roberta Conner, interview with the author, July 21, 2009, Pendleton.

20. David Greene to Marcus Whitman, February 25, 1842, ABCFM Archives.

21. Narcissa Whitman to Marcus Whitman, October 4 and 5, 1842, in *Letters of Narcissa Whitman*.

22. Narcissa Whitman to Marcus Whitman, October 7, 1842, in *Letters of Narcissa Whitman*.

23. Jeffrey, *Converting the West*, 172.

24. Henry Spalding to Dudley Allen, September 15, 1845, in Drury, *Henry Harmon Spalding*, 322–24.

25. Narcissa Whitman to Marcus Whitman in care of David Greene, March 29, 1843, ABCFM Archives.

26. Narcissa Whitman to Mary Walker, Tshimakain, April 11, 1843, in Eells, *Marcus Whitman*, 262 (original at Yale University).

27. Drury, *Henry Harmon Spalding*, 296; and Gray, *History of Oregon*, 228.

28. Hines, *Life on the Plains of the Pacific*, 178–9, 181. As with many Indian names, spellings vary widely. PeoPeoMoxMox is preferred by the Confederated Tribes of the Cayuse, Umatilla, and Walla Walla. Other variations include Peo-peo-mox-mox, Piupiumaksmaks, and Peu-peu-mox-mox.

29. Elijah White to Secretary of War J. M. Porter, April 1, 1843, in White, *Concise View of Oregon Territory*, 12–13.

30. Hines, *Life on the Plains of the Pacific,* 185.

31. West, *Last Indian War*, 33.

32. Elijah White, "The Wallawalla Indians, a Report to the Secretary of War," reprinted from *The Californian*, published in *The Polynesian* (Honolulu), October 31, 1846.

33. The reference to the "beating tumour" is in Narcissa Whitman to Laura Brewer, January 30, 1844, in *Letters of Narcissa Whitman*.

34. Jeffrey, *Converting the West*, 162.

35. Narcissa Whitman to her father, April 12, 1844, in *Letters of Narcissa Whitman*.

36. Narcissa Whitman to her parents, August 11, 1843, in *Letters of Narcissa Whitman*.

37. Narcissa Whitman to her father, April 12, 1844, in *Letters of Narcissa Whitman*.

38. Narcissa Whitman to Jane Prentiss, July 11, 1843, in *Letters of Narcissa Whitman*.

39. Narcissa Whitman to her father, April 12, 1844, in *Letters of Narcissa Whitman*.

40. Narcissa Whitman to her father, April 12, 1844, in *Letters of Narcissa Whitman*.

41. David Greene, undated memo, in Drury, *Mountains We Have Crossed*, 284–85.

42. Horace Greeley, "Arrival from Oregon," *New York Daily Tribune*, March 29, 1843.

43. Marcus Whitman to Jonas Galusha Prentiss, May 28, 1843, in *Letters of Narcissa Whitman*.

44. Burnett later became a member of the Oregon Provisional Legislature and eventually the first governor of California.

45. West, *Last Indian War*, 46–47.

46. Marcus Whitman to Stephen and Clarissa Prentiss, May 16, 1844, in *Letters of Narcissa Whitman*.

CHAPTER SEVEN

Epigraph: Narcissa Whitman to her sister Clarissa, May 20, 1844, in *Letters of Narcissa Whitman*.

1. Antone Minthorn, "Wars, Treaties, and the Beginning of Reservation Life," in Karson, *Wiyaxayxt / Wiyaakaa'awn / As Days Go By*, 61–89, quote on 64.

2. Marcus Whitman to Stephen Prentiss, May 18, 1844, in *Letters of Narcissa Whitman*, 173.

3. Elwood Evans, citing an undated letter from Robert Newell, in *Transactions of the Oregon Pioneer Association* 5 (1877): 23.

4. Marcus Whitman to David Greene, April 8, 1844, ABCFM Archives.

5. Marcus Whitman to David Greene, October 18, 1847, ABCFM Archives.

6. *Cleveland Plain Dealer*, March 8, 1843; *Boston Daily Evening Transcript*, April 4, 1843; and *Ohio Statesman*, April 26, 1843.

7. Narcissa Whitman to her sister Harriet, April 13, 1846, in *Letters of Narcissa Whitman*.

8. Catherine Sager Pringle, "Account of Overland Journey to Oregon in 1844: Life at the Whitman Mission: The Whitman Massacre," manuscript written ca. 1860, in Clarke, *Pioneer Days of Oregon History*, 2: 508.

9. Narcissa Whitman to Elvira Perkins, January 1, 1840; and Narcissa Whitman to her parents, October 6, 1841, in *Letters of Narcissa Whitman*.

10. Narcissa Whitman to her mother, November 3, 1846, in *Letters of Narcissa Whitman*.

11. Delaney, *Survivor's Recollections*, 8.

12. Narcissa Whitman to Laura Brewer, August 9, 1845, in *Letters of Narcissa Whitman*.

13. Catherine Sager quoted in Drury, *Marcus and Narcissa Whitman*, 2: 129.

14. Marcus Whitman to David Greene, September 8, 1846, ABCFM Archives.

15. Marcus Whitman to David Greene, April 8, 1845, ABCFM Archives.

16. "Notice," *Oregon Spectator*, July 9, 1846.

17. Henry K. W. Perkins to Jane Prentiss, October 19, 1840, in Drury, *Marcus Whitman, M.D.*, 460.

18. Marcus Whitman to David Greene, September 13, 1847, ABCFM Archives.

19. Marcus Whitman to David Greene, November 3, 1846, ABCFM Archives; Marcus Whitman to Lyman Judson, November 5, 1846, in *Letters of Narcissa Whitman*; and Marcus Whitman to Asa Bowen Smith, Honolulu, May 31, 1844, in Drury, *Mountains We Have Crossed*.

20. In the fall of 1846, Whitman warned Greene in a September 8, 1846, letter (in ABCFM Archives) that he would probably not sell enough to travelers that year to cover his bills: "As the Immigrants have not called on me this year for any supplies, I shall have no means to meet the small bill I have made at [Fort] Vancouver therefore I shall need to draw upon the Board."

21. Marcus Whitman to David Greene, April 8, 1845, ABCFM Archives.

22. Marcus Whitman to David Greene, April 7, 1843, ABCFM Archives.

23. David Greene to Marcus Whitman, October 22, 1847, ABCFM Archives.

24. Jeffrey, *Converting the West*, 208.

25. Marcus Whitman to David Greene, April 8, 1845, ABCFM Archives. Narcissa also wrote about these events, telling her parents in an undated letter in late October 1844: "We have had some serious trials this spring with the Indians. Two important Indians have died and they have ventured to say and intimate that the doctor has killed them by his magical power, in the same way they accuse their own sorcerers and kill them for it" (in *Letters of Narcissa Whitman*).

26. Statement of John Toupin, former interpreter at Fort Walla Walla, September 24, 1848, in Brouillet, *Authentic Account of the Murder*, 27–28.

27. Pringle, "Account of Overland Journey," 256.

28. Marcus Whitman to David Greene, May 20, 1845, ABCFM Archives.

29. Marcus Whitman to Elkanah Walker and Cushing Eells, November 25, 1845, in Elkanah and Mary Richardson Walker Papers, Box 2, Manuscripts, Archives, and Special Collections, Washington State University Libraries, Pullman (hereafter WSU Archives).

30. Narcissa Whitman to her parents, August 23, 1847, in *Letters of Narcissa Whitman*.

31. Marcus Whitman to David Greene, April 1, 1847, ABCFM Archives.

32. Marcus Whitman to David Greene, from The Dalles, September 13, 1847, ABCFM Archives.

33. Narcissa Whitman to her parents, August 23, 1847, in *Letters of Narcissa Whitman*.

34. Boyd, *Coming of the Spirit of Pestilence*, 146–47. See also Robert Heizer, "Walla Walla Indian Expeditions to the Sacramento Valley," *California Historical Society Quarterly* 21, no. 1 (March 1942): 1–7; and Barbara Alice Mann, *The Tainted Gift: The Disease Method of Frontier Expansion* (Santa Barbara, CA: Praeger, 2009).

35. "About 30 souls of the Cayuse tribe, died, one after another, who eventually believed the Doctor poisoned them. . . . As far as I have been able to learn, this has been the sole cause of the dreadful butchery" (William McBean, Fort Walla Walla, to James Douglas, Fort Vancouver, November 30, 1847, published in *Oregon Spectator*, December 9, 1847).

36. Testimony of William Craig, July 11, 1848, in Brouillet, *Authentic Account of the Murder,* 35–36.

37. Henry Spalding, *Oregon American and Evangelical Unionist*, July 19, 1848, in Drury, *Henry Harmon Spalding*, 332; and Henry Spalding to Dudley Allen, Hinsman, Ohio, March 16, 1848, published in *Christian Observer*, October 28, 1848.

38. Nancy Osborn Jacobs, paper read at Walla Walla, May 29, 1912, reprinted in *Waitsburg* (Washington) *Times*, February 2, 1934, clipping in Marcus and Narcissa Whitman Collection, Whitman College Archives.

39. Marcus Whitman to Alanson Hinman, November 8, 1847, in Drury, *More about the Whitmans*.

40. "Statements of Principal Chiefs of the Cayuses," December 20, 1847, in Brouillet, *Authentic Account of the Murder*, 63. See also Statement of William Craig, July 11, 1848, in Brouillet, *Authentic Account of the Murder,* 35. Tauitau accused Whitman of "having poison to kill the people with" in the spring of 1845; Whitman to Walker and Eells, November 25, 1845, in Elkanah and Mary Richardson Walker Papers, Box 2, WSU Archives.

41. Camaspelo as reported in *Oregon Spectator*, April 20, 1848.

42. Brouillet, *Authentic Account of the Murder*, 49.

43. William McBean report to Board of Management, Fort Vancouver, November 30, 1847, published in *Oregon Spectator*, December 9, 1847.

44. Statement of John Mix Stanley, Oregon City, March 10, 1848, in Brouillet, *Authentic Account of the Murder*, 77.

45. Brouillet to Gilliam, March 2, 1848, in Brouillet, *Authentic Account of the Murder*, 51.

46. Garth, "Report on the Second Season's Excavations at Waiilatpu," 309.

47. Statement of Lorinda Bewley, February 7, 1849, in Gray, *History of Oregon*, 500.

48. Affidavit by Lorinda Bewley, December 12, 1848, recorded by G. Walling, Justice of the Peace, Clackamas County, Oregon Territory, in Gray, *History of Oregon*, 497.

49. Statement of Lorinda Bewley, February 7, 1849, in Gray, *History of Oregon*, 500.

50. Sager, Sager, and Sager, *Whitman Massacre*, 76.

51. Sager, Sager, and Sager, *Whitman Massacre*, 77–79; and Stern, *Chiefs and Change in the Oregon Country*, 180.

52. Saunders, *Whitman Massacre,* 40–41.

53. Brouillet, *Authentic Account of the Murder*, 57, 64.

54. Brouillet, *Authentic Account of the Murder*, 61–62.

55. Translated statement signed by "Tikokate, Camaspalo, Tawatoe, Achekai, at the Place of Tawatoe, Youmatilla," December 20, 1847, forwarded to Provisional Gov. George Abernethy by Bishop Blanchet, December 21, 1847, published in *Oregon Spectator*, January 20, 1848.

56. Brouillet, *Authentic Account of the Murder*, 65–66; and James Douglas, Fort Vancouver, to George Abernethy, December 7, 1847, published in *Oregon Spectator*, December 9, 1847.

57. Brouillet, *Authentic Account of the Murder*, 66.

58. The passengers included John Mix Stanley, an American artist who had arrived at Fort Walla Walla shortly after the attack, Bishop Blanchet, and two other Catholic priests; see Thomas Lowe, "Private Journal Kept at Fort Vancouver, Columbia River [1843–1850]," entry dated January 8, 1848, typescript in Provincial Archives of British Columbia, Victoria, BC, 63–64.

59. Narcissa Whitman to her family, entry dated March 21, 1842, in *Letters of Narcissa Whitman*.

60. Matilda Sager as cited in Delaney, *Survivor's Recollections*, 17.

CHAPTER EIGHT

Epigraph: "The Massacre at Waiilatpu," *Oregon Spectator*, January 20, 1848.

1. William McBean report to Board of Management, Fort Vancouver, November 30, 1847, published in *Oregon Spectator*, December 9, 1847.

2. George Abernethy as quoted in *Oregon Spectator*, December 9, 1847.

3. James Douglas to George Abernethy, December 7, 1847, published in *Oregon Spectator*, December 9, 1847.

4. US Army Captain Walter W. DeLacy, who was traveling with the militia as an adjutant, counted twenty-seven dead immediately, and at least thirty-four others chased down and killed by the end of the day. The Indians' winter provisions "and in fact everything they possessed" were destroyed; see *Diary of the Yakima Indian War Kept by W. W. DeLacy, Captain, Engineers, and Acting Adjutant, Washington Territorial Volunteers*, entry dated July 17, 1856, www.nachestrail.org/media /pdf/DELACY%20Indian%20War%20reports%201856.pdf (accessed November 2019). See also Ruby and Brown, *Cayuse Indians*, 238–39.

5. Minthorn, "Wars, Treaties, and the Beginning of Reservation Life," 64.

6. Stern, *Chiefs and Change in the Oregon Country*, 61.

7. A.M.A. Blanchet to George Abernethy, December 21, 1847, in *Oregon Spectator*, January 20, 1848.

8. "Oregon Indians: Letter from Mr. Spalding, January 8, 1848," *Missionary Herald* 44, no. 7 (July 1848): 237–41. Spalding provided even more salacious accounts in a series of lectures published in the *Albany* (Oregon) *Democrat* in 1867 and 1868, reprinted in Warren, *Memoirs of the West*, 118–30. Examples: "Helpless wives and daughters, with their husbands and fathers dead or dying in sight; girls so young that the knife had to be used, subjected to the brutalities of the naked, painted demons—four or five at a time glutting their hell-born passions upon one of these most to be pitied of our fellow mortals. They kept up the scalp dance all night, the screams of our helpless women, writhing in the hands of the unrestrained demons, in plain hearing."

9. "The Massacre at Waiilatpu," *Oregon Spectator*, January 20, 1848.

10. "Interview with Perrin B. Whitman, Lewiston, Idaho, April 27, 1898," *Whitman College Quarterly* 2, no. 3 (October 1898): 36.

11. "By Authority," *Oregon Spectator*, January 6, 1848.

12. Thompson, *Shallow Grave at Waiilatpu*, 10.

13. "By Authority," *Oregon Spectator*, January 6, 1848.

14. James Douglas to George Abernethy, January 4, 1848, published in *Oregon Spectator*, February 10, 1848; and Stern, *Chiefs and Change in the Oregon Country*, 186–87.

15. "The thunders of war have commenced! Let them be continued until American *property*, and American *life* shall be secure upon American *soil*!" in *Oregon Spectator*, February 10, 1848 (emphasis in original).

16. Cornelius Gilliam to Asa Lovejoy, adjunct general, February 7, 1848, published in *Oregon Spectator*, February 24, 1848.

17. Newell's journal, entry dated March 5, 1848, in Johansen, *Robert Newell's Memoranda*, 112.

18. Weather journal, November 1847–January 1848, in *Oregon Spectator*, February 10, 1848.

19. A few days after the bodies were buried for the first time, Joe Stanfield, Whitman's French Canadian employee, told the hostages that wolves were digging up the bodies. Elizabeth Sager said she had gone with Joe to the gravesite. "The wolves had scratched the earth away from Mrs. Whitman's body and eaten all of the flesh from one leg from the knee to the ankle," she said. Joe "put her back in the grave with the others and shoveled earth over her" (in Lockley, *Oregon Trail Blazers,* 341).

20. "Report of the Peace Commissioners," *Oregon Spectator*, April 6, 1848.

21. "Mr. Newell's Remarks," *Oregon Spectator*, April 6, 1848.

22. According to Charles McKay, a lieutenant in the company led by Thomas McKay, "'Five Crows,' the fellow who took one of the girls was shot in two places, smashing his left arm into splinters, by myself. He dropped his gun, which I obtained, and if my horse had been good he would not have escaped me," in "News from the Army," *Oregon Spectator*, March 23, 1848.

23. As recounted in Bancroft, *History of Oregon,* 1: 718.

24. Quoted in *Oregon Spectator*, April 20, 1848.

25. Glassley, *Pacific Northwest Indian Wars*, 29. Gilliam and his troops left Fort Waters on March 10 and "proceeded in search of the enemy"; H.A.G. Maxon to Lovejoy, March 28, 1848, published in *Oregon Spectator*, April 6, 1848.

26. From Bancroft, *History of Oregon,* 1: 722, 724.

27. Glassley, *Pacific Northwest Indian Wars*, 32.

28. Glassley, *Pacific Northwest Indian Wars*, 34–35.

29. Report by James Waters, commander of the First Regiment of the Oregon Riflemen, from the Headquarters of the Army, Oregon City, published in *Oregon Spectator*, July 27, 1848. See also editorial note, Baird, Mallickan, and Swagerty, *Encounters with the People*, 271.

30. Roberta Conner, interview with the author, July 21, 2009, Pendleton.

31. Meek as quoted in Victor, *River of the West*, 443.

32. "Message to the Territorial Legislature, from Governor Joseph Lane," May 7, 1850, Oregon State Archives, Oregon Provisional and Territorial Records, 1850, Calendar No. 10571, https://sos.oregon.gov/archives/Documents/records/governors/governor-joseph-lane.pdf (accessed May 2019).

33. Baird, Mallickan, and Swagerty, *Encounters with the People*, 35. Provisional governor George Abernethy received several reports that the Yakama had refused to join the militant Cayuse, even when offered horses and cattle; see *Oregon Spectator*, March 23, 1848, and April 6, 1848.

34. Joseph Lane to the Nez Perce, November 8, 1848, and to the Young Chief of the Cayuse Nation, November 9, 1849, in Stern, *Chiefs and Change in the Oregon Country*, 219–20.

35. Stern, *Chiefs and Change in the Oregon Country*, 172.

36. Pringle manuscript, cited in Drury, *Marcus and Narcissa Whitman,* 2: 371.

37. As told in Bancroft, *History of Oregon,* 2: 95.

38. "Message to the Territorial Legislature, from Governor Joseph Lane," May 7, 1850, Oregon State Archives.

39. Reprinted in Lansing, *Juggernaut*, 16.

40. Clackamas County, US District Court Records, *U.S.* vs. *Telakite et al.*, Motion #40–41, https://sos.oregon.gov/archives/exhibits/highlights/Documents/demurrer-challenge-court-authority.pdf (accessed May 2019).

41. "Trial of Cayuse Murderers," *Oregon Spectator,* May 30, 1850.

42. "Trial of Cayuse Murderers," *Oregon Spectator,* May 30, 1850.

43. Lansing, *Juggernaut*, 46.

44. "Trial of Cayuse Murderers," *Oregon Spectator,* May 30, 1850.

45. *Oregon Spectator*, June 27, 1850. See also Lansing, *Juggernaut*, 96–98; and Warren, *Memoirs of the West*, 32.

46. Anson Dart, Annual Report, September 1851, cited in Stern, *Chiefs and Change in the Oregon Country*, 244.

47. Young Chief as recorded on June 7, 1855, in *Certified Copy of the Original Minutes of the Official Proceedings at the Council in Walla Walla Valley, Which Culminated in the Stevens Treaty of 1855* (Portland, OR: Bureau of Indian Affairs, 1953), https://www.lib.uidaho.edu/mcbeth/governmentdoc/1855council.htm (accessed May 2019).

48. Palmer as recorded on June 2, 1855, in *Original Minutes of the Official Proceedings*.

49. West, *Last Indian War*, 64–65.

50. Young Chief as recorded on June 7, 1855, in *Original Minutes of the Official Proceedings*.

51. A writer for the *New York Times* pointed out that whites had been moving onto the ceded Indian lands even though the treaty had not been ratified and the Indians had not been given what they had been promised in money, goods, or services ("Latest by Telegraph / The Indian Troubles in Washington and Oregon / Synopsis of Treaties with the Different Tribes," *New York Times*, July 7, 1858).

52. The newspaper editorial is quoted in Karson, *Wiyaxayxt / Wiyaakaa'awn / As Days Go By*, 115.

CHAPTER NINE

Epigraph: "Harding Says Whitman Tale Is Appealing / Would Like To Believe Story of the Pioneer Missionary Whether It Is True or Not, He Declares," *Statesman Journal* (Salem, Oregon), July 4, 1923.

1. Nixon, *How Marcus Whitman Saved Oregon*, first and second editions, 1895.

2. Nixon, *How Marcus Whitman Saved* Oregon, fifth and sixth editions, 1895.

3. Woodbridge, "Are These the Whitmans?" Kane was more interested in Indians than in missionaries or settlers, but he sketched at least twelve obviously Caucasian men and at least five obviously white women during his time in Oregon Country. See Lister, *Paul Kane, the Artist*.

4. Matilda Sager Delaney to Mrs. Edmund Bowden, March 26, 1928, Sager Family Collection, Box 6, Whitman College Archives.

5. Morrow, *We Must March*, esp. 12–14.

6. Drury as quoted in "Centennial Pays Tribute to First Pioneer Mother," *Spokesman-Review* (Spokane), August 15, 1936.

7. Arch Merrill, "Missionary Martyrs," in Merrill, *Upstate Echoes*, 48.

8. "Golden Haired Hymn Singing Beauty First Woman to Cross the Continent / the Full Story of Narcissa Whitman, Who As Missionary's Bride of 1836 Rode Sidesaddle to Oregon Territory Is Told in Two New Books," *Milwaukee Journal*, August 1, 1952.

9. Lavender, *Land of Giants*, 174.

10. "Whitman's Life and Death: Historical Data Concerning the Hero's Adventures," *Walla Walla Union*, Dr. Marcus Whitman Memorial Edition, December 1, 1897.

11. Marcus Whitman to Lyman Judson, November 5, 1846, in *Letters of Narcissa Whitman*. Whitman made similar claims in a letter to David Greene, April 1, 1847, ABCFM Archives.

12. "Join Indian Tribe," *Statesman Journal*, July 4, 1923.

13. "President Joins Indian Powwow," *New York Times*, July 5, 1923.

14. *Address of the President of the United States on the Oregon Trail at Meacham* (Washington, DC: Government Printing Office, 1923), 2, 4.

15. "Harding Says Whitman Tale Is Appealing," *Statesman Journal*, July 4, 1923. Frederick V. Holman, president of the Oregon Historical Society, publicly scolded the president in a letter to the editor of the *Sunday Oregonian*, published on July 8, 1923: "Warren G. Harding, as a private citizen, may believe in such historical myths as he chooses, and he may teach them to his family and to his friends as charming fictions. But as president of the United States, in a public historical address, he should not give his approval to discredited myths and traditions."

16. Peter Boag, "Death and Oregon's Settler Generation," *Oregon Historical Quarterly* 113, no. 3 (Fall 2014): 344–79, quotes on 349.

17. George Ludington Weed, "When Dr. Whitman Added Three Stars to Our Flag / How Oregon Was Saved for the Union," *Ladies Home Journal* 14, no. 11 (November 1897): 9–10.

18. Penrose, "Romance of a College," 9.

19. Edwards, *Triumph of Tradition*, 145.

20. "Whitman's Bones To Be Glass-Cased for a Public Inspection," *Los Angeles Herald*, October 22, 1897.

21. "Description of the Remains Found in the Whitman Mound, October 21st, 1897," Marcus and Narcissa Whitman Collection, Box 19, W-13, AG-1, Whitman College Archives.

22. "Skulls Cut in Two / Whitman Remains as Viewed by the Exhuming Party," *Spokesman-Review* (Spokane), October 28, 1897.

23. Catherine Sager Pringle, "Not the Skull of Whitman," *Spokesman-Review* (Spokane), October 30, 1897.

24. "Interview with Perrin B. Whitman, Lewiston, Idaho, April 27, 1898," *Whitman College Quarterly* 2, no. 3 (October 1898): 36.

25. Marcus and Narcissa Whitman Collection, Box 19, Folders labeled W-16 H 2 R-C Mss 105, Whitman College Archives.

26. "Story of Fifty Years Ago: Eloquent Address by Rev. L. H. Hallock, D.D.," *Walla Walla Union*, Dr. Marcus Whitman Memorial Edition, December 1, 1897.

27. "Life, Death and Work of Whitman," *Walla Walla Union*, Dr. Marcus Whitman Memorial Edition, December 1, 1897.

28. "Whitman's Grave No Longer Unkept / Vast Throngs Do Honor to His Memory / Entire Northwest Represented in Gathering of Pioneers at Waiilatpu, Where the Missionary Band Was Butchered Fifty Years Ago," *Seattle Post-Intelligencer*, December 1, 1897.

29. "Placed in New Vault: Remains of Dr. and Mrs. Whitman Again Interred," *Seattle Post-Intelligencer,* January 30, 1898.

30. "Completing Next Month a Century of Development since Marcus Whitman Established Its First Hearthstone, Washington Still Breathes Fire and Brimstone of the Frontier," *Spokane Chronicle*, July 26, 1936.

31. "Centennial Pays Tribute to First Pioneer Mother," *Spokesman-Review* (Spokane), August 15, 1936.

32. Whitman Centennial Celebration Official Program, dedication, Centennial Collection, Box 00, Whitman College Archives.

33. Whitman Centennial Celebration Official Program, pp. 7–15, Whitman College Archives.

34. Vi Forrest as quoted in Keiko Morris, "Uncomfortable History: The Whitman 'Massacre,'" *Seattle Times,* November 16, 1997.

35. National Park Service, "Whitman National Monument," Washington, DC, 1958; copy in possession of the author.

36. "Master Plan for Whitman National Monument, 1959, revised 1960," in Crabtree, *Whitman Mission Administrative History,* 134.

37. Drury, *Marcus and Narcissa Whitman,* 2: 382.

38. "Indians Coming to City for Motion Picture," *Oregon City Enterprise*, May 23, 1919; "Whitman Massacre Players in Wreck; Two Meet Death," *Spokane Daily Chronicle*, May 28, 1919; and "Martyrs of Yesterday," Oregon City on Film, https://sites.google.com/site /oregoncityonfilm/home/martyrs-of-yesterday (accessed August 2019).

39. See, for example, Johansen, *Empire of the Columbia*; Avery, *Washington*; Rinker Buck, *The Oregon Trail: A New American Journey* (New York: Simon & Schuster, 2015); and Gwartney, *I Am a Stranger Here Myself*.

40. Edwards, *Triumph of Tradition*, 147.

41. Penrose first claimed that the Whitmans had been scalped in an article in the *Whitman College Quarterly* 1, no. 1 (January 1897): 15. He repeated it in *Walla Walla Valley: The Cradle of the Pacific Northwest* (Walla Walla, WA: Inland Printing, 1935), 5; and in *Whitman: An Unfinished Story* (Walla Walla: Whitman Publishing Company, 1935), 24. The story circulated nationally. See, for example, Penrose, "Marcus Whitman, Pioneer," *New York Times*, March 4, 1936; and Neuberger, *Our Promised Land*, 4.

42. Edwards, *Triumph of Tradition*, 147.

43. US Code, Title 2, Chapter 30, Part D, Section 2131, "National Statuary Hall," www.law.cornell.edu/uscode/text/2/2131 (accessed November 2019).

44. "Whitman Statue Movement Gains," *Spokesman-Review* (Spokane), September 16, 1947.

45. Drury, *Marcus and Narcissa Whitman,* 2: 393.

46. *Acceptance of the Statue of Marcus Whitman,* 1.

47. Douglas's remarks are in *Acceptance of the Statue of Marcus Whitman*, 53–59.

CHAPTER TEN

Epigraph: Stephanie Martin, park ranger, Whitman Mission National Historic Site, email to author, October 5, 2019; "Cayuse, Umatilla and Walla Walla Homeland Heritage Corridor," Tamástslikt Cultural Institute, 2002 brochure in possession of the author.

1. Elizabeth Miller, Whitman College, email to author, May 13, 2019.

2. Rachel Needham, "Narcissa Whitman Painting Defaced," *Whitman Wire*, October 31, 2017.

3. Lisa Uddin, "White Unsettlement 101," *Whitman Wire*, March 1, 2018.

4. Holland Cotter, "Half-Measures Won't Erase the Painful Past of Our Monuments," *New York Times*, January 12, 2018.

5. Daniela Blei, "San Francisco's 'Early Days' Statue Is Gone. Now Comes the Work of Activating Real History," *Smithsonian*, October 4, 2018, www.smithsonianmag.com/smithsonian-institution/san-francisco-early -days-statue-gone-now-comes-work-activating-real-history-180970462.

6. "Mascots, Myths, Monuments and Memory," Smithsonian Institution news release, March 1, 2018, www.si.edu/newsdesk/releases /mascots-myths-monuments-and-memory-symposium-examines -racist-mascots-fate-confederate-statu.

7. Richard White as quoted in Kelman, *Misplaced Massacre,* 211–12.

8. Crabtree, *Whitman Mission Administrative History*, 136.

9. Marjorie Waheneka as quoted in Timothy Egan, "Offspring of Indians and Settlers Edit Histories of the West of Old," *New York Times*, May 31, 1993.

10. Morris, "Uncomfortable History."

11. Morris, "Uncomfortable History."

12. Jim Simon, "Layers of Pork Help Grease State's Capital Budget," *Walla Walla Union-Bulletin*, April 25, 1991.

13. "Too Bad Attention Just on Marcus Whitman," letter to the editor, *Walla Walla Union-Bulletin*, June 7, 1992; Bryan Corliss, "Marcus Whitman Statue May Be in Place This Week," *Walla Walla Union-Bulletin,* September 14, 1992; and "Statue Dedication Deserved Coverage," letter to the editor, *Walla Walla Union-Bulletin*, November 25, 1992. See also Grace Elise Fritzke, "When (That) Secularism Meets (Our) Memory Politics: Repression and Representation at Whitman College," honors thesis, Whitman College, 2018, https://arminda.whitman.edu /theses/393, 44–45.

14. Jonathan Martin, "Editorial Notebook: Whom to Memorialize in Statuary Hall from Washington State?" *Seattle Times*, June 25, 2014.

15. SB 5237, 66th Legislature of Washington State, 2019 reg. sess.

16. *Acceptance of the Statue of Marcus Whitman*, 63.

17. Tom Banse, "Proposal to Replace Marcus Whitman Statues Stokes Anger in Olympia," *Northwest News Network*, January 30, 2019, www .nwnewsnetwork.org/post/proposal-replace-marcus-whitman-statues -stokes-anger-olympia.

18. Roger Harnack, "Bill Targets Marcus Whitman's Significance, and Our Heritage," *Statesman-Examiner* and *Deer Park Tribune,* February 7, 2019.

19. Dr. G. Thomas Edwards to Donald Sampson, October 1, 1996, cited in Delaney Hardin Hanon, "The Whitman Legend: The Intertwining of History and Memorial in the Narrative of Marcus and Narcissa Whitman," honors thesis, Whitman College, 2017, https://arminda .whitman.edu/theses/344, 133–34.

20. Limerick, *Legacy of Conquest*, 41, 54.

21. Morris, "Uncomfortable History."

22. Jeffrey Kettleman et al., "John Chau Aced Missionary Boot Camp. Reality Proved a Harsher Test," *New York Times*, November 30, 2018. See also Ruth Graham, "Martyr or 'American Dickhead': Why Missionary John Chau's Death Off a Remote Indian Island Is So Unsettling to Christians," *Slate.com*, December 3, 2018.

23. Andrew Millman, *New York Times,* Reader Center, November 11, 2018, www.nytimes.com/2018/11/30/reader-center/john-allen-chau -missionaries.html.

24. Bonnie Sue Lewis, introduction to the Bison Books edition of Drury, *Mountains We Have Crossed,* 6–7.

25. Narcissa Whitman to Stephen Prentiss, October 10, 1840, in *Letters of Narcissa Whitman*.

26. Rev. Henry K. W. Perkins, Hallowell, Maine, to Jane Prentiss, Alleghany County, New York, October 19, 1849, in Drury, *Marcus Whitman, M.D.*, 458–60.

27. There were more than 150 wineries in the Walla Walla Valley as of 2020. One of the most acclaimed (and least accessible) was Cayuse Vineyards, established in 1997, the sesquicentennial of the Cayuse attack on the Whitman Mission. Cayuse wines are sold only to a few select restaurants and to consumers who get on a limited mailing list and buy "futures" a year in advance.

28. Kit Oldham, "First Ring-Necked Pheasants Introduced in the U.S. Arrive at Port Townsend on March 13, 1881," *HistoryLink.org: Online Encyclopedia of Washington State History*, December 31, 2007, www .historylink.org/File/8444 (accessed March 30, 2019).

29. National Park Service, Whitman Mission National Historic Site, homepage, www.nps.gov/whmi/index.htm (accessed September 2019).

30. Brouillet, *Authentic Account of the Murder*, 62–63. Suspicions about Whitman and poison persisted among Indian people for decades. Smoholla, a Wanapum spiritual leader and founder of what became known as the Dreamer religion, told an interviewer in 1885 that Whitman had gone East "to get a bottle of poison for us." See Eli L. Huggins, "Smohalla, the Prophet of Priest Rapids," *Overland Monthly* 17, no. 98 (February 1891): 214. The photographer Edward S. Curtis heard a similar story in the early 1900s from Yellow Bull, a Nez Perce, and his Cayuse wife, a daughter of Tomahas (accused of killing Whitman); see Curtis, *North American Indian*, 8: 81.

31. William Johnson, Confederated Tribes of the Umatilla Indian Reservation (CTUIR) tribal judge and attorney, has described the trial of the "Cayuse Five" as "the first gross violation of our inherent sovereignty." It remains, he wrote, "an underlying factor in the Umatilla, Walla Walla, and Cayuse peoples' reluctance to trust law enforcement and other officials in positions of authority." In Karson, *Wiyaxayxt / Wiyaakaa'awn / As Days Go By*, 172.

32. Samuel Black, "Report by Chief Trader Samuel Black to the Governor and Committee of the Hudson's Bay Company, dated 'Walla Walla,' March 25, 1829," quoted in Stern, *Chiefs and Chief Traders*, 66.

33. Archibald McKinlay to W. Fraser Tolmie, May 12, 1884, in *Transactions of the Oregon Pioneer Association* 12 (1884): 35.

34. Narcissa Whitman to her parents, May 2, 1837, in *Letters of Narcissa Whitman*.

35. Roberta Conner, interview with the author, July 21, 2009, Pendleton.

36. Karson, *Wiyaxayxt / Wiyaakaa'awn / As Days Go By*, 117, 165, 168–69. See also "History of CTUIR," Confederated Tribes of the Umatilla Indian Reservation website, https://ctuir.org/history-culture/history-ctuir (accessed September 2019).

37. Karson, *Wiyaxayxt / Wiyaakaa'awn / As Days Go By*, 86–87.

38. Oregon Cultural Trust, "The Museum at Tamástslikt Cultural Institute: A Whole World Unfolds," video short, 2012, www.youtube.com /watch?v=NcUMJL6XtJI (accessed September 2019).

39. Stern, *Chiefs and Change in the Oregon Country*, 347.

40. Roberta Conner, "Round-Up Reminiscences," in *Pendleton Round-Up at 100: Oregon's Legendary Rodeo,* edited by Michael Bales and Ann Terry Hill (Portland, OR: Graphic Arts Books, 2009), 45–65, quote on 47.

41. Trafzer, *Yakima, Palouse, Cayuse, Umatilla, Walla Walla, and Wanapum Indians*, 7.

42. "About Us," Confederated Tribes of the Umatilla Indian Reservation, https://ctuir.org/about-us (accessed September 2019).

43. Confederated Tribes of the Umatilla Indian Reservation, 2018 annual report, pp. 1, 8, https://ctuir.org/sites/default/files/CTUIR%20AR18 %20FINAL.pdf (accessed September 2019).

44. Roberta Conner, interview with David E. Hall, 2007, "Native Perspectives on Sustainability," transcript retrieved from the Native Perspectives on Sustainability project, www.nativeperspectives.net (accessed May 2018).

SELECTED
BIBLIOGRAPHY

MANUSCRIPT SOURCES

Every writer who delves into the history of the Whitman Mission stands on the shoulders of Clifford M. Drury, a Presbyterian minister who was stationed in Moscow, Idaho, in the 1930s, when he began researching the lives of the members of the Oregon Mission of the American Board of Commissioners for Foreign Missions. Drury was indefatigable in tracking down letters, documents, and ephemera—from a pair of Marcus Whitman's saddlebags to a charred doorsill from the burned Mission House at Waiilatpu. Parts of his treasure trove ended up in the Marcus and Narcissa Whitman Collection and the Sager Family Collection at Whitman College and Northwest Archives, Walla Walla. Whitman College holds Narcissa's original journal, along with five samples of hair said to have come from her head, one sample said to have come from Marcus, and two said to have come from Marcus's mother, Alice.

Reading the original letters and journals is a visceral experience, a way of literally touching the past, but published versions have the advantage of being easier to read and infinitely more accessible.

Many of Narcissa's letters were published in *Transactions of the Oregon Pioneer Association*, beginning in the 1880s. Digitized, searchable editions of the *Transactions* are available through the Hathi Trust Digital Library (https://catalog.hathitrust.org/Record/008376302). Volumes 19 through 23 of the *Transactions* are particularly useful. I also relied on *The Letters of Narcissa Whitman, 1836–1847* (Fairfield, WA: Ye Galleon Press, 1996).

Drury edited several important published collections of missionary diaries and letters, including the three-volume *First White Women over the Rockies* (Glendale, CA: Arthur H. Clark Company, 1963, 1966); reissued as *Where Wagons Could Go: Narcissa Whitman and Eliza Spalding* (Lincoln: University of Nebraska Press, 1997); *On to Oregon: The Diaries of Mary Walker and Myra Eells* (Lincoln: University of Nebraska Press, 1998); and *The Mountains We Have Crossed: Diaries and Letters of the Oregon Mission, 1838* (Lincoln: University of Nebraska Press, 1999). Drury also edited *More about the Whitmans: Four Hitherto Unpublished Letters of Marcus and Narcissa Whitman* (Tacoma: Washington State Historical Society, 1979), and *The Diaries and Letters of Henry H. Spalding and Asa Bowen Smith Relating to the Nez Perce Mission, 1838–1842* (Glendale, CA: Arthur H. Clark, 1958).

While living in Moscow, Drury cultivated a special relationship with the president of nearby Washington State University in Pullman. As a result, the Manuscripts, Archives, and Special Collections Department at WSU holds a wealth of missionary materials. I made particular use of the Marcus and Narcissa Whitman Papers, the Clifford Merrill Drury Papers, the Henry Harmon Spalding Papers, and the Elkanah and Mary Richardson Walker Papers.

The vast records of the American Board of Commissioners for Foreign Missions (ABCFM) are housed at Houghton Library, Harvard University. The collection includes eighty-three boxes of correspondence regarding the board's North American Indian missions from 1803 to 1883. I focused on ABC 18.5.3, "Mission to the Oregon Indians," and ABC 18.5.5, "Oregon Indians, Miscellaneous." All quotations from the collection are used with permission from the Houghton Library and the United Church of Christ Wider Church Ministries. The ABCFM's Annual Reports were published in the *Missionary Herald*. Digitized, searchable editions are available through the Hathi Trust (HathiTrust.org). Archer Butler Hulbert and Dorothy Printup Hulbert included letters from Marcus Whitman, Samuel Parker, and others involved in the missionary enterprise in their three-volume *Marcus Whitman, Crusader* (Denver: Stewart Commission of Colorado College and the Denver Library, 1936, 1938, 1941), part of their eight-volume *Overland to the Pacific*.

OTHER SOURCES

Acceptance of the Statue of Marcus Whitman Presented by the State of Washington. Washington, DC: Government Printing Office, 1955. https://babel.hathitrust.org/cgi/pt?id=uc1.aa0011977105&view=1up&seq=9.

Addis, Cameron. "The Whitman Massacre: Religion and Manifest Destiny on the Columbia Plateau, 1809–1958." *Journal of the Early Republic* 25, no. 2 (Summer 2005): 221–58.

Avery, Mary W. *Washington: A History of the Evergreen State.* Seattle: University of Washington Press, 1965.

Baird, Dennis, Diane Mallickan, and W. R. Swagerty, eds. *Encounters with the People: Written and Oral Accounts of Nez Perce Life to 1858.* Pullman: Washington State University Press, 2015.

Bancroft, Hubert Howe. *The Works of Hubert Howe Bancroft, Volume 29: History of Oregon, Volume 1, 1834–1848.* San Francisco: History Co., 1886.

———. *The Works of Hubert Howe Bancroft, Volume 30: History of Oregon, Volume 2, 1848–1883.* San Francisco: History Co., 1888.

Boyd, Robert T. *The Coming of the Spirit of Pestilence: Introduced Infectious Diseases and Population Decline among Northwest Indians, 1774–1874.* Seattle: University of Washington Press, 1999.

———. *People of The Dalles: The Indians of Wascopam Mission.* Lincoln: University of Nebraska Press, 1996.

Brouillet, J.B.A. *Authentic Account of the Murder of Dr. Whitman and Other Missionaries, by the Cayuse Indians of Oregon*. Portland, OR: S.J. McCormick, second edition, 1869. https://archive.org/details/authenticaccount00brou.

Catlin, George. *Letters and Notes on the Manners, Customs, and Condition of the North American Indians*, 2 volumes. London: Tosswill and Myers, 1841.

———. *My Life amongst the Indians*. London: William Clowes and Sons, 1867.

Cebula. Larry. *Plateau Indians and the Quest for Spiritual Power, 1700–1850*. Lincoln: University of Nebraska Press, 2003.

Clarke, Samuel A. *Pioneer Days of Oregon History*. Volume 2. Portland, OR: J.K. Gill Company, 1905. https://archive.org/stream/pioneerdaysofore02clar#page/n3/mode/2up.

Crabtree, Jennifer. *Whitman Mission Administrative History*. Seattle: US Department of the Interior, 1988.

Curtis, Edward S. *The North American Indian*. Volume 8. Norwood, MA: Plimpton Press, 1911.

Delaney, Matilda J. Sager. *A Survivor's Recollections of the Whitman Massacre*. Spokane, WA: Esther Reed Chapter, Daughters of the American Revolution, 1920.

Dietrich, William. *Northwest Passage: The Great Columbia River*. New York: Simon and Schuster, 1995.

Douglas, David. *Journal Kept by David Douglas during His Travels in North America, 1823–1827*. London: W. Wesley & Son, 1914.

Drury, Clifford M. *Henry Harmon Spalding*. Caldwell, ID: Caxton Printers, Ltd., 1936.

———. *Marcus Whitman, M.D.: Pioneer and Martyr*. Caldwell, ID: Caxton Printers, Ltd., 1937.

———. *Marcus and Narcissa Whitman and the Opening of Old Oregon*. 2 volumes. 1973; reprint, Seattle: Northwest Interpretive Association, 2005.

———. *On to Oregon: The Diaries of Mary Walker and Myra Eells*. Lincoln: University of Nebraska Press, 1998.

———. *Where Wagons Could Go: Narcissa Whitman and Eliza Spalding*. Lincoln: University of Nebraska Press, 1997.

Edwards, G. Thomas. *The Triumph of Tradition: The Emergence of Whitman College, 1859–1924*. Walla Walla: Whitman College, 1992.

Eells, Myron. *Marcus Whitman, Pathfinder and Patriot*. Seattle: Lowman and Hanford Co., 1909.

Farnham, Thomas J. *Travels in the Great Western Prairies, the Anahuac and Rocky Mountains and in the Oregon Territory*. 2 volumes. London: Richard Bentley, 1843.

Feathers, Joseph J. S. *These Are the Nez Perce Nation*. Lewiston, ID: Lewis-Clark Normal Press, 1970.

Furtwangler, Albert. *Bringing Indians to the Book*. Seattle: University of Washington Press, 2005.

Garth, Thomas R. "A Report on the Second Season's Excavations at Waiilatpu." *Pacific Northwest Quarterly* 40, no. 4 (October 1949): 295–315.

Glassley, Ray Hoard. *Pacific Northwest Indian Wars*. Portland, OR: Binfords & Mort, 1953.

Gray, William H. *A History of Oregon, 1792–1849, Drawn from Personal Observation and Authentic Information*. Portland, OR: Harris and Holman, 1870.

Gwartney, Debra. *I Am a Stranger Here Myself*. Albuquerque: University of New Mexico Press, 2019.

Harmon, Alexandra. *Indians in the Making: Ethnic Relations and Indian Identities around Puget Sound*. Berkeley: University of California Press, 2000.

Hines, Gustavus. *Life on the Plains of the Pacific; Oregon: Its History, Condition and Prospects*. Buffalo, NY: Geo. H. Derby, 1852.

Hulbert, Archer Butler, and Dorothy Printup Hulbert, eds. *Marcus Whitman, Crusader*. 3 volumes. Denver: Stewart Commission of Colorado College and the Denver Library, 1936, 1938, 1941. Part of *Overland to the Pacific*. 8 volumes. 1932–41.

Hunn, Eugene S. *Nch'i-Wana "The Big River": Mid-Columbia Indians and Their Land*. Seattle: University of Washington Press, 1990.

———, ed. *Čáw Pawá Láakni / They Are Not Forgotten: Sahaptian Place Names Atlas of the Cayuse, Umatilla, and Walla Walla*. Seattle: University of Washington Press and Tamástslikt Cultural Institute, 2015.

Jeffrey, Julie Roy. *Converting the West: A Biography of Narcissa Whitman*. Norman: University of Oklahoma Press, 1991.

Johansen, Dorothy O. *Empire of the Columbia: A History of the Pacific Northwest*. Second edition. New York: Harper & Row, 1967.

———, ed. *Robert Newell's Memoranda: Travles in the Teritory of Missourie; Travle to the Kayuse War; Together with A Report on the Indians South of the Columbia River*. Portland, OR: Champoeg Press, Inc., 1959.

Jones, Nard. *The Great Command: The Story of Marcus and Narcissa Whitman and the Oregon Country Pioneers*. Boston: Little, Brown and Company, 1959.

Josephy, Alvin M., Jr. *The Nez Perce Indians and the Opening of the Northwest*. New Haven, CT: Yale University Press, 1965; reprint, Boston: Houghton Mifflin, 1997.

Kane, Paul. *Wanderings of an Artist among the Indians of North America*. London: Longman, Brown, Green, Longmans, and Roberts, 1859.

Karson, Jennifer, ed. *Wiyaxayxt / Wiyaakaa'awn / As Days Go By: Our History, Our Land, and Our People: The Cayuse, Umatilla, and Walla Walla*. Pendleton: Oregon Historical Society Press and Tamástslikt Cultural Institute, 2006.

Kelman, Ari. *A Misplaced Massacre: Struggling over the Memory of Sand Creek*. Cambridge, MA: Harvard University Press, 2013.

Lansing, Ronald B. *Juggernaut: The Whitman Massacre Trial, 1850*. Portland, OR: Ninth Judicial Circuit Historical Society, 1993.

Lavender, David. *Land of Giants: The Drive to the Pacific Northwest*. 1956; reprint, Lincoln: University of Nebraska Press, 1979.

Lee, Daniel, and Joseph Frost. *Ten Years in Oregon*. New York: J. Collard, 1844.

Limerick, Patricia. *The Legacy of Conquest: The Unbroken Past of the American West*. New York: W.W. Norton & Company, 1987.

Lister, Kenneth R. *Paul Kane the Artist: Wilderness to Studio*. Toronto: Royal Ontario Museum Press, 2010.

Lockley, Fred. *Oregon Trail Blazers*. New York: Knickerbocker Press, 1929.

Mann, Barbara Alice. *The Tainted Gift: The Disease Method of Frontier Expansion*. Santa Barbara, CA: Praeger, 2009.

Merrill, Arch. *Upstate Echoes*. New York: American Book–Knickerbocker Press, Inc., 1950.

Miller, Christopher L. *Prophetic Worlds: Indians and Whites on the Columbia Plateau.* Seattle: University of Washington Press, 2003.

Mithun, Marianne. *The Languages of Native North America.* New York: Cambridge University Press, 1999.

Morrison, Dorothy N. *Outpost: John McLoughlin and the Far Northwest.* Portland: Oregon Historical Society Press, 1999.

Morrow, Honore Willsie. *We Must March: A Novel of the Winning of Oregon.* New York: Frederick A. Stokes Company, 1925.

Moulton, Gary, ed. *The Journals of the Lewis and Clark Expedition.* Electronic Text Center, Lincoln Libraries, University of Nebraska. Lincoln: University of Nebraska Press, 2005. http://lewisandclarkjournals.unl.edu/journals.php?id=1806-09-04.

Mowry, William A. *Marcus Whitman and the Early Days of Oregon.* New York: Silver, Burdett and Company, 1901.

Neuberger, Richard L. *Our Promised Land.* New York: Macmillan Company, 1938.

Nixon, Oliver W. *How Marcus Whitman Saved Oregon: A True Romance of Patriotic Heroism, Christian Devotion and Final Martyrdom.* Chicago: Star Publishing Company, 1895.

———. *Whitman's Ride through Savage Lands.* Chicago: Winona Publishing Company, 1905.

Original Minutes of the Official Proceedings at the Council in Walla Walla Valley, Which Culminated in the Stevens Treaty of 1855. Portland, OR: US Department of the Interior, Bureau of Indian Affairs, 1953. www.lib.uidaho.edu/mcbeth /governmentdoc/1855council.htm.

Palmer, Joel. *Journal of Travels over the Rocky Mountains, 1845–1846.* Volume 30 of Reuben G. Thwaites, ed., *Early Western Travels, 1748–1846.* Cleveland, OH: Arthur H. Clark Company, 1906.

Parker, Samuel. *Journal of an Exploring Tour beyond the Rocky Mountains.* Published by the author. Ithaca, NY, 1840.

Penrose, Stephen B. "The Romance of a College." Whitman College, Walla Walla, 1894. https://arminda.whitman.edu/object/arminda30156.

Pringle, Catherine Sager. "Account of Overland Journey to Oregon in 1844: Life at the Whitman Mission: the Whitman Massacre," ca. 1860. Originally published as "On the Plains in 1844." In S. A. Clarke, *Pioneer Days of Oregon History.* Volume 2. Portland, OR: J. K. Gill, 1905. Republished as *Across the Plains in 1844*, multiple publishers and editions.

Ross, Alexander. *Adventures of the First Settlers on the Oregon or Columbia River.* London: Smith, Elder & Co., 1849.

———. *The Fur Hunters of the Far West.* Edited by Milo Milton Quaife. 1855; reprint, Chicago: Lakeside Press, 1924.

Ruby, Robert H., and John A. Brown. *The Cayuse Indians: Imperial Tribesmen of Old Oregon.* 1972; reprint, Norman: University of Oklahoma Press, 2005.

———. *The Spokane Indians: Children of the Sun.* 1970; expanded edition, Norman: University of Oklahoma Press, 2006.

Sager, Catherine, Elizabeth, and Matilda. *The Whitman Massacre of 1847.* Fairfield, WA: Ye Galleon Press, 1981.

Saunders, Mary. *The Whitman Massacre: A True Story by a Survivor of This Terrible Tragedy Which Took Place in Oregon in 1847*. 1916; reprint, Fairfield, WA: Ye Galleon Press, 1977.

Stark, Peter. *Astoria: Astor and Jefferson's Lost Pacific Empire: A Tale of Ambition and Survival on the Early American Frontier*. New York: HarperCollins Publishers, 2015.

Stern, Theodore. *Chiefs and Change in the Oregon Country: Indian Relations at Fort Nez Percés, 1818–1855*. Corvallis: Oregon State University Press, 1996.

——. *Chiefs and Chief Traders: Indian Relations at Fort Nez Percés, 1818–1855*. Corvallis: Oregon State University Press, 1993.

Thompson, David. *David Thompson's Narrative*. New York: Greenwood Press, 1968. Originally published as *David Thompson's Narrative of His Explorations in Western America, 1784–1812*. Toronto: Champlain Society, 1916.

Thompson, Erwin N. *Shallow Grave at Waiilatpu: The Sagers' West*. Portland: Oregon Historical Society, 1969.

Thornton, Russell. *American Indian Holocaust and Survival: A Population History since 1492*. 1987; reprint, Norman: University of Oklahoma Press, 1990.

Townsend, John K. *Narrative of a Journey across the Rocky Mountains to the Columbia River and a Visit to the Sandwich Islands, Chili, &c. with a Scientific Appendix*. Philadelphia: Henry Perkins, 1839.

Trafzer, Clifford E. *Yakima, Palouse, Cayuse, Umatilla, Walla Walla, and Wanapum Indians: An Historical Bibliography*. Metuchen, NJ: Scarecrow Press, 1992.

Vibert, Elizabeth. *Traders' Tales: Narratives of Cultural Encounters in the Columbia Plateau, 1807–1846*. Norman: University of Oklahoma Press, 2000.

Victor, Frances Fuller. *The River of the West*. Hartford, CT: Columbian Book Company, 1871.

Warren, Eliza Spalding. *Memoirs of the West: The Spaldings*. Portland, OR: March Printing Company, 1916.

West, Elliott. *The Last Indian War: The Nez Perce Story*. New York: Oxford University Press, 2009.

White, Elijah. *Concise View of Oregon Territory and Its Colonial and Indian Relations*. Washington, DC: T. Bernard, 1846.

Whitman, Narcissa. *The Letters of Narcissa Whitman, 1836–1847*. Fairfield, WA: Ye Galleon Press, 1996.

Wilkes, Charles. *Narrative of the United States Exploring Expedition, during the Years 1838, 1839, 1840, 1841, 1842*. Volume 4. Philadelphia: C. Sherman, 1844.

Woodbridge, Ross. "Are These the Whitmans?" *The Whitman Alumnus: Whitman College Bulletin* 73, no. 5 (February 1970): 2–6.

Young, F. G., ed. "Journal and Report by Dr. Marcus Whitman of His Tour of Exploration with Rev. Samuel Parker in 1835 beyond the Rocky Mountains." *Oregon Historical Quarterly* 28, no. 3 (September 1927): 239–57. www.jstor.org /stable/20610386.

INDEX

Photo by Glenn A. Drosendahl

ABOUT THE AUTHOR

Cassandra Tate worked as a journalist for twenty-five years before earning a PhD in history at the University of Washington in 1995. A former Nieman Fellow at Harvard University, she is the author of *Cigarette Wars: The Triumph of "The Little White Slaver."* She contributes to a wide range of print and electronic media, including HistoryLink.org, the online encyclopedia of Washington State history.